JBoss® Seam

JBoss® Seam

Simplicity and Power Beyond Java™ EE

Michael Yuan
Thomas Heute

PRENTICE
HALL

Upper Saddle River, NJ • Boston • Indianapolis • San Francisco
New York • Toronto • Montreal • London • Munich • Paris • Madrid
Cape Town • Sydney • Tokyo • Singapore • Mexico City

The publisher offers excellent discounts on this book when ordered in quantity for bulk purchases or special sales, which may include electronic versions and/or custom covers and content particular to your business, training goals, marketing focus, and branding interests. For more information, please contact:

U.S. Corporate and Government Sales
(800) 382-3419
corpsales@pearsontechgroup.com

For sales outside the United States, please contact:

International Sales
international@pearsoned.com

Visit us on the Web: www.prenhallprofessional.com

Library of Congress Cataloging-in-Publication Data:

Yuan, Michael Juntao.

JBox seam : simplicity and power beyond Java EE / Michael Yuan, Thomas Heute. — 1st ed.

p. cm.

ISBN 0-13-134796-9 (pbk. : alk. paper) 1. JBoss. 2. Web servers—Management. 3. Java (Computer program language) I. Heute, Thomas. II. Title.

TK5105.8885.J42Y83 2007

005.2'762—dc22

2007005043

ISBN 0-13-134796-9
Text printed in the United States on recycled paper at RR Donnelley in Crawfordsville, Indiana.
Second Printing, June 2007

 This Book Is Safari Enabled

The Safari™ Enabled icon on the cover of your favorite technology book means the book is available through Safari Bookshelf. When you buy this book, you get free access to the online edition for 45 days.

Safari Bookshelf is an electronic reference library that lets you easily search thousands of technical books, find code samples, download chapters, and access technical information whenever and wherever you need it.

To gain 45-day Safari Enabled access to this book:

- Go to http://www.prenhallprofessional.com/safarienabled.
- Complete the brief registration form.
- Enter the coupon code SZJQ-XMTK-HT8N-W5KR-XX37.

If you have difficulty registering on Safari Bookshelf or accessing the online edition, please email customer-service@safaribooksonline.com.

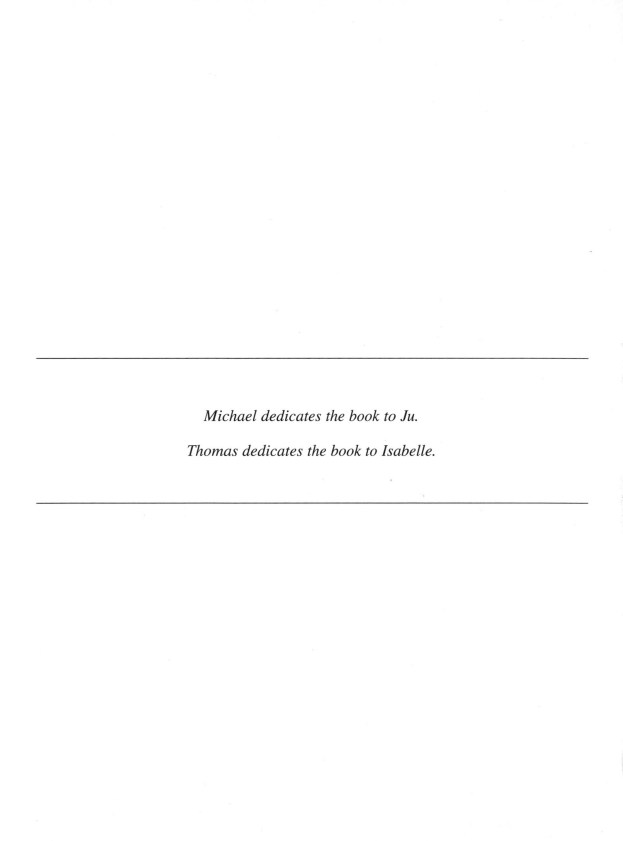

Michael dedicates the book to Ju.

Thomas dedicates the book to Isabelle.

Table of Contents

I

Getting Started

In this part, we provide an overview of JBoss Seam and its key features and benefits. A simple Hello World example illustrates how Seam ties together the database, the web UI, and the transactional business logic to form an application. We discuss the JSF enhancements Seam and Facelets provide that make JSF one of the best web application frameworks around and ideal for Seam applications. For readers who do not want to waste time setting up common Seam/Java EE configuration files, we introduce a tool called Seam Gen. Seam Gen generates projects with complete Eclipse and NetBeans IDE support. It's the best way to jump-start your Seam application.

1

What Is Seam?

According to the official JBoss web site, JBoss Seam is a "lightweight framework for Java EE 5.0." What does that mean? Isn't Java EE (Enterprise Edition) 5.0 itself a collection of "frameworks?" Why do you need another one that is outside the official specification? Well, we view Seam as the "missing framework" that should have been included in Java EE 5.0. It sits on top of Java EE 5.0 frameworks to provide a consistent and easy-to-understand programming model for all components in an enterprise web application. It also makes stateful applications and business process-driven applications a breeze to develop. In other words, Seam is all about developer productivity and application scalability.

In this book, we show you how Seam can make development easier for you. We cover several web application examples to make our case. But before we get into concrete code examples, let's first explain what exactly Seam does and introduce its key design principles. This will help you better understand how Seam works in applications throughout the book.

1.1. Integrate and Enhance Java EE Frameworks

The core frameworks in Java EE 5.0 are EJB (Enterprise JavaBeans) 3.0 and JSF (JavaServer Faces) 1.2. EJB 3.0 (EJB3, hereafter) is a lightweight framework based on Plain Old Java Objects (POJO) for business services and database persistence. JSF is a Model-View-Controller (MVC) component framework for web applications. Most Java EE 5.0 web applications have both EJB3 modules for business logic and JSF modules for the web front end. However, although EJB3 and JSF are complementary to each other, they are designed as separate frameworks, each with its own philosophy. For instance, EJB3 uses annotations to configure services, whereas JSF makes use of XML files. Furthermore, EJB3 and JSF components are not aware of each other at the framework level. To make EJB3 and JSF work together, you need artificial facade objects (i.e., JSF backing beans) to tie business components to web pages, and boilerplate code (a.k.a. plumbing code) to make method calls across framework boundaries. Gluing those technologies together is part of Seam's responsibilities.

application with code that is unrelated to the core business logic, but it also brings on an array of performance issues.

In Seam, all the basic application components are inherently stateful. They are much easier to use than the HTTP session because Seam declaratively manages their states. No need exists to write distracting state-management code in a Seam application—just annotate the component with its scope, lifecycle methods, and other stateful properties, and Seam takes over the rest. Seam stateful components also provide much finer control over user states than the plain HTTP session does. For instance, you can have multiple "conversations," each consisting of a sequence of web requests and business method calls, in an HTTP session. For more on Seam stateful components, refer to Chapter 5, *An Introduction to Stateful Framework*.

Furthermore, database caches and transactions can be automatically tied with the application state in Seam. Seam automatically holds database updates in memory and commits to the database only at the end of a conversation. The in-memory cache greatly reduces database load in complex stateful applications. Refer to Chapter 9, *Transactions*, for more on conversation-based database transactions.

In addition to everything we've mentioned, Seam takes state management in web applications a big step further by supporting integration with the open source JBoss jBPM business process engine. You can now specify the work flows of different people in the organization (customers, managers, technical support, etc.) and use the work flow to drive the application instead of relying on the UI event handlers and databases. See Chapter 18, *Managing Business Processes*, for more on Seam and jBPM integration.

Declarative Contextual Components

Each stateful component in Seam has a scope or context. For instance, a shopping cart component is created at the start of a shopping conversation and is destroyed at the end of the conversation when all items are checked out. Hence, this component lives in a conversation context. Your application simply declares this context via annotations on the component, and Seam automatically manages the component creation, state, and removal.

Seam provides several levels of stateful contexts, ranging from a single web request to a multipage conversation, an HTTP session, or a long-running business process.

1.4. Web 2.0 Ready

Seam is fully optimized for Web 2.0 style applications. It provides multiple ways for AJAX (Asynchronous JavaScript and XML, a technology to add interactivity to web pages) support, from drop-in JavaScript-less AJAX components (see Chapter 15, *Custom and AJAX UI Components*), to AJAX-enabling existing JSF components (see Chapter 16, *Enabling AJAX for Existing Components*), to a custom JavaScript library (see Chapter 17, *Direct JavaScript Integration*) that provides direct access to Seam server components from the browser. Internally, Seam provides an advanced concurrency model to efficiently manage multiple AJAX requests from the same user.

A big challenge for AJAX applications is the increased database load. An AJAX application makes much more frequent requests to the server than its non-AJAX counterpart does. If all those AJAX requests had to be served by the database, the database would not be able to handle the load. The stateful persistence context in Seam acts as an in-memory cache. It can hold information throughout a long-running conversation and, hence, help to reduce the database round-trips.

Web 2.0 applications also tend to employ complex relational models for data (e.g., a social network site is all about managing and presenting the relationships between "users"). For those sites, lazy loading in the ORM layer is crucial. Otherwise, a single query could cascade to loading the entire database. As we discussed earlier, Seam is the only web framework today that supports lazy loading correctly for web applications.

1.5. POJO Services via Dependency Bijection

Seam is a "lightweight framework" because it promotes the use of Plain Old Java Objects (POJO) as service components. No framework interfaces or abstract classes exist to "hook" components into the application. The question, of course, is, how do those POJOs interact with each other to form an application? How do they interact with container services (e.g., the database persistence service)?

Seam wires POJO components together using a popular design pattern known as dependency injection (DI). Under this pattern, the Seam framework manages the lifecyle of all the components. When a component needs to use another, it declares this dependency to Seam using annotations. Seam determines where to get this dependent component based on the application's current state and "injects" it into the asking component.

Expanding on the dependency injection concept, Seam component A can also create another component B and "outject" the created component B back to Seam for other components, such as C, to use later.

This type of bidirectional dependency management is widely used in even the simplest Seam web applications (e.g., the Hello World example in Chapter 2, *Seam Hello World*). In Seam terms, we call this dependency bijection.

1.6. Configuration by Exception

The key design principle that makes Seam so easy to use is configuration by exception. The idea is to have a set of common-sense default behavior for the components. The developer needs to configure the component explicitly only when the desired behavior is not the default. For instance, when Seam injects component A as a property of component B, the Seam name of component A defaults to the recipient property name in component B. Many little things like that are true in Seam. The overall result is that configuration metadata in Seam is much simpler than that in competing Java frameworks. As a result, most Seam applications can be adequately configured with a small number of simple Java annotations. Developers benefit from reduced complexity and, in the end, fewer lines of code for the same functionalities developed in competing frameworks.

1.7. Avoid XML Abuse

As you have probably noticed, Java annotations play a crucial role in expressing and managing Seam configuration metadata. That is done by design to make the framework easier to work with.

In the early days of J2EE, XML was viewed as the "holy grail" for configuration management. Framework designers threw all kinds of configuration information, including Java class and method names, in XML files without much thought about the consequence to developers. In retrospect, that was a big mistake. XML configuration files are highly repetitive. They have to repeat information already in the code to connect the configuration to the code. Those repetitions make the application prone to minor errors (e.g., a misspelled class name would show up as a hard-to-debug error at runtime). The lack of reasonable default configuration settings further compounds this problem. In fact, in some frameworks, the amount of boilerplate code disguised as XML might rival or even exceed the amount of actual Java code in the application. For Java developers, this abuse of XML is commonly known as the "XML hell" in J2EE.

The enterprise Java community recognizes this problem with XML abuse and has successfully attempted to replace XML files with annotations in Java source code. EJB3 is the effort by the official Java standardization body to promote the use of annotations in enterprise Java components. EJB3 makes XML files completely optional, and it is definitely a step in the right direction. Seam adds to EJB3 annotations and expands the annotation-based programming model to the entire web application.

Of course, XML is not entirely bad for configuration data. Seam designers recognize that XML is well suited to specifying wcb application pageflows or defining business process work flows. The XML file enables us to centrally manage the work flow for the entire application, as opposed to scattering the information around in Java source files. The work flow information has little coupling with the source code—hence, the XML files do not need to duplicate typed information already available in the code. For more details on this subject, see Chapter 19, *Stateful Pageflows*.

1.8. Designed for Testing

Seam was designed from ground up for easy testing. Because all Seam components are just annotated POJOs, they are easy to unit-test. You can just create instances of the POJOs using the regular Java new keyword and then run any methods in your testing framework (e.g., JUnit or TestNG). If you need to test interaction among multiple Seam components, you can instantiate those components individually and then set up their relationships manually (i.e., use the setter methods explicitly instead of relying on Seam's dependency injection features). In Chapter 21, *Unit Testing*, we explain how to set up unit tests for your Seam applications, and how to mock database service for the test cases.

Integration testing in Seam is perhaps even simpler than unit testing. With the Seam testing framework, you can write simple scripts to simulate web user interaction, and then test the outcome. You can use the JSF Expression Language (EL) to reference Seam components in the test script just as you do on a JSF web page. Like unit tests, the integration tests run directly from the command-line in the Java SE environment. There is no need to start the application server just to run the tests. Refer to Chapter 22, *Integration Testing* for more details.

1.9. Great Tools Support

Tools support is crucial for an application framework that focuses on developer productivity. Seam is distributed with a command-line application generator called Seam Gen (see Chapter 4, *Rapid Application Development Tools*). Seam Gen closely resembles the tools available in Ruby on Rails. It supports features such as generating complete CRUD applications from a database, quick developer turnaround for web applications via the edit/save/reload browser actions, testing support, and more.

But more importantly, Seam Gen-generated projects work out of the box with leading Java IDEs such as Eclipse and NetBeans. With Seam Gen, you can get started with Seam in no time.

1.10. Let's Start Coding!

In a nutshell, Seam simplifies the developer overhead for Java EE applications and, at the same time, adds powerful new features beyond Java EE 5.0. But do not take our word for it. Starting with the next chapter, we show you some real code examples to illustrate how Seam works.

You can find the source code download for all example applications in the book from the book's web site `http://www.michaelyuan.com/seam/`.

2

Seam Hello World

The most basic and widely used functionality of JBoss Seam is to be the glue between EJB3 and JSF. Seam allows seamless (no pun intended!) integration between the two frameworks through managed components. It extends the EJB3 annotated Plain Old Java Objects (POJO) programming model to the entire web application. There's no more artificially required JNDI lookup, verbose JSF backing bean declaration, excessive facade business methods, or painstakingly passing objects between tiers.

> **Continue to Use Java EE Patterns in Seam**
>
> In traditional Java EE applications, some design patterns, such as JNDI lookup, XML declaration of components, value objects, and business facade, are mandatory. Seam eliminates those artificial requirements with annotated POJOs. However, you are still free to use those patterns when your Seam applications truly need them.

Writing a Seam web application is conceptually very simple. You just need to code the following components:

- Entity objects represent the data model. The entity objects could be entity beans in the Java Persistence API (JPA, a.k.a. EJB3 persistence) or Hibernate POJOs. They are automatically mapped to relational database tables.

- JSF web pages display the user interface. The pages capture user input via forms and display result data. The data fields on the page are mapped to the backend data model via the JSF Expression Language (EL).

- EJB3 session beans or annotated Seam POJOs act as UI event handlers for the JSF web pages. They update the data model based on the user input.

Seam manages all these components and automatically injects them into the right pages/objects at runtime. For instance, when the user clicks a button to submit a JSF form, Seam automatically parses the form fields and constructs an entity bean. Then Seam passes the entity bean into the event handler session bean, which Seam also creates, for processing. You do not need to manage component lifecycles and relationships between components in your own code. There is no boilerplate code and no XML file for dependency management.

In this chapter, we use a Hello World example to show exactly how Seam glues together a web application. The example application works like this: The user can enter her name on a web form to "say hello" to Seam. After she submits this, the application saves her name to a relational database and displays all the users who have said hello to Seam. The example project is in the `helloworld` folder in the source code download for this book. To build it, you must have Apache ANT 1.6+ (`http://ant.apache.org/`) installed. Enter the `helloworld` directory and run the command `ant`. The build result is the `build/jars/helloworld.ear` file, which you can directly copy into your JBoss AS instance's `server/default/deploy` directory. Now start JBoss AS; the application is available at the URL `http://localhost:8080/helloworld/`.

Install JBoss AS

To run examples in the book, we recommend that you use the JBoss Enterprise Middleware Suite (JEMS) GUI installer to install a Seam-compatible version of JBoss AS. You can download the JEMS installer from `http://labs.jboss.com/portal/jemsinstaller/downloads`. Refer to Appendix A, *Installing and Deploying JBoss AS*, if you need further help on JBoss AS installation and application deployment.

You are welcome to use the sample application as a template to jump-start your own Seam projects (see Appendix B, *Using Example Applications as Templates*). Or you can use the command-line tool Seam Gen (see Chapter 4, *Rapid Application Development Tools*) to automatically generate project templates, including all configuration files, for you. In this chapter, we do not spend much time explaining the details of the directory structure in the source code project. Instead, we focus on the code and configuration artifacts a developer must write or manage to build a Seam application. This way, you can apply the knowledge to any project structure without being confined to our template.

> **Source Code Directories**
>
> A Seam application consists of Java classes and XML/text configuration files. In the book's example projects, the Java source code files are in the `src` directory, the web pages are in the `view` directory, and all configuration files are in the `resources` directory. See more in Appendix B, *Using Example Applications as Templates*.

2.1. Create a Data Model

The data model in the Hello World application is simply a `Person` class with a `name` and an `id` property. The `@Entity` annotation tells the container to map this class to a relational database table, with each property a column in the table. Each `Person` instance corresponds to a row of data in the table. Because Seam is "configuration by exception," the container simply uses the class name property name for the table name and column name. The `@Id` and `@GeneratedValue` annotations on the `id` property indicate that the `id` column is for the primary key and that the application server automatically generates its value for each `Person` object saved into the database.

```
@Entity
@Name("person")
public class Person implements Serializable {

  private long id;
  private String name;

  @Id @GeneratedValue
  public long getId() { return id;}
  public void setId(long id) { this.id = id; }

  public String getName() { return name; }
  public void setName(String name) {
    this.name = name;
  }
}
```

The most important annotation in the `Person` class is the `@Name` annotation. It specifies the string name the `Person` bean should be registered by under Seam. In other Seam components (e.g., JSF web pages and session beans), you can reference the managed `Person` bean for this component using the `person` name.

2.2. Map the Data Model to a Web Form

In the JSF page, we use the `Person` bean to back the form input text field. The `#{person.name}` symbol refers to the `name` property on the Seam component named `person`, which is an instance of the `Person` entity bean as we just discussed. The `#{...}` notation to reference Java objects is called JSF Expression Language (EL). It is widely used in Seam.

```
<h:form>
Please enter your name:<br/>
<h:inputText value="#{person.name}" size="15"/><br/>
<h:commandButton type="submit" value="Say Hello"
                 action="#{manager.sayHello}"/>
</h:form>
```

Below the entry form, the JSF page displays all people who have said "hello" to Seam in the database. The list of people is stored in a Seam component named `fans`. The `fans` component is a `List <Person>` object. The JSF `dataTable` iterates through the list and displays each `Person` object in a row. The `fan` symbol is the iterator for the `fans` list. Figure 2.1., "The Hello World web page" shows the web page.

```
<h:dataTable value="#{fans}" var="fan">
  <h:column>
    <h:outputText value="#{fan.name}"/>
  </h:column>
</h:dataTable>
```

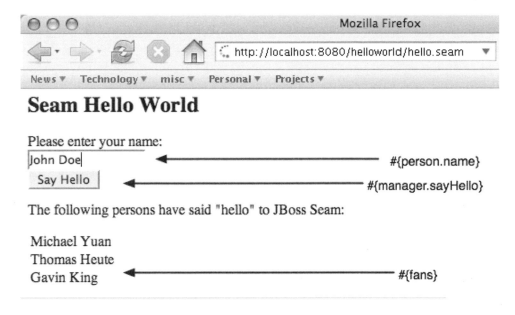

Figure 2.1. The Hello World web page

When the user clicks on the Say Hello button to submit the form, Seam creates the `person` managed component with the input data. It then invokes the `sayHello()` method on the Seam component named `manager` (i.e., EL notation `#{manager.sayHello}` references the UI event handler for the form submit button), which saves the `person` object to the database and refreshes the `fans` list. The `manager` component is an EJB3 session bean, which we discuss in the next section.

2.3. Handle Web Events

The `manager` component in Seam is the `ManagerAction` session bean, as specified by the `@Name` annotation on the class. The `ManagerAction` class has `person` and `fans` fields annotated with the `@In` and `@Out` annotations.

```
@Stateless
@Name("manager")
public class ManagerAction implements Manager {

  @In @Out
  private Person person;
```

```
@Out
private List <Person> fans;
```

The @In and @Out annotations are at the heart of the Seam programming model. Let's look at exactly what they do here.

- The @In annotation tells Seam to assign the person component, which is composed from the JSF form data, to the person field (dependency injection) before executing any method in the session bean. You can specify an arbitrary name for the injected component in @In(value="anyname"). But if no name is specified, as it is here, Seam just injects the component with the same type and same name as the receiving field variable.

- The @Out annotations tell Seam to assign values of the fans and person fields to the managed components of the same names after any method execution. We call this action dependency outjection in Seam. This way, in the ManagerAction.sayHello() method, we simply need to update the fans and person field values to make them automatically available on the web page.

> **What is Bijection**
>
> Seam documentation sometimes includes the term bijection. That refers to the two-way injection and outjection interaction between Seam components and the Seam managed context.

Because the person field already contains the form data via injection, the sayHello() method simply saves it to the database via the JPA EntityManager, which is injected via the @PersistenceContext annotation. Then it refreshes the fans and person objects, which are outjected after the method exits. The sayHello() method returns null to indicate that the current JSF page will be redisplayed with the most up-to-date model data after the call.

```
@PersistenceContext
private EntityManager em;

public String sayHello () {
   em.persist (person);
   person = new Person ();
```

```
    fans = em.createQuery("select p from Person p")
        .getResultList();
    return null;
}
```

We're almost done, except for one little thing. As you probably noticed, the `ManagerAction` bean class implements the `Manager` interface. To conform to the EJB3 session bean specification, we need an interface that lists all public methods in the bean. The following is the code for the `Manager` interface. Fortunately, it is easy to automatically generate this interface from any modern IDE tool.

```
@Local
public interface Manager {
  public String sayHello ();
}
```

That's all the code you need for the Hello World example. In the next two sections, we cover alternative ways to do things and the configuration of Seam applications. You can skip the rest of the chapter for now if you want to jump right into the code and customize the `hello-world` project for your own small database application.

2.4. More on the Seam Programming Model

Now we have rushed through the Hello World example application. But we have left off some important topics, such as alternative ways to do things and important features not covered by the previous code. In this section, we go through those topics; they help you gain a deeper understanding of Seam. But for the impatient, you can skip this section and come back later.

2.4.1. Seam POJO Components

In the previous example, we used an EJB3 session bean to implement the application logic. But we're not limited to using EJB3 components in Seam. In fact, in Seam, any POJO with an `@Name` annotation can be turned into a managed component.

For instance, we can make `ManagerAction` a POJO instead of an EJB3 session bean.

```
@Name("manager")
public class ManagerAction {

  @In (create=true)
  private EntityManager em;


  ... ...
}
```

Using POJOs to replace EJB3 beans has pros and cons. POJOs are slightly simpler to program because they do not require EJB3-specific annotations and interfaces (see preceding code listing). If all your business components are Seam POJOs, you can run your Seam application outside the EJB3 application server (see Chapter 24, *Seam Without EJB3*).

However, POJOs also have fewer features than EJB3 components because POJOs cannot get EJB3 container services. Examples of EJB3 services that you lose in non-EJB3 Seam POJOs include the following.

• The `@PersistenceContext` injection no longer works in POJOs. To obtain an `EntityManager` in a Seam POJO, you must initialize the `EntityManager` in the Seam configuration file and then use the Seam `@In` annotation to inject it into the POJO. See Chapter 24, *Seam Without EJB3*, for more details.

• No support exists for declarative method-level transaction in POJOs. Instead, you can configure Seam to demarcate a database transaction from when the web request is received until the response page is rendered. See Section 9.3., "Atomic Conversation (Web Transaction)" for more details.

• Seam POJOs cannot be message-driven components.

• No support for `@Asynchronous` methods exists.

• No support for container managed security exists.

• No transaction or component level persistence context exists. All persistence contexts in Seam POJOs are "extended" (see Section 7.1., "The Default Conversation Scope" for more details).

- No integration into the container's management architecture (ie. JMX console services) exists.

- No Java remoting (RMI) into Seam POJO methods exists.

- Seam POJOs cannot be `@WebService` components.

- No JCA integration exists.

So why would anyone want to use POJO components when deploying in an EJB3 container? Well, POJO components are good for pure "business logic" components, which delegate data access, messaging, and other infrastructure functionalities to other components. For instance, we can use POJO components to manage Seam data access objects, discussed in Chapter 13, *The Seam CRUD Application Framework*. The "business logic" POJO is useful because it can be reused in other frameworks. But the application of POJO components is much smaller than EJB3 components, especially in small to middle-size applications. So in most examples throughout this book, we use EJB3 components.

2.4.2. Seam Built-in Components

Aside from named application components (i.e., classes with `@Name` annotation), Seam maintains a set of built-in components to provide the application access to the runtime context and infrastructure. The `@In` annotation injects Seam's built-in components, and the JSF EL enables you to reference Seam built-in components from a web page.

For instance, the Seam `FacesMessages` component provides access to the JSF messages (displayed by the `<h:messages>` tags) in the current JSF context. You can inject the `FacesMessages` component into any Seam component.

```
@Name("manager")
public class ManagerAction implements manager {

  @In
  Person person;

  @In
  FacesMessages facesMessages;

  public String sayHello () {

    try {
    // ... ...
```

```
    } catch (Exception e) {
      facesMessages.add(
          "Has problem saving #{person.name}");
      return null;
    }
    ... ...
  }
}
```

Another example is the Seam conversation list component, which gives the user an easy way to switch between workspaces. All you need is to reference the #{conversationList} component from the web page. See Chapter 8, *Workspaces and Concurrent Conversations*, for more details.

You can initialize and configure Seam built-in components in the components.xml file. We discuss configuration files later in this chapter, and you can see more elaborate component configuration examples in Chapter 13, *The Seam CRUD Application Framework*, and Chapter 24, *Seam Without EJB3*.

2.4.3. Ease of Testing

As we mentioned in Chapter 1, *What Is Seam?*, Seam was built from ground up to enable easy and out-of-the-container testing. In the helloworld example project, we included two test cases, for unit testing and integrated JSF testing respectively, in the test folder. The Seam testing infrastructure mocks the database, JSF, Seam context, and other application server services in plain Java SE environment. Just run ant test to run those tests. To learn more about how to test Seam applications, refer to Chapter 21, *Unit Testing*, and Chapter 22, *Integration Testing*.

2.4.4. Getter/Setter-Based Bijection

In the Hello World example, we demonstrated how to biject Seam components against field variables. You can also biject components against getter and setter methods. For instance, the following code would work just fine.

```
private Person person;
private List <Person> fans;
```

```
@In
public void setPerson (Person person) {
  this.person = person;
}
@Out
public Person getPerson () {
  return person;
}
@Out
public List <Person> getFans () {
  return fans;
}
```

Although these getter/setter methods are trivial, the real value of bijection via getter/setter methods is that you can add custom logic to manipulate the bijection process. For instance, you can validate the injected object or retrieve the outjected object on the fly from the database.

2.4.5. Avoid Excessive Bijection

Dependency bijection is a very useful design pattern. However, as with any other design pattern, there is always a danger of overusing it. Too much dependency bijection can make the code harder to read because the developer must mentally figure out where each component is injected from. Too much bijection could also add performance overhead because the bijection happens at runtime.

In the Hello World example, there's a simple way to reduce and even eliminate the bijection: Just make the data components properties of the business component. This way, in the JSF pages, we need only reference the business component; no bijection is needed to tie together the business and data components. For instance, we can change the `ManagerAction` class to the following.

```
@Stateless
@Name("manager")
public class ManagerAction implements Manager {

  private Person person;
  public Person getPerson () {return person;}
  public void setPerson (Person person) {
    this.person = person;
  }
```

```
    private List <Person> fans;
    public List<Person> getFans () {return fans;}

    ... ...
}
```

Then, on the web page, we reference the bean properties as follows.

```
<h:form>
Please enter your name:<br/>
<h:inputText value="#{manager.person.name}"/>
<br/>
<h:commandButton type="submit" value="Say Hello"
                 action="#{manager.sayHello}"/>
</h:form>
... ...
<h:dataTable value="#{manager.fans}" var="fan">
  <h:column>
    <h:outputText value="#{fan.name}"/>
  </h:column>
</h:dataTable>
```

The bottom line is that Seam is versatile when it comes to dependency management. It's generally a good practice to encapsulate the data component within its data access component. This is especially the case for stateful business components (see more in Section 6.1.2., "Stateful Session Bean").

2.4.6. Page Navigation in JSF

In this example, we have a single-page application. After each button click, JSF rerenders the page with updated data model values. Obviously, most web applications have more than one page. In JSF, an UI event handler method can determine which page to display next by returning the string name of a navigation rule. For instance, you can define the following navigation rule in the `navigation.xml` file (see Section 2.5., "Configuration and Packaging").

```
<navigation-case>
  <from-outcome>anotherPage</from-outcome>
  <to-view-id>/anotherPage.jsp</to-view-id>
</navigation-case>
```

Then if the `sayHello()` method returns the string value `anotherPage`, JSF would display the `anotherPage.jsp` page next. This gives us programmatic control over which page to display next from inside the UI event handler method. For a more detailed example, see Section 6.2., "Page Navigation Flow", or refer to the JSF documentation.

2.4.7. Access Database via the EntityManager

The Java Persistence API (JPA, a.k.a. EJB3 Entity Bean Persistence) `EntityManager` manages the mapping between relational database tables and entity bean objects. The `EntityManager` is created by the application server at runtime. You can inject an `EntityManager` instance using the `@PersistenceContext` annotation.

The `EntityManager.persist()` method saves an entity bean object as a row in its mapped relational table. The `EntityManager.query()` method runs an SQL-like query to retrieve data from the database in the form of a collection of entity bean objects. Refer to the JPA documentation for more on how to use the `EntityManager` and the query language. In this book, we only use the simplest queries.

By default, the `EntityManager` saves data to the embedded HSQL database. If you are running the application in JBoss AS on the local machine, you can open a GUI console for the HSQL database via the following steps: Go to the page `http://localhost:8080/jmx-console/`, click on the `database=localDB,service=Hypersonic` MBean, and then click on the Invoke button under the `startDatabaseManager` method. You can execute any SQL commands against the database from the console. See Chapter 26, *Using a Production Database*, for how to use databases other than the HSQL with your Seam application.

2.5. Configuration and Packaging

Next, let's move on to configuration files and application packaging. You can actually generate almost all the configuration files and build script via the Seam Gen command-line utility (see Chapter 4, *Rapid Application Development Tools*), or you can simply reuse the ones in the sample application source project (see Appendix B, *Using Example Applications as Templates*). So if you want to learn Seam programming techniques first and worry about configuration/deployment later, that's fine. *You can safely skip this section and come back later when you need it.*

In this section, we focus on the Seam EJB3 component configuration. For Seam POJO configuration (and to potentially deploy outside JBoss AS), see Chapter 24, *Seam Without EJB3*. Most Seam configuration files are XML files. But wait! Hadn't we just promised that Seam would get us out of the XML hell in J2EE and Spring? Why does it have XML files, too? Well, as it turns out, XML files have some good uses. XML files are good for deployment time configuration (e.g., the root URL of the web application and the location of the back-end database) because they enable us to make deploy-time changes without changing and recompiling the code. They're also good for gluing together different subsystems in the application server (e.g., to configure how JSF components interact with Seam EJB3 components), and they're good for presentation-related content (e.g., web page and page-navigation flow).

What we try to avoid is replicating information that already exists in the Java source code to XML files. We do not want to repeat the same information in both Java source code and XML files. We just need one place to express the information so that it is easier to maintain. As you will soon see, this simple Seam application has several XML configuration files. All of them are very short, and none concerns information that is already available in the Java code. In other words, no "XML code" exists in Seam.

Furthermore, most content in those XML files is fairly static, so you can easily reuse those files for your own Seam applications. Refer to Appendix B, *Using Example Applications as Templates*, for instructions on how to use the sample application as a template for your own applications.

We use the next several pages to detail the configuration files and packaging structure of the sample application. If you are impatient and are happy with the application template, you can skip those.

JBoss AS 4.2.x and 5.x

The information given in this section applies to deployment in JBoss AS 4.0.5. For JBoss AS 4.2.x and 5.x., see changes you need to make in Section 23.2., "JBoss AS 4.2.x and 5.x".

Without further ado, let's look into how the Hello World example application is configured and packaged. To build a deployable Seam application for JBoss AS, we have to package all the previous Java classes and configuration files in an Enterprise Application aRchive (EAR) file. In this example, the EAR file is `helloworld.ear`. It contains three JAR files and two XML configuration files.

```
helloworld.ear
|+ app.war        // Contains web pages etc.
|+ app.jar        // Contains Seam components
|+ jboss-seam.jar // The Seam library
|+ META-INF
   |+ application.xml
   |+ jboss-app.xml
```

> **Source Code Directories**
>
> In the source code project, thc `resources/WEB-INF` directory contains the configuration files that go into `app.war/WEB-INF`, the `resources/META-INF` directory contains files that go into `app.jar/META-INF` and `helloworld.ear/META-INF`, the `resources` directory root has files that go into the root directory of `app.jar`. See more in Appendix B, *Using Example Applications as Templates*.

The `application.xml` file lists the JAR files in the EAR and specifies the root URL for this application.

```
<application>
  <display-name>Seam Hello World</display-name>

  <module>
    <web>
      <web-uri>app.war</web-uri>
      <context-root>/helloworld</context-root>
    </web>
  </module>

  <module>
    <ejb>app.jar</ejb>
  </module>

  <module>
    <java>jboss-seam.jar</java>
  </module>

</application>
```

The `jboss-app.xml` file specifies the class loader for this application. Each EAR application should have a unique string name for the class loader. Here, we use the application name in the class loader name to avoid potential conflicts (see Appendix B, *Using Example Applications as Templates* for more on this).

```
<jboss-app>
  <loader-repository>
    helloworld:archive=helloworld.ear
  </loader-repository>
</jboss-app>
```

The `jboss-seam.jar` file is the Seam library JAR file from the Seam distribution. The `app.war` and `app.jar` files are built by us; let's look them next.

2.5.1. The WAR File

The `app.war` file is a JAR file packaged to the Web Application aRchive (WAR) specification. It contains the web pages as well as standard JSF/Seam configuration files. You can also put JSF-specific library files in the `WEB-INF/lib` directory (e.g., the `jboss-seam-ui.jar` — see Chapter 7, *Conversations*).

```
app.war
|+ hello.jsp
|+ index.html
|+ WEB-INF
   |+ web.xml
   |+ faces-config.xml
   |+ components.xml
   |+ navigation.xml
```

All Java EE web applications require the `web.xml` file. JSF uses it to configure the JSF controller servlet and Seam uses it to intercept all web requests. The configuration in this file is pretty standard.

```
<web-app version="2.4"
    xmlns="http://java.sun.com/xml/ns/j2ee"
    xmlns:xsi="..."
```

```
    xsi:schemaLocation="...">

  <!-- Seam -->
  <listener>
    <listener-class>
      org.jboss.seam.servlet.SeamListener
    </listener-class>
  </listener>

  <!-- MyFaces -->
  <listener>
    <listener-class>
org.apache.myfaces.webapp.StartupServletContextListener
    </listener-class>
  </listener>

  <context-param>
    <param-name>
      javax.faces.STATE_SAVING_METHOD
    </param-name>
    <param-value>client</param-value>
  </context-param>

  <servlet>
    <servlet-name>Faces Servlet</servlet-name>
    <servlet-class>
      javax.faces.webapp.FacesServlet
    </servlet-class>
    <load-on-startup>1</load-on-startup>
  </servlet>

  <!-- Faces Servlet Mapping -->
  <servlet-mapping>
    <servlet-name>Faces Servlet</servlet-name>
    <url-pattern>*.seam</url-pattern>
  </servlet-mapping>

  <context-param>
    <param-name>javax.faces.CONFIG_FILES</param-name>
    <param-value>/WEB-INF/navigation.xml</param-value>
  </context-param>

</web-app>
```

The `faces-config.xml` file is a standard configuration file for JSF. Seam uses it to add the Seam interceptor into the JSF lifecycle.

```
<faces-config>
  <lifecycle>
```

```
     <phase-listener>
        org.jboss.seam.jsf.SeamPhaseListener
     </phase-listener>
   </lifecycle>
</faces-config>
```

The `navigation.xml` file contains JSF page navigation rules for multipage applications. Because the Hello World example has only a single page, this file is empty here (see Section 6.2., "Page Navigation Flow", for more on this).

The `components.xml` file contains Seam-specific configuration options. It is also pretty much application-independent with the exception of the `jndi-pattern` property, which must include the EAR file's base name for Seam to access EJB3 beans by their full JNDI name.

```
<components ...>

  <core:init
    jndi-pattern="helloworld/#{ejbName}/local"
    debug="false"/>

  <core:manager conversation-timeout="120000"/>

</components>
```

2.5.2. The Seam Components JAR

The `app.jar` file contains all EJB3 bean classes (both entity beans and session beans), as well as EJB3-related configuration files.

```
app.jar
|+ Person.class        // entity bean
|+ Manager.class       // session bean interface
|+ ManagerAction.class // session bean
|+ seam.properties     // empty file but needed
|+ META-INF
   |+ ejb-jar.xml
   |+ persistence.xml
```

The `seam.properties` file is empty here but it is required. The Seam runtime searches for this file in all JAR files. If it is found, Seam would load the classes in the corresponding JAR file and process all the Seam annotations.

The `ejb-jar.xml` file contains extra configurations that can override or supplement the annotations on EJB3 beans. In a Seam application, it adds the Seam interceptor to all EJB3 classes. We can reuse the same file for all Seam applications.

```
<ejb-jar>
  <assembly-descriptor>
    <interceptor-binding>
      <ejb-name>*</ejb-name>
      <interceptor-class>
        org.jboss.seam.ejb.SeamInterceptor
      </interceptor-class>
    </interceptor-binding>
  </assembly-descriptor>
</ejb-jar>
```

The `persistence.xml` file configures the back-end database source for the `EntityManager`. In this example, we just use the default HSQL database embedded inside JBoss AS (i.e., the `java:/DefaultDS` data source). Refer to Chapter 26, *Using a Production Database*, for more details on this file and how to change to another database backend (e.g., MySQL).

```
<persistence>
  <persistence-unit name="helloworld">
    <provider>
      org.hibernate.ejb.HibernatePersistence
    </provider>
    <jta-data-source>java:/DefaultDS</jta-data-source>
    <properties>
      <property name="hibernate.dialect"
          value="org.hibernate.dialect.HSQLDialect"/>
      <property name="hibernate.hbm2ddl.auto"
          value="create-drop"/>
      <property name="hibernate.show_sql"
          value="true"/>
    </properties>
  </persistence-unit>
</persistence>
```

So that's all the configuration and packaging a simple Seam application needs. We cover more configuration options and library files as we move to more advanced topics in this book. Again, the simplest way to start your Seam application is not to worry about those configuration files at all and start from a ready-made application template (see Chapter 4, *Rapid Application Development Tools*, or Appendix B, *Using Example Applications as Templates*).

2.6. How Is This Simple?

That's it for the Hello World application. With three simple Java classes, a JSF page, and a bunch of largely static configuration files, we have a complete database-driven web application. The entire application requires fewer than 30 lines of Java code and no "XML code." However, if you are coming from a PHP background, you might still be asking, "How is this simple? I can do that in PHP with less code!"

Well, the answer is that Seam applications are conceptually much simpler than PHP (or any other scripting language) applications. The Seam component model enables us to add more functionalities to the application in a controlled and maintainable manner. As you will soon see, Seam components make it a breeze to develop stateful and transactional web applications. The object-relational mapping framework (i.e., entity beans) enables us to focus on the abstract data model without having to deal with database-specific SQL statements.

In the rest of this book, we discuss how to develop increasingly complex Seam applications using Seam components. In the next chapter, we start with improving the Hello World example with Facelets and Seam UI libraries.

3

Recommended JSF Enhancements

The Hello World example in Chapter 2, *Seam Hello World*, demonstrates how to build a Seam application on standard EJB3 and JSF. Seam chooses JSF for its "web framework" for many reasons. JSF is the standard technology in Java EE 5.0 and has a large ecosystem of users and vendors. All Java application servers support it. JSF is fully component based and has a vibrant vendor community for components. JSF also has a powerful and unified expression language (EL—e.g., the #{...} notation) that can be used in web pages, work flow description, and component configuration files throughout the application. JSF also has great support for visual GUI tools in leading Java IDEs.

However, JSF also has its share of problems and awkwardness. JSF has been criticized for being too verbose and too "component centric" (i.e., not transparent to HTTP requests). Being a standard framework, JSF innovates more slowly than grass-root open source projects such as Seam itself and, hence, is less agile when it comes to correcting design issues and adding new features. As such, Seam works with other open source projects to improve and enhance JSF. For Seam applications, we strongly recommend that you use the following JSF enhancements.

- Use the Facelets framework for web pages. Write your web pages in Facelets XHTML files instead of JSP files. Facelets provides many benefits over the standard JSP in JSF. Please see Section 3.1.1., "Why Facelets?" for more details.

- Use the Seam JSF component library for special JSF tags that take advantage of Seam-specific UI features, as well as Seam's extended EL for JSF.

- Setup Seam filters to capture and manage JSF redirect, error messages, debugging information etc.

Throughout the rest of the book, we assume that you already have these three JSF enhancements installed and enabled (see Section 3.3., "Add Facelets and Seam UI Support" for instructions). In Section 7.1., "The Default Conversation Scope", we explain how Seam supports lazy loading in JSF page rendering and expands the use of JSF messages beyond simple error messages. In Part III, "Integrating Web and Data Components", we cover how to integrate the data components directly into the JSF web pages. Such direct integration allows Seam to add important features to JSF, such as end-to-end validators (see Chapter 10, *Validating Input Data*), easy-to-use data tables (see Chapter 11, *Clickable Data Tables*), bookmarkable URLs (see Chapter 12, *Bookmarkable Web Pages*), and custom error pages (see Chapter 14, *Failing Gracefully*). In Part IV, "AJAX Support", we discuss how to incorporate third-party AJAX UI widgets in Seam applications. In Chapter 19, *Stateful Pageflows*, we discuss how to use the jBPM business process to manage pageflows in JSF/Seam applications. This enables us to use EL expressions in page navigation rules and have navigation rules that are dependent on the application state.

In this chapter, we first explain how those additional frameworks improve your JSF development experience. We show you how to develop applications with Facelets and Seam UI libraries. Then in Section 3.3., "Add Facelets and Seam UI Support", we list changes you need to make from the Hello World example to support the Facelets and Seam UI components. The new example is in the `betterjsf` project in the book's source code bundle. Feel free to use it as a starting point for your own applications.

3.1. An Introduction to Facelets

JavaServer Pages (JSP) is the de-facto "view" technology in JavaServer Faces (JSF). In a standard JSF application, the web pages containing JSF tags and visual components are typically authored in JSP files. However, JSP is not the only choice for authoring JSF web pages. An open source project called Facelets (`https://facelets.dev.java.net/`) enables us to write JSF web pages in XHTML files with significantly improved page readability, developer productivity, and runtime performance, compared with equivalent pages authored in JSP. Although Facelets is not yet a Java Community Process (JCP) standard, we highly recommend that you use it in your Seam applications whenever possible.

3.1.1. Why Facelets?

First, Facelets improves JSF performance by 30 percent to 50 percent by bypassing the JSP engine and using XHTML pages directly as the view technology. By avoiding JSP, Facelets also avoids potential conflicts between JSF 1.1 and JSP 2.4 specifications, which are the specifications supported in JBoss AS 4.x (see the accompanying sidebar for more).

The Potential Conflict between JSF and JSP

In our Hello World series of examples, we used JSP files (e.g., the `hello.jsp` file) to create the web pages in the JSF application. The JSP container processes those files at the same time they are processed by the JSF engine. That raises some potential conflicts between the JSP 2.0 container and JSF 1.1 runtime in JBoss AS 4.x. For a detailed explanation of the problems and examples, refer to Hans Bergsten's excellent article "Improving JSF by Dumping JSP" (see `www.onjava.com/pub/a/onjava/2004/06/09/jsf.html`).

Those conflicts are resolved in JBoss AS 5.x, which supports JSP 2.1+ and JSF 1.2+. But if you need to use JBoss 4.x for now, the best solution is to avoid JSP altogether and use Facelets instead.

Second, you can use any XHTML tags in Facelets pages. It eliminates the need to enclose XHTML tags and free text in the `f:verbatim` tags. The `f:verbatim` tags are tedious to write and they make JSP-based JSF pages hard to read.

Third, Facelets provides nice debugging support from the browser. If an error occurs when Facelets renders a page, it gives you the exact location of that error in the source file and provides context information around the error (see Section 14.5., "Debug Information Page"). It is much nicer than digging into stack trace when a JSP/JSF error occurs.

Last, and perhaps more important, Facelets provides a template framework for JSF. With Facelets, you can use a Seam-like dependency injection model to assemble pages, instead of manually including page header, footer, and sidebar components in each page.

The Case for JSP

If Facelets is this good, why do we bother to use JSP with JSF at all? Well, JSP is a standard technology in the Java EE stack, whereas Facelets is not yet a standard. That means JSP is supported everywhere, while Facelets might have integration issues with third-party JSF components. In the meantime, the JSP spec committee is certainly learning lessons from Facelets. The next-generation JSPs will work a lot better with JSF.

3.1.2. A Facelets Hello World

As we discussed, the basic Facelets XHTML page is not all that different from the equivalent JSP pages. To illustrate this point, we ported the Hello World sample application (see Chapter 2, *Seam Hello World*) from JSP to Facelets. The new application is in the `betterjsf` project. Below is the JSP version of the `hello.jsp` page.

```
<%@ taglib uri="http://java.sun.com/jsf/html" prefix="h" %>
<%@ taglib uri="http://java.sun.com/jsf/core" prefix="f" %>

<html>
<body>
<f:view>

<f:verbatim>
<h2>Seam Hello World</h2>
</f:verbatim>

<h:form>
<f:verbatim>
Please enter your name:<br/>
</f:verbatim>

<h:inputText value="#{person.name}" size="15"/><br/>
<h:commandButton type="submit" value="Say Hello"
                 action="#{manager.sayHello}"/>
</h:form>

<f:subview id="fans"
           rendered="#{!empty(fans)}">
<f:verbatim>
<p>The following fans have said "hello" to JBoss Seam:</p>
</f:verbatim>

<h:dataTable value="#{fans}" var="fan">
  <h:column>
    <h:outputText value="#{fan.name}"/>
  </h:column>
</h:dataTable>
</f:subview>

</f:view>
</body>
</html>
```

Now, let's compare it with the Facelets XHTML version of the `hello.xhtml` page.

```
<html xmlns="http://www.w3.org/1999/xhtml"
        xmlns:ui="http://java.sun.com/jsf/facelets"
        xmlns:h="http://java.sun.com/jsf/html"
      xmlns:f="http://java.sun.com/jsf/core">
<body>

<h2>Seam Hello World</h2>

<h:form>
Please enter your name:<br/>
<h:inputText value="#{person.name}" size="15"/>
<br/>
<h:commandButton type="submit" value="Say Hello"
                 action="#{manager.sayHello}"/>
</h:form>

<f:subview id="fans"
           rendered="#{!empty(fans)}">
<p>The following fans have said "hello"
     to JBoss Seam:</p>
<h:dataTable value="#{fans}" var="fan">
  <h:column>
    <h:outputText value="#{fan.name}"/>
  </h:column>
</h:dataTable>
</f:subview>

</body>
</html>
```

It is pretty obvious that the Facelets XHTML page is cleaner and easier to read than the JSP page since the XHTML page does not get cluttered up with `<f:verbatim>` tags. The namespace declaration in the Facelets XHTML page conforms to the XHTML standard. But other than that, the two pages look similar. All the JSF component tags are identical.

3.1.3. Use Facelets as a Template Engine

For most developers, the ability to use XHTML templates is probably the most appealing feature of Facelets. Let's see how it works.

A typical web application consists of multiple web pages with a common layout. They typically have the same header, footer, and sidebar menu. Without a template engine, you must repeat all those elements in each page. That's a lot of duplicated code with complex HTML formatting tags. Worse, if you need to make a small change to any of the elements (e.g., change a word in the header), you have to edit all pages. From all we know about the software-development processes, this type of copy-and-paste editing is very inefficient and error prone.

The solution, of course, is to abstract out the layout information into a single source and, hence, avoid the spread and duplication of the same information on multiple pages. In Facelets, the template page is a single source of layout information. The `template.xhtml` file in the Seam Hotel Booking example (the `booking` project in source code) is a template page.

```
<html xmlns="http://www.w3.org/1999/xhtml"
    xmlns:ui="http://java.sun.com/jsf/facelets"
    xmlns:h="http://java.sun.com/jsf/html">
<head>
  <title>JBoss Suites: Seam Framework</title>
  <link href="css/screen.css"
        rel="stylesheet" type="text/css" />
</head>
<body>

<div id="document">
  <div id="header">
    <div id="title">...</div>
    <div id="status">
      ... Settings and Log in/out ...
    </div>
  </div>
  <div id="container">
    <div id="sidebar">
      <ui:insert name="sidebar"/>
    </div>
    <div id="content">
      <ui:insert name="content"/>
    </div>
  </div>
  <div id="footer">...</div>
</div>
</body>
</html>
```

The `template.xhtml` file defines the layout of the page header, footer, sidebar, and main content area (see Figure 3.1., "The template layout"). Obviously, the sidebar and main content area have different contents for each page, so we use the `<ui:insert>` tags as placeholders in the template. In each Facelets page, we tag UI elements accordingly to tell the engine how to fill contents into the template placeholders.

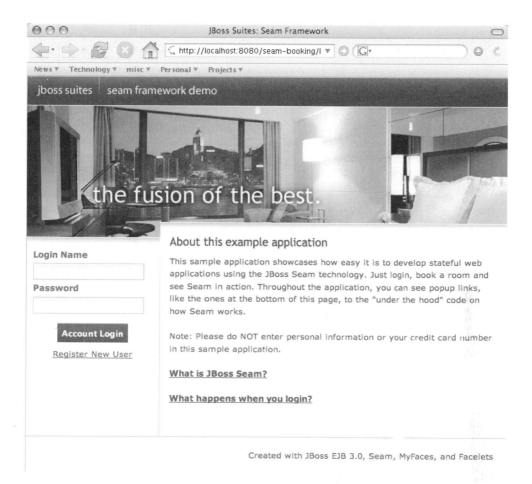

Figure 3.1. The template layout

Multiple Template Pages

Actually, we were not entirely accurate when we mentioned that the template is a "single" source for layout knowledge in the application. Facelets is flexible in managing template pages. In a Facelets application, you can have multiple template pages for alternative themes (or for different sections) of the web site. Yet the basic idea of abstracting layout information to avoid duplicated code still applies.

> **Extensive use of CSS**
>
> All pages in the Seam Hotel Booking example, including the `template.xhtml` page, are styled using CSS. We highly recommend using CSS in Seam/Facelet applications because it's concise and easy to understand. Even more important, CSS separates the styling from the page content. With CSS, the web designer does not need to understand the JSF/Seam symbols and tags in the page.
>
> Of course, if you still prefer to use XHTML tables to lay out your page, you can still do so in the `template.xhtml` file. Just make sure that you place the `<ui:insert>` tags in the right places in the nested tables.

Each Facelets page corresponds to a web page. It "injects" contents for the `<ui:insert>` placeholders in the template. Below is the `main.xhtml` page in the Seam Hotel Booking example application.

```
<ui:composition
    xmlns="http://www.w3.org/1999/xhtml"
    xmlns:ui="http://java.sun.com/jsf/facelets"
    xmlns:h="http://java.sun.com/jsf/html"
    xmlns:f="http://java.sun.com/jsf/core"
    template="template.xhtml">

  <ui:define name="content">
    <ui:include src="conversations.xhtml" />

    <div class="section">
      <h:form>
          <h1>Search Hotels</h1>
          ... ...
      </h:form>
    </div>

    <div class="section">
      <h:dataTable value="#{hotels}" ...>
        ... ...
      </h:dataTable>
    </div>

    <div class="section">
      <h1>Current Hotel Bookings</h1>
    </div>
```

```
   <div class="section">
     <h:dataTable value="#{bookings}" ...>
       ... ...
     </h:dataTable>
   </div>
 </ui:define>

 <ui:define name="sidebar">
   <h1>Stateful and contextual components</h1>
   <p>... ...</p>
 </ui:define>

</ui:composition>
```

At the beginning of the `main.xhtml` file, the code declares that the `template.xhtml` template is used to format the layout. The `<ui:define>` elements correspond to the `<ui:insert>` placeholders of the same names in the template. You can arrange those `<ui:define>` elements in any order, and the Facelets engine renders the web pages according to the template at runtime.

3.1.4. Data List Component

One of the biggest omissions in the current JSF specification is that it lacks a standard component to iterate over a data list. The `<h:dataTable>` component displays a data list in an HTML table, but it is not a generic iteration component.

Facelets remedies this problem by providing a `<ui:repeat>` component to iterate over any data list. For instance, the following Facelets page snippet displays a list in a table-less format.

```
<ui:repeat value="#{fans} var="fan">
  <div class="faninfo">#{fan.name}</div>
</ui:repeat>
```

In Section 3.4.1., "Generate PDF Reports" and Section 3.4.2., "Template-Based Email", you will see that the Facelets `<ui:repeat>` component can be used in completely non-HTML environments.

In this section, we just scratched the surface of what Facelets can do. We encourage you to explore Facelets (`https://facelets.dev.java.net/`) and make the most out of this excellent framework.

3.2. Seam JSF Enhancements

Seam provides its own JSF enhancements that work with both Facelets XHTML and JSP pages. You can use Seam UI tags in your JSF view pages, use Seam's special extension to the JSF EL, and use the Seam filter to make Seam work better with the JSF URL redirecting and error-handling mechanisms. Those Seam JSF components work with Seam framework features not yet discussed in the book. In this section, we just provide an overview of those enhancements and leave the details to later chapters of the book. Impatient readers can safely skip to Section 3.3., "Add Facelets and Seam UI Support", for instructions on how to install those Seam JSF components.

3.2.1. Seam UI Tags

The Seam UI tags give regular JSF UI components access to Seam managed runtime information. They help integrate Seam business and data components more tightly with the web UI components. Seam UI tags can be roughly divided into the following categories.

* Validation — The Seam validation tags enable us to use Hibernate validator annotations on entity beans to validate JSF input fields. They also enable us to decorate the entire invalid (or valid) fields when the validation fails. See Chapter 10, *Validating Input Data*, for more on how use those components.

* Conversation management — A key concept in Seam is the long-running web conversation (see Chapter 7, *Conversations*). Normally, the web pages in a conversation are connected via hidden fields in HTTP POST operations. But what if you want to click on a regular hyperlink and still stay in the same conversation? Seam provides tags that can generate conversation-aware proper hyperlinks. See Section 7.2.5., "Links and Buttons", and Section 8.3., "Carry a Conversation Across Workspaces", for more.

* Business process management — Seam provides tags that can associate web page content with business processes in the background (see Chapter 18, *Managing Business Processes*).

- Performance — The `<s:cache>` tag encloses page content that should be cached on the server. When the page is rendered again, the cached region is retrieved from the cache instead of being dynamically rendered (see Chapter 27, *Performance Tuning and Clustering*).

- JSF replacement tags — Some Seam tags are a direct replacement for JSF tags to fix certain deficiencies in JSF. Right now, the only such tag is `<s:convertDateTime>`, which fixes JSF's annoying default time zone problem.

- Alternative display output — In addition to the standard HTML output, Seam provides JSF tags that render PDF and email outputs based on Facelets templates. It also provides tags to render wiki text snippets into HTML elements. Refer to Section 3.4., "PDF, Email, and Rich Text", for more details on those alternative display technologies supported by the Seam tag library.

Later chapters cover the use of these Seam UI tags when we discuss specific Seam features related to them. Here, we use the `<s:convertDateTime>` tag as an example to demonstrate how Seam UI tags are used. The `<s:convertDateTime>` tag replaces JSF's convertor tag `<f:convertDateTime>` to convert the back-end `Date` or `Time` objects to formatted output/input strings in the server's local time zone. The JSF tag is insufficient because it converts the time stamp to the UTC time zone by default. The sensible default time zone in the Seam tag makes life a lot easier for developers. To use the Seam UI tags in a web page, you need to declare the Seam taglib namespace, as follows.

```
<html xmlns:ui="http://java.sun.com/jsf/facelets"
  xmlns:h="http://java.sun.com/jsf/html"
  xmlns:f="http://java.sun.com/jsf/core"
  xmlns:s="http://jboss.com/products/seam/taglib">

... ...

The old hello date is:<br/>
<h:outputText value="#{manager.helloDate}">
    <s:convertDateTime/>
</h:outputText>

Please enter a new date:<br/>
<h:inputText value="#{manager.helloDate}">
    <s:convertDateTime/>
</h:inputText>

</html>
```

web pages from Facelets template and pages. This is the relevant snippet from the `faces-config.xml` file.

```
<faces-config>

  ... ...

  <application>
    <view-handler>
org.jboss.seam.ui.facelet.SeamFaceletViewHandler
    </view-handler>
  </application>
<faces-config>
```

Facelets and Ajax4jsf

The Ajax4jsf framework requires special configuration to avoid conflicts with the Facelets view handler. Please see Section 16.6., "Configuring Ajax4jsf", for more details.

In a Facelets application, we typically use the `.xhtml` file suffix for web pages since they are now XHTML files, not JSP pages. We have to tell the JSF runtime this change in the `web.xml` file (in the same directory as the `faces-config.xml` file).

```
<web-app>

  ... ...

  <context-param>
    <param-name>
      javax.faces.DEFAULT_SUFFIX
    </param-name>
    <param-value>.xhtml</param-value>
  </context-param>
</web-app>
```

Finally, let's set up the Seam filter and resource servlet in the same `web.xml`. The `SeamFilter` provides support for error pages, JSF redirect, and file upload. The Seam resource servlet provides access to images and CSS files in `jboss-seam-ui.jar`, which are required by Seam

UI components. The resource servlet also enables direct JavaScript access to Seam components (see Chapter 17, *Direct JavaScript Integration*).

```
<web-app>

  ... ...

  <servlet>
    <servlet-name>Seam Resource Servlet</servlet-name>
    <servlet-class>
      org.jboss.seam.servlet.ResourceServlet
    </servlet-class>
  </servlet>

  <servlet-mapping>
    <servlet-name>Seam Resource Servlet</servlet-name>
    <url-pattern>/seam/resource/*</url-pattern>
  </servlet-mapping>

  <filter>
    <filter-name>Seam Filter</filter-name>
    <filter-class>
      org.jboss.seam.web.SeamFilter
    </filter-class>
  </filter>

  <filter-mapping>
    <filter-name>Seam Filter</filter-name>
    <url-pattern>/*</url-pattern>
  </filter-mapping>

</web-app>
```

3.4. PDF, Email, and Rich Text

So far, we have discussed JSF enhancements provided by Facelets and the `jboss-seam-ui.jar` library. Those are important usability and integration features required by almost all Seam web applications. In this section, we discuss several additional UI features Seam provides. To use those features, you need to bundle more library JAR files in your application and provide extra configuration as described below. You can choose and mix the UI feature sets you want in the application while keeping the footprint/configuration complexity to a minimum.

3.4.1. Generate PDF Reports

The Facelets XHTML files generate HTML web pages by default. But a real-world web application sometimes need to generate PDF output for printer-ready documents such as reports, legal documents, tickets, receipts, etc. The Seam PDF library leverages the open source iText toolkit to generate PDF documents. Below is a simple Facelets file, `hello.xhtml`, to render a PDF document.

```
<p:document
    xmlns:p="http://jboss.com/products/seam/pdf"
    title="Hello">
  <p:chapter number="1">
    <p:title>
      <p:paragraph>Hello</p:paragraph>
    </p:title>
    <p:paragraph>Hello #{user.name}!</p:paragraph>
    <p:paragraph>The time now is
      <p:text value="#{manager.nowDate}">
        <f:convertDateTime style="date"
                           format="short"/>
      </p:text>
    </p:paragraph>
  </p:chapter>

  <p:chapter number="2">
    <p:title>
      <p:paragraph>Goodbye</p:paragraph>
    </p:title>
    <p:paragraph>Goodbye #{user.name}.</p:paragraph>
  </p:chapter>
</p:document>
```

While the `hello.xhtml` file has the `xhtml` suffix, it is really an XML file with Seam PDF UI tags. When the user loads the `hello.seam` URL, Seam generates the PDF document, and redirects the browser to `hello.pdf`. The browser then displays the `hello.pdf` file in its PDF reader plugin or prompts the user to save the PDF file. By passing the `pageSize` HTTP parameter to the URL, you can specify the page size of the generated PDF document. For instance, the `hello.seam?pageSize=LETTER` URL produces a letter-sized `hello.pdf` document. Other `pageSize` options include `A4`, `LEGAL` and more.

You can use any JSF EL expression in the `xhtml` page; the EL expressions are resolved on-the-fly when the PDF document is rendered, just as EL expressions on web pages. You can also use JSF convertors to control text formating, the `<f:facet>` tag to control table formatting, or the Facelets `<ui:repeat>` tag to render a list or PDF table from dynamic data. Refer to the Seam reference documentation for more details on the tags.

To use the Seam PDF tags, you need to include the `jboss-seam-pdf.jar` and `itext-x.y.z.jar` files in the `WEB-INF/lib` directory of your WAR application archive.

```
mywebapp.ear
|+ app.war
   |+ web pages
   |+ WEB-INF
      |+ web.xml
      |+ faces-config.xml
      |+ other config files
      |+ lib
         |+ jsf-facelets.jar
         |+ jboss-seam-ui.jar
         |+ jboss-seam-debug.jar
         |+ jboss-seam-pdf.jar
         |+ itext-x.y.z.jar
|+ app.jar
|+ el-api.jar
|+ el-ri.jar
|+ jboss-seam.jar
|+ META-INF
```

Then, you need to configure the PDF-related Seam component in the `components.xml` file. The `useExtensions` property indicates whether the `hello.seam` URL should redirect to the `hello.pdf` URL. If the `useExtensions` property is set to `false`, the redirection would not happen and the web application would serve PDF data directly to the browser from a `.seam` URL, which could cause usability problems in some browsers.

```
<components
    xmlns:pdf="http://jboss.com/products/seam/pdf"
    xmlns:core="http://jboss.com/products/seam/core">

  <pdf:documentStore useExtensions="true"/>

  ... ...

</components>
```

Finally, you need to set up servlet filters for the `.pdf` files. Those filters are only needed when you have the `useExtensions` property set to `true` in the `components.xml` configuration shown previously.

```
<web-app ...>

  ... ...

  <filter>
    <filter-name>Seam Servlet Filter</filter-name>
    <filter-class>
       org.jboss.seam.servlet.SeamServletFilter
    </filter-class>
  </filter>

  <filter-mapping>
    <filter-name>Seam Servlet Filter</filter-name>
    <url-pattern>*.pdf</url-pattern>
  </filter-mapping>

  <servlet>
    <servlet-name>
      Document Store Servlet
    </servlet-name>
    <servlet-class>
       org.jboss.seam.pdf.DocumentStoreServlet
    </servlet-class>
  </servlet>

  <servlet-mapping>
    <servlet-name>
      Document Store Servlet
    </servlet-name>
    <url-pattern>*.pdf</url-pattern>
  </servlet-mapping>
</web-app>
```

The Seam PDF library supports generating digitally signed PDF documents. The public key configuration, however, is beyond the scope of this book. Refer to the Seam reference documentation and iText documentation for more details.

3.4.2. Template-Based Email

Sending email from your web application is not hard but it can be a messy task. The standard JavaMail API requires developers to embed the email messages as literal strings inside Java code. That makes it very difficult to write rich email (i.e., HTML email with elaborate text formatting and embedded images), and makes it nearly impossible for non-developers to design and compose the email messages. The lack of design and branding in email messages is a major weakness in many web applications.

In Seam, we provide a template-based approach to handle email. A business person or a page designer writes the email as if it is a web page. Here is an example email template page `hello.xhtml`.

```
<m:message xmlns="http://www.w3.org/1999/xhtml"
    xmlns:m="http://jboss.com/products/seam/mail"
    xmlns:h="http://java.sun.com/jsf/html">
  <m:from name="Michael Yuan"
      address="myuan@redhat.com"/>
  <m:to name="#{person.firstname} #{person.lastname}">
    #{person.address}
  </m:to>
  <m:subject>Try out Seam!</m:subject>
  <m:body>
      <p>Dear #{person.firstname},</p>
      <p>You can try out Seam by visiting
      <a href="http://labs.jboss.com/jbossseam">
        http://labs.jboss.com/jbossseam
  </a>.</p>
      <p>Regards,</p>
      <p>Michael</p>
  </m:body>
</m:message>
```

When a web user needs to send out the `hello.xhtml` message, she clicks on a button or a link to invoke a Seam backing bean method to render the `hello.xhtml` page. Below is an example method to send the `hello.xhtml` email. The message recipient is dynamically determined at runtime via the `#{person.address}` EL expression. Similarly, you can dynamically determine the sender address, or any content in the message via EL expressions.

```
public class ManagerAction implements Manager {

  @In(create=true)
  private Renderer renderer;

  public void send() {
    try {
      renderer.render("/hello.xhtml");
```

```
          facesMessages.add("Email sent successfully");
      } catch (Exception e) {
          facesMessages.add("Email sending failed: "
                           + e.getMessage());
      }
   }
}
```

If a message has multiple recipients, you can repeat multiple `<m:to>` tags within the Facelets `<ui:repeat>` tag. You can also use the Facelets `<ui:insert>` tag to compose messages from a template.

To use the Seam email support tags, you first bundle the `jboss-seam-mail.jar` file in the `WEB-INF/lib` directory of your WAR archive.

```
mywebapp.ear
|+ app.war
   |+ web pages
   |+ WEB-INF
      |+ web.xml
      |+ faces-config.xml
      |+ other config files
      |+ lib
         |+ jsf-facelets.jar
         |+ jboss-seam-ui.jar
         |+ jboss-seam-debug.jar
         |+ jboss-seam-mail.jar
|+ app.jar
|+ el-api.jar
|+ el-ri.jar
|+ jboss-seam.jar
|+ META-INF
```

Then, you need to configure an SMTP server to actually send the email. That is done via the Seam `mailSession` component in `components.xml`. You can specify the host name, port number, and login credentials for the SMTP server. The following listing is an example SMTP configuration.

```
<components
    xmlns="http://jboss.com/products/seam/components"
    xmlns:core="http://jboss.com/products/seam/core"
    xmlns:mail="http://jboss.com/products/seam/mail">
```

```
    <mail:mailSession host="smtp.example.com"
                      port="25"
                      username="myuan"
                      password="mypass" />

    ... ...

</components>
```

3.4.3. Display Rich Text

A community oriented web application often needs to display user contributed content (e.g., forum posts, comments etc.). However, a big issue is how to allow rich text formatting in user contributed content. Allowing the web user to submit arbitrary HTML formatted text is out of the question, as un-sanitized HTML is insecure and prone to various cross-site scripting attacks.

One solution is to use a WYSIWYG rich text editor widget to capture user input. The widget transforms its content to sanitized HTML when the form is submitted to the server. Refer to Section 17.3.2., "Input Widgets", for more on this subject.

Another solution, which we cover here, is to provide the web user a simple set of non-HTML markup tags they can use to format the content. When the application displays the content, it automatically converts the markup to HTML tags. A popular non-HTML text markup language is Wikitext. Wikitext is widely used on wiki community sites (e.g., the `Wikipedia.com` site). The Seam `<s:formattedText>` UI component converts Wikitext to HTML formatted text. For instance, suppose that the `#{user.post}` Seam component contains the following text.

```
It's easy to make *bold text*, /italic text/,
|monospace|, -deleted text-, super^scripts^
or _underlines_.
```

UI element `<s:formattedText  value="#{user.post}"/>` would produce the following HTML text on the web page.

```
<p>
It's easy to make <b>bold text</b>,
<i>italic text</i>, <tt>monospace</tt>
<del>deleted text</del>, super<sup>scripts</sup>
or <u>underlines</u>.
</p>
```

Support for the `<s:formattedText>` tag is already included in the `jboss-seam-ui.jar` file. But it depends on the ANTLR (ANother Tool for Language Recognition, see `http://www.antlr.org/`) parser to process the Wikitext grammar. In order to use the `<s:formattedText>` tag, you need to bundle the ANTLR JAR in your WAR archive.

```
mywebapp.ear
|+ app.war
   |+ web pages
   |+ WEB-INF
      |+ web.xml
      |+ faces-config.xml
      |+ other config files
      |+ lib
         |+ jsf-facelets.jar
         |+ jboss-seam-ui.jar
         |+ jboss-seam-debug.jar
         |+ antlr-x.y.z.jar
|+ app.jar
|+ el-api.jar
|+ el-ri.jar
|+ jboss-seam.jar
|+ META-INF
```

With the ANTLR parser, Seam would potentially support other markup languages beyond the Wikitext. For instance, it might support sanitized HTML (i.e., HTML text with all potential security loopholes removed), BBCode (widely used in online forms), and others. Refer to Seam documentation for the latest update on this subject.

4

Rapid Application Development Tools

In the previous two chapters, we have seen that Seam applications are very easy to code but there are several configuration files to manage. To be fair, the configuration files are simple (i.e., no "XML code") and they are about 90% the same across different projects. But still, the developers need to keep track of them. That is where development tools can really help us!

Seam Gen is a rapid application generator shipped with Seam distribution. With a few command line commands, Seam Gen generates an array of artifacts for Seam projects. In particular, we often use Seam Gen to do the following.

- Automatically generate an empty Seam project with common configuration files, a build script, and directories for Java code and JSF view pages.

- Automatically generate complete Eclipse and NetBeans project files for the Seam project.

- Reverse-engineer entity bean objects from relational database tables.

- Generate template files for common Seam components.

The command-line script-based approach allows Seam Gen to work in any development environment, in much the same successful approach Ruby on Rails took. But the difference is that Seam Gen also works with IDEs. In particular, it provides excellent integration support for Eclipse and NetBeans. In this chapter, we show you how to start a project with Seam Gen.

4.1. Prerequisites

Seam Gen requires Apache Ant 1.6+. In fact, all the build scripts in this book's examples require Apache Ant. Please download Ant and install it from `http://ant.apache.org/`, if you have not done so.

Seam Gen generates code and configuration files for deployment in the `ejb3` profile of the JBoss Application Server 4.0.5+ (see Appendix A, *Installing and Deploying JBoss AS*, for installation instructions). It does not work with J2EE 1.4 or plain Tomcat deployment options (see more in Chapter 24, *Seam Without EJB3*, and Chapter 25, *Tomcat Deployment*).

Seam Gen projects use Facelets (see Section 3.1., "An Introduction to Facelets") as the view framework. You must author your JSF web pages in XHTML files.

4.2. A Quick Tutorial

The `seam` (Linux, Unix and Mac) and `seam.bat` (Windows) scripts in the Seam distribution are the main scripts for Seam Gen. On a Linux/Unix machine, you might need to adjust the permission of the `seam` file to make it executable from the command line.

In the rest of this section, we will go over the steps to use Seam Gen to generate and build the complete `betterjsf` example application we discussed in Chapter 3, *Recommended JSF Enhancements*.

4.2.1. Set Up Seam Gen

First, you need to tell Seam Gen about the project you are about to generate. Just type the following in your Seam distribution's root directory.

```
seam setup
```

The script asks you a few questions about the project, such as the project name, JBoss AS location, Eclipse workspace, and database server. Following is an example conversation. You can simply enter RETURN to accept the default value in the square brackets for each question.

```
[echo] Welcome to seam-gen :-)
[input] Enter your Java project workspace
        [C:/Projects]
/home/juntao/projects

[input] Enter your JBoss home directory
```

```
            [C:/Program Files/jboss-4.0.5.GA]
/usr/local/jboss-4.0.5-GA

[input] Enter the project name [myproject]
helloseamgen

[input] Is this project deployed as an EAR
        (with EJB components) or a WAR
        (with no EJB support) [ear] (ear,war,)
ear

[input] Enter the Java package name for your
        session beans [com.mydomain.MyFirstProject]
book.helloseamgen

[input] Enter the Java package name for your
        entity beans [com.mydomain.MyFirstProject]
book.helloseamgen

[input] Enter the Java package name for your
        test cases [com.mydomain.MyFirstProject.test]
book.helloseamgen.test

[input] What kind of database are you using? [hsql]
    (hsql,mysql,oracle,postgres,mssql,db2,sybase,)

[input] Enter the Hibernate dialect for your database
        [org.hibernate.dialect.HSQLDialect]

[input] Enter the filesystem path to the
        JDBC driver jar [lib/hsqldb.jar]

[input] Enter JDBC driver class for your database
        [org.hsqldb.jdbcDriver]

[input] Enter the JDBC URL for your database
        [jdbc:hsqldb:.]

[input] Enter database username [sa]

[input] Enter database password []

[input] Enter the database schema name
        (it is OK to leave this blank) []

[input] Enter the database catalog name
        (it is OK to leave this blank) []

[input] Are you working with tables that already
        exist in the database? [y] (y,n,)
n
[input] Do you want to drop and recreate the
```

- EJB3 entity beans that map to the tables. Each table has a corresponding bean with the same name as the table name. The associations and relationships between the tables are properly generated in the entity bean classes. Refer to Hibernate or JPA documentation on how relational associations are expressed in the entity objects via annotations. All the NOT NULL constraints on data columns are also translated into Hibernate validators (see Chapter 10, *Validating Input Data*).

- Seam POJOs to access the database. Those Data Access Objects (DAOs) are based on Seam's built-in CRUD component framework (see Chapter 13, *The Seam CRUD Application Framework*). Each generated entity bean has a corresponding DAO. The DAO provides methods for CRUD operations using the EntityManager. In Chapter 24, *Seam Without EJB3*, we explain how to use the EntityManager from Seam POJOs.

- Facelets XHTML files for presentation. Each table has a corresponding XHTML file to search and display rows in the table, an XHTML file to display a row of data, as well as an XHTML file to edit a selected row or create a new row. For each "edit" XHTML file, there is also a *.page.xml file to define page parameters so that RESTful URLs can be supported for those view files (see Chapter 12, *Bookmarkable Web Pages*).

Figure 4.6., "The Seam Gen-generated CRUD application home page", to Figure 4.8., "The Seam Gen-generated row edit page", show an example Seam CRUD application generated from a database. All the pages have a default CSS-based style. You can easily alter the look and feel by changing the CSS or editing the XHTML files directly in your favorite IDE.

Figure 4.6. The Seam Gen-generated CRUD application home page

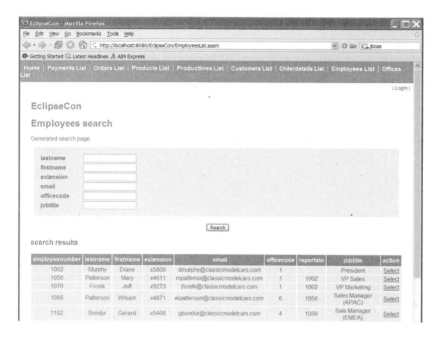

Figure 4.7. The Seam Gen-generated table content search and display page

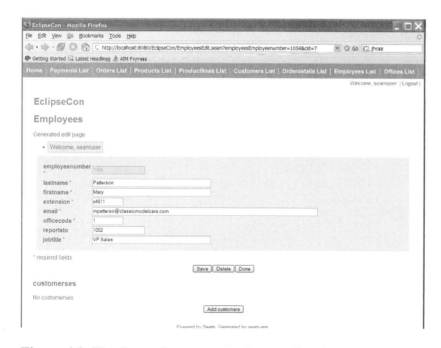

Figure 4.8. The Seam Gen-generated row edit page

The Seam Gen `generate-entities` task is really powerful and fun to use. Try it on one of your databases and see how well it works!

Stateful Applications Made Easy

A key innovation in Seam is the declarative management of POJO-based stateful components. In this part, we explain why stateful components are crucial for today's database-driven web applications. We show how the components are constructed and how their lifecycles are managed. We cover useful features such as multiple conversations in an HTTP session and multiple independent workspaces for a single user. Finally, we discuss how to perform database transactions for Seam conversations.

5

An Introduction to Stateful Framework

In the previous part, we have demonstrated how Seam simplifies Java EE 5.0 application development by integrating annotated EJB3 session beans (Chapter 2, *Seam Hello World*) into JSF. However, as you learn more about Seam, you will realize that the simple Java EE 5.0 integration just barely scratches the surface of what Seam can do. The real jewel of Seam is its support for sophisticated application state management that is not available in any other web application frameworks today. That is what we mean when we call Seam the "next generation" web application framework.

The state management facility in Seam is independent of JSF or EJB3. That makes Seam useful in a variety of environments. For instance, Chapter 17, *Direct JavaScript Integration* discusses how to use client JavaScript to access Seam objects directly. Those AJAX UI examples work outside of the JSF framework yet they can still take advantage of Seam's stateful components.

Since state management is such a crucial feature in Seam, we dedicate this short chapter to explain why you should seriously consider using it in your applications. We will focus on the concepts in this chapter and you will see ample code examples in the next several chapters!

5.1. Correct Usage of ORM

Consider that Seam is invented by Gavin King—of the Hibernate ORM (Object-Relational Mapping) framework fame. It is not surprising that one of the primary goals of Seam is to make it work better with ORM solutions. And a stateful framework is key to the correct usage of an ORM solution.

One of the chief challenges of ORM is to bridge the paradigm rift between the object world and the relational world. A key concept here is "lazy loading". When the framework loads an object from the relational database, it does not necessarily loads all its associated objects. To understand lazy loading, let's look at an example. Below is the code snippet from a typical data model: A `Teacher` object might be associated with a number of `Student` objects, and each `Student` object might be associated with a number of `Assignment` objects, etc.

```
@Entity
public class Teacher implements Serializable {

  protected Long id;
  protected String name;
  protected List <Student> students;

  // getter and setter methods
}
@Entity
public class Student implements Serializable {

  protected Long id;
  protected List <Assignment> assignments;

  // getter and setter methods
}
@Entity
public class Assignment implements Serializable {
  // ... ...
}
```

If the ORM framework loads all associated `Student` and `Assignment` objects when it loads a `Teacher` object (known as "eager loading"), it would issue 2 SQL JOIN commands and might end up loading a sizable chunk of the database into this single object. But of course, when the application actually uses the `Teacher` object, it might not use the `students` property at all. It might change the teacher's name and save the object right back to the database. Eager loading is a huge waste of resources in this case.

The ORM framework deals with this problem by "lazy loading" the `Teacher` object. That is not to load any of the `Student` objects at all initially. Then, when the application calls `Teacher.getStudents()` explicitly, it goes back to the database to load the `students` list.

Okay, so far so good. But the real problem arises when the data access layer of the web application is "stateless". For instance, let's look at how the data is loaded in the very popular Spring framework. When the HTTP request comes in, it is dispatched to the Spring / Hibernate integration template and Hibernate lazy loads the `Teacher` object, which is returned to the web presentation layer. Now, if the web page displays a list of student names associated with the teacher, the web presentation layer will need to lazy load the `students` list as it renders the page. But here is the problem: since Spring is a stateless framework, it destroys the persistence context when the `Teacher` object is passed back to the presentation layer in preparation for the next "stateless" data query. As far as Spring is concerned, the data loading is done. If the web presentation layer attempts to lazy load associated objects after Spring returns, an exception will be thrown. In fact, this lazy loading exception is one of the most encountered Hibernate exceptions of all time.

To avoid the nasty lazy loading exceptions, developers have to work around the framework using hacks like the Data Transfer Objects (DTO) or messing with the database query / schema.

But with a stateful framework like Seam, this lazy loading problem is solved once and for all. By default, a Seam component keeps the persistence context valid from the time when the HTTP request is submitted to the time when the response page is fully rendered (see Section 7.1., "The Default Conversation Scope"). If needed, we can configure the Seam component to keep the persistence context valid across an entire HTTP session or even beyond. Seam can do that because it is stateful and remembers which request / response cycle or HTTP session it is associated with.

So, in a Seam application, we can focus our attention and effort working with objects rather than messing with the data queries or massaging the database schema. We can pass entity objects (i.e., EJB3 entity beans) directly across the business layer and the presentation layer without the need to wrap them in DTOs. Those are significant productivity gains from the simple fact that Seam finally allows us to use ORM in the "correct" way.

In the Relational World ...

The lazy loading versus eager loading problem does not exist in the relational world since you can always tweak your JOIN statement to select only the data you know the application would actually use. But in the object world, the data query has no concept of "join" (those are objects, not relational tables after all). This problem represents a fundamental rift between the two worlds.

5.2. Better Performance

A nice "side effect" of keeping the persistence context valid beyond a single stateless method call is improved database performance. Now we already know that lazy loading saves the database performance, but we are talking about *another* performance improvement in a somewhat opposite direction here: the reduction of database round trips.

A major performance problem with database driven web applications is that many of those applications are "chatty". A chatty web application saves information to the database whenever the user changes anything as opposed to queue database operations and execute them in a bench. Since a round trip to the database, potentially over the network, is much slower than a method call inside the application server, it slows down the application significantly.

For instance, a shopping cart application can save every order into the database as the user adds products into the cart. But then, if the user abandons the shopping cart, the application would have to clean up the database. Wouldn't it be much better if the orders are never saved into the database in the first place? The application should only save orders in a bench when the user checks out the shopping cart.

Before Seam, application developers needed to develop a rather sophisticated caching mechanism to hold the database updates for each user session in memory. But with the extended persistence context in Seam, you get all that for free! A Seam stateful component can stay valid across several web pages (i.e., a web wizard or a shopping cart). It is known as a "long running conversation" in Seam. The component only dirty checks objects and flushes changes to the database from its persistence context at the end of the conversation.

Those are all accomplished with no explicit API calls or elaborate XML files. Just a few annotations on your component class would do the trick. Please see Section 7.2., "Long-Running Conversations", for the exact syntax on how to define a long running conversation, and Section 9.3., "Atomic Conversation (Web Transaction)", on how such bench database update works.

But I Heard Stateful Frameworks Are Not Scalable ...

To be fair, the argument has its merits: The more state data you have, the more work the server must do to replicate it to other nodes in a cluster environment (see Chapter 27, *Performance Tuning and Clustering*). However, the argument is only true if Seam requires

---

you to manage substantially more state data than other "stateless" frameworks. In fact, in most so-called "stateless" architecture, the application simply puts all the state data in an HTTP session, which requires the exact same amount of work in clusters as the equivalent state data Seam manages. Seam does not necessarily increase your stateful data. It just makes your existing state data a lot easier to manage.

Furthermore, the HTTP session approach is prone to memory leak (see later in this chapter). Once the memory leaks, the scalability of the "stateless" + HTTP session approach would be much much worse than Seam.

5.3. Better Browser Navigation Support

Before Seam, almost all web application frameworks save the per-user application state in HTTP sessions. It works fine until the user clicks on the browser's BACK button or simply opens up another browser window / tab for the same application. Why? Because the view displayed in the browser is now out of sync with the application state on the server!

What is an HTTP Session

The HTTP protocol used in web applications is fundamentally stateless. Each HTTP request is independent from other requests. In order to distinguish requests from multiple users, the server will generate a unique session ID for each user and ask the user (i.e., the web browser) to embed the ID in all subsequent HTTP requests. The web browser can choose to append the ID at the end of the request URL or embed it in the `Cookie` field of the HTTP header. On the server side, each session ID is associated with an `HttpSession` object, which holds the application state data as properties. This setup allows the server to provide stateful services to each individual user. `Session` scoped Seam components have the same lifecycle as the `HttpSession` object in the servlet container.

Figure 6.1. The three-page stateful Hello World

6.1. Stateful Components

For an application like `stateful`, the backend components must maintain their state across multiple pages. For instance, the `person` component is referenced on all three web pages. It must retain its value across multiple HTTP page requests so that all pages for the same user can display the same `person`.

```
< -- Snippet from hello.xhtml -->
Please enter your name:<br/>
<h:inputText value="#{person.name}" size="15"/>
```

```
... ...

< -- Snippet from warning.xhtml -->
<p>You just entered the name
<i>#{person.name}</i>
... ...


< -- Snippet from fans.xhtml -->
<p>Hello,
<b>#{person.name}</b></p>
... ...
```

Similarly, the `manager` component must also track whether the user has previously confirmed that she wants to input an "invalid" name: The `manager.sayHello` method is invoked directly or indirectly on both `hello.xhtml` and `warning.xhtml` pages. The outcome of the method (i.e., which page to display next) depends on the `confirmed` field variable inside `manager`. All pages must access the same object instance when they reference the `manager` component.

```java
public class ManagerAction implements Manager {

  @In @Out
  private Person person;

  private boolean confirmed = false;

  ... ...

  // Called from the hello.xhtml page
  public String sayHello () {
    if (person.getName()
           .matches("^[a-zA-Z.-]+ [a-zA-Z.-]+")
        || confirmed) {

      em.persist (person);
      confirmed = false;
      find ();
      return "fans";

    } else {
      return "warning";
    }
  }

  // Called from the warning.xhtml page
  public String confirm () {
```

```
    confirmed = true;
    return sayHello ();
  }
}
```

> **Multi-page Navigation**
>
> If the `sayHello()` method returns `fans`, JSF renders the `fans.xhtml`
> page to the user. If it returns `warning`, JSF navigates the user to the
> `warning.xhtml` page. More explanations on the JSF page naviga-
> tion rules are provided in Section 6.2., "Page Navigation Flow".

Experienced web developers know that we probably need to store the `person` and `manager`
objects inside the HTTP session to retain states across page requests from the same user. That
is exactly what we are going to do here (in fact, we store proxies of those Seam components
in the HTTP session, but that is functionally equivalent to storing those components themselves in the session). Seam allows us to declaratively manage the HTTP session, and hence
eliminate the boilerplate code for getting objects into/out of the HTTP session. Seam also
supports lifecycle methods in stateful components, which allow us to properly instantiate and
destroy those components with minimal effort.

> **Beyond HTTP Session**
>
> Stateful management is a core feature in Seam. Seam supports sev-
> eral stateful contexts beyond the HTTP session, which truly distin-
> guish it from previous generations of web frameworks. In this ex-
> ample, we discuss the HTTP session scope since it is already a fa-
> miliar concept for most web developers. We will discuss additional
> Seam stateful contexts later in this chapter, and then in Chapter 7,
> *Conversations*, and Chapter 18, *Managing Business Processes*.

6.1.1. Stateful Entity Bean

To declare the `person` component in the session context, all we need is to annotate the entity bean class with the `@Scope` annotation. All the injection and outjection of this component will automatically happen in the session context.

```
import static org.jboss.seam.ScopeType.SESSION;

... ...

@Entity
@Name("person")
@Scope (SESSION)
public class Person implements Serializable {

  ... ...

}
```

6.1.2. Stateful Session Bean

To declare the `manager` component in the session context, you have to first declare the `ManagerAction` class as a stateful session bean via the `@Stateful` annotation, and then specify the scope via the `@Scope` annotation. Now, since the `manager` component is stateful, it can expose its state as properties to the JSF web pages. To illustrate this point, we use the `manager.fans` property to represent the list of Seam fans who said "hello." This way, we no longer need to outject the `fans` component. See more in Section 2.4.5., "Avoid Excessive Bijection".

```
@Stateful
@Name("manager")
@Scope (SESSION)
public class ManagerAction implements Manager {

  private List <Person> fans;

  public List <Person> getFans () {
    return fans;
  }

  ... ...

}
```

Seam POJO Component

If we use a Seam POJO component to replace the EJB3 session bean here (see Chapter 24, *Seam Without EJB3*), we would not need the `@Stateful` annotation on the POJO. Seam POJO components are stateful by default. And it has the default conversation scope (see Chapter 7, *Conversations*) if the `@Scope` is not specified.

In the `fans.xhtml` page, you can just reference the stateful `manager` component.

```
<h:dataTable value="#{manager.fans}" var="fan">
  <h:column>
    #{fan.name}
  </h:column>
</h:dataTable>
```

How to Decouple Seam Components

The stateful session bean component integrates data and business logic in the same class. In this example, we just showed that the `fans` list is now a property in the `manager` component and no longer needs to be outjected.

But what about the `person` data field in the `ManagerAction` class? Should we make it a property of the `manager` component as well (i.e., `#{manager.person}`, see Section 2.4.5., "Avoid Excessive Bijection")? Well, we could do that but we decide not to. The reason is that we'd like to decouple the `person` component from the `manager` component. This way, we can update the `person` value without involving the `manager`. The `person` and `manager` can have different scopes and lifecycles. And we do not need to create `person` instance in the `ManagerAction` constructor (the instance is created by Seam and then injected).

The moral is that you can choose the level of coupling between stateful components in Seam. With stateful session beans and

> bijection, you have the ultimate flexibility to archive the optimal coupling between components in the application.

6.1.3. Stateful Component Lifecycle

One of the challenges to use stateful components is to make sure that the component has the proper state when it is created. For instance, in our example, a user might load the `fans.xhtml` page as the first page in the session to see who has said hello. A `manager` component would be created for this user session. However, since the `sayHello()` method had never been invoked on this component, the `manager.fans` property would be `null` even if there were people in the database. To fix this problem, we need to run the database query right after the `manager` component is created. In a Seam stateful component, any method marked with the `@Create` annotation would be executed right after the component creation. So, below is the fix we need for `manager` to behave correctly.

```
@Stateful
@Name("manager")
@Scope (SESSION)
public class ManagerAction implements Manager {

  private List <Person> fans;

  @Create
  public void find () {
    fans = em.createQuery("select p from Person p")
                        .getResultList();
  }

  ... ...
}
```

Why Not Use the Class Constructor?

The class constructor is called before the component object is created while the `@Create` method is called after the component creation. The constructor would not have access to Seam injected objects such as the `EntityManager`.

contains one or several navigation cases (`navigation-case` element). Each navigation case has a unique string name (`from-outcome` element) and it specifies a possible page transition (`to-view-id` element) from the rule's target pages (`from-view-id` element). Then, in the web UI event handler method (i.e., the EJB3 session bean method), you can return the string name for a case (`from-outcome` element). JSF uses this case to determine which page to forward to next.

In the `stateful` application, we define one rule that applies to all pages. It has three navigation cases. According to those cases, the server forwards to the `fans.xhtml` page if the event handler method returns `"fans"`, to the `warning.xhtml` page for return value `"warning"`, and to the `hello.xhtml` page for return value `"hello"`. The `redirect` element makes sure that the browser displays the URL of the forwarded page.

```
<faces-config>

  ... ...

 <navigation-rule>
   <from-view-id>*</from-view-id>

   <navigation-case>
     <from-outcome>fans</from-outcome>
     <to-view-id>/fans.xhtml</to-view-id>
     <redirect />
   </navigation-case>

   <navigation-case>
     <from-outcome>hello</from-outcome>
     <to-view-id>/hello.xhtml</to-view-id>
     <redirect />
   </navigation-case>

   <navigation-case>
     <from-outcome>warning</from-outcome>
     <to-view-id>/warning.xhtml</to-view-id>
     <redirect />
   </navigation-case>
 </navigation-rule>

</faces-config>
```

Visual Navigation Rule Editor

You can develop very complex navigation rules for JSF using the XML language. But writing all that XML by hand can be tedious. What happens to Seam's promise of getting rid of the XML hell? Well, in reality, you do not need to write those page flow XML files by hand! Many modern Java IDEs (e.g., NetBeans and Eclipse) provide support for a visual editor for JSF navigation rules. You can develop the page navigation flow on a diagram and then have the tool export to an XML file.

Then, in the web UI event handler methods, we simply return the string names for the applicable navigation cases.

```
... ...
@Name("manager")
public class ManagerAction implements Manager {

  // Event handler for the
  // "Say Hello" button on the hello.xhtml page
  // and the
  // "Yes ..." button on the warning.xhtml page
  public String sayHello () {
    // If the person name matches pattern
    // Or, the user confirmed the spelling
      em.persist (person);
      ... ...
      return "fans";

    // If the person name does not match pattern
    // and the user has not confirmed
      return "warning";
  }

  // Event handler for the "Go to Hello page"
  // button on the fans.xhtml page
  public String startOver () {
    person = new Person ();
    return "hello";
  }
  ... ...
}
```

request/response cycle is also a conversation because it involves two pages: the form page submitted as request and the response page. Multiple conversations can exist in the same HTTP session. Actually, Seam even supports multiple concurrent conversations, each contained inside its own browser window or tab (see Chapter 8, *Workspaces and Concurrent Conversations*). Seam database transactions can also be tied to conversations (see Chapter 9, *Transactions*).

Stateful conversation is a core concept in Seam. Let's see how it works.

7.1. The Default Conversation Scope

By default (i.e., if you omit the @Scope annotation on the component class), a Seam stateful component has a conversation scope. The default conversation scope spans only two pages: The component is instantiated when the first page is submitted, and it is destroyed after the response page is fully rendered. Consider the following stateful session bean class.

```
@Stateful
@Name("manager")
public class ManagerAction implements Manager {

  @In @Out
  private Person person;

  private String mesg;

  @PersistenceContext (type=EXTENDED)
  private EntityManager em;

  public String sayHello () {
    // save person
    // update mesg
  }

  @Remove @Destroy
  public void destroy() {}

  public String getMesg () {
    return mesg;
  }
  public void setMesg (String mesg) {
    this.mesg = mesg;
  }
}
```

When the user submits the form, the `ManagerAction` object is instantiated with the user input captured in its `person` property. JSF invokes the `sayHello()` method as the UI event handler. The `sayHello()` method saves the `person` object to the database and updates the `mesg` property. Now, on the response page, we display the `mesg` to inform the user that `person` has been successfully saved to the database. After the response page is completely rendered, the `ManagerAction` component is removed from the stateful context and is garbage-collected.

Notice that the `ManagerAction` object stays valid after the `sayHello()` method exists so that the `mesg` property can propagate back to the response page; that is a major difference between Seam and stateless frameworks. In addition, we gave the `EntityManager` an `EXTENDED` type, which allows it to lazy load more data from the database as needed when the `sayHello()` method exists (see a discussion on lazy loading in Section 5.1., "Correct Usage of ORM").

HTTP GET Request

An HTTP GET request also breaks out a new conversation. Components associated with this conversation last only one page; they are destroyed after the GET response page is rendered.

Redirect

In JSF, you can choose to redirect the response page to its own URL instead of using the request page's URL. With the Seam filter (see Section 3.2.4., "Seam Filter"), Seam conversation components can live until the redirect page is fully rendered.

Seam POJO Component

Without any annotations (except for `@Name`), a Seam POJO component is stateful and has the default conversation scope. Refer to Section 2.4.1., "Seam POJO Components", and Chapter 24, *Seam Without EJB3*, for more on Seam POJO components.

The default conversation scope should suffice for most web interactions. But the power of the conversation concept is that it can be easily expanded to handle more than two pages. Seam provides a very clever mechanism to declaratively manage stateful components across a series of related pages (e.g., a wizard or a shopping cart). In the rest of the chapter, we discuss how to manage such long-running conversations.

7.1.1. Display JSF Messages

Besides correct ORM lazy loading, the Seam default conversation scope helps improve JSF by expanding JSF support for error messages.

One of the most useful features in JSF is its message facility. When an operation fails, the JSF backing bean method could add a message to the JSF context and return `null`. The JSF runtime then can redisplay the current page with error messages added to the page. In Seam, such operation is simplified because you can directly inject a `FacesMessages` object into the Seam component. Thus, you can easily add JSF error messages from a Seam event handler using the `FacesMessages.add()` method. You can add global JSF messages or messages to JSF components with specific IDs. The error message is displayed anywhere on the page where you have the `<h:messages>` tags. With Seam, you can even use the EL expressions in the messages. The following is an example.

```java
@Name("manager")
public class ManagerAction implements manager {

  @In
  Person person;

  @In
  FacesMessages facesMessages;

  public String sayHello () {

    try {
      // ... ...
    } catch (Exception e) {
      facesMessages.add(
          "Has problem saving #{person.name}");
      return null;
    }
    return "fans";
  }
}
```

However, if the operation succeeds, the message system in plain JSF cannot display the "success message" on the next page. That is because the next page is out of the current JSF request context (as with lazy-loaded entity objects) and often requires a redirect. But in Seam, the next page is still within the default conversation scope, so Seam can easily display a success message through the JSF message system as well. That is a great enhancement to JSF. The following is an example on how to add a success message to a Seam UI event handler.

```
@Name("manager")
public class ManagerAction implements manager {

  @In
  Person person;

  @In
  FacesMessages facesMessages;

  public String sayHello () {
    // ... ...

    facesMessages.add(
        "#{person.name} said hello!");

    return "fans";
  }
}
```

7.2. Long-Running Conversations

In a web application, a long-running conversation usually consists of a series of web pages the user must go through to accomplish a business task. The application data generated from the task is permanently committed to the database at the end of the conversation. For instance, in an e-commerce application, the checkout process is a conversation, with a page for order confirmation, a page for billing information, and a final page for the confirmation code.

The example application we use in this chapter is the Seam Hotel Booking example in the booking project in the book's source code bundle. The Hotel Booking example directory is set up the same way as the directory for the hello world examples in the previous chapters (see Appendix B, *Using Example Applications as Templates*, for the application template).

Figure 7.1., "main.xhtml — click on Find Hotels to start a conversation", to Figure 7.5., "confirm.xhtml — click on the Confirm button to end the conversation", show a conversation in action. On the `main.xhtml` page, the user clicks the Find Hotels button to start a conversation. In the conversation, you can click on any of the View Hotel links in the search result list to view the hotel details on the `hotel.xhtml` page. Click on the Book Hotel button to load the `book.xhtml` page to enter booking dates and credit card information. Click on the Proceed button to load the confirmation page `confirm.xhtml`. Click the Confirm button to confirm the booking and end the conversation. Seam then loads the `confirmed.xhtml` page to display the confirmation number.

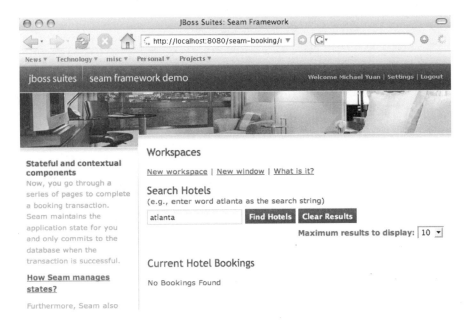

Figure 7.1. `main.xhtml` — **click on Find Hotels to start a conversation**

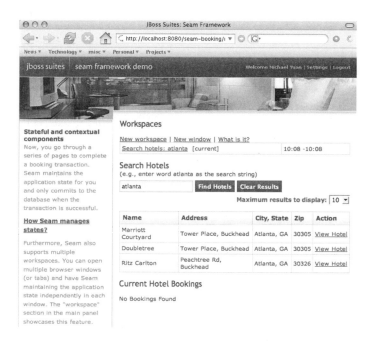

Figure 7.2. `main.xhtml` — click on View Hotel for any item in the search result

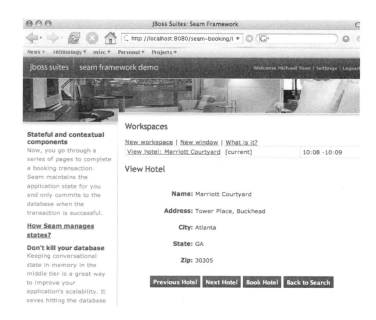

Figure 7.3. `hotel.xhtml` — click on the Previous Hotel or Next Hotel button to navigate the search result. Click on the Book Hotel button to move ahead with the conversation.

Figure 7.4. `book.xhtml` — enter dates and a 16-digit credit card number

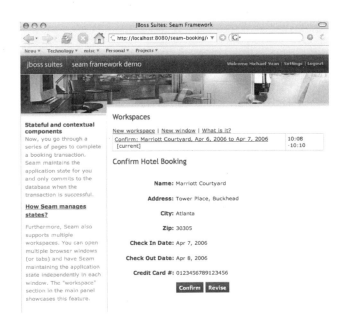

Figure 7.5. `confirm.xhtml` — click on the Confirm button to end the conversation

> **The Back Button Just Works**
>
> Within the conversation, you can use the browser's Back button to navigate to any previous page; the application state then reverts to that page. For instance, from the `confirmed.xhtml` page, you can click the Back button several times and go back to the `hotel.xhtml` page. From there, you can select another hotel and book it. No "invalid state" error is thrown. You can back into an interrupted conversation or a finished conversation. The incomplete bookings are not saved to the database, and no booking is saved twice by accident. Later in this chapter and in Chapter 8, *Workspaces and Concurrent Conversations*, we include more sidebars to discuss various Back button scenarios that are hard to deal with in pre-Seam stateless web frameworks.

The search results, current hotel selection, reservation dates, and credit card number are all associated with the conversation. Stateful objects that hold that data have the conversational scope. They are automatically created when conversation starts and are destroyed when the conversation ends. You do not need to manage them in the long-running HTTP session. As you will see in Chapter 8, *Workspaces and Concurrent Conversations*, you can even have multiple concurrent conversations in a same session. Now let's dig into the code and see how the conversation is implemented.

7.2.1. Define a Long-Running Conversational Component

In the Hotel Booking conversation described earlier, the `HotelBookingAction` bean is the long-running conversation component and the following listing shows its structure.

```
@Stateful
@Name("hotelBooking")
@Conversational(ifNotBegunOutcome="main")
@LoggedIn
public class HotelBookingAction
      implements HotelBooking, Serializable {

  @Begin(join=true)
  public String find() {
    // Initialize the conversation state
  }
```

```
<div class="section">
  <div class="entry">
    <div class="label">Name:</div>
    <div class="output">#{hotel.name}</div>
  </div>
  <div class="entry">
    <div class="label">Address:</div>
    <div class="output">#{hotel.address}</div>
  </div>
  ... ...
</div>

<div class="section">
  <h:form>
    <fieldset class="buttonBox">
      <h:commandButton
        action="#{hotelBooking.lastHotel}"
        value="Previous Hotel"
        class="button"/>
      <h:commandButton
        action="#{hotelBooking.nextHotel}"
        value="Next Hotel" class="button"/>
      <h:commandButton
        action="#{hotelBooking.bookHotel}"
        value="Book Hotel" class="button"/>
      <h:commandButton action="main"
        value="Back to Search" class="button"/>
    </fieldset>
  </h:form>
</div>
```

The `bookHotel()` method creates a new `Booking` object for this conversation. The booking object has default reservation dates and is displayed on the `booking.xhtml` page for you to edit.

```
public class HotelBookingAction
    implements HotelBooking, Serializable {

  @Out(required=false)
  private Hotel hotel;

  @In(required=false)
  @Out(required=false)
  @Valid
  private Booking booking;

  public String bookHotel() {
```

```
   booking = new Booking(hotel, user);
   Calendar calendar = Calendar.getInstance();
   booking.setCheckinDate( calendar.getTime());
   calendar.add(Calendar.DAY_OF_MONTH, 1);
   booking.setCheckoutDate(calendar.getTime());

   return "book";
 }
 // ... ...
}
```

Except for the @Begin find() method, all the bean methods in HotelBookingAction are designed to be invoked after the long-running conversation starts. However, in real life, there is no guarantee of that. The user might load the hotel.seam page first and then click on the Book Hotel button. Because no valid conversation context exists here, the application would fail. To avoid this, we have this @Conversational(ifNotBegunOutcome="main") tag on the bean class. That means if any bean method is invoked outside an active long-running conversation, the application should forward to the page corresponding to the navigation destination "main" (i.e., the main.xhtml page in our example).

```
@Stateful
@Name("hotelBooking")
@Conversational(ifNotBegunOutcome="main")
@LoggedIn
public class HotelBookingAction
      implements HotelBooking, Serializable {
  ... ...
}
```

This is why you are forwarded to main.xhtml when you move back to a conversation page after the conversation has ended and you click on a button on that page.

7.2.4. End the Conversation

When the @End method is called, Seam destroys the stateful session bean instance. You can save the conversation data to the database and clean up any loose ends here. In this example, we have two @End methods for two possible endings of the conversation. The confirm() method is invoked after the user creates a reservation and clicks on the Confirm button on the confirm.xhtml page.

```
<h:form>
  <fieldset>
    <div class="entry">
      <div class="label">Name:</div>
      <div class="output">#{hotel.name}</div>
    </div>

    ... Hotel and reservation details ...

    <div class="entry">
      <div class="label"> </div>
      <div class="input">
        <h:commandButton value="Confirm"
          action="#{hotelBooking.confirm}"
          class="button"/>
        <h:commandButton value="Revise"
          action="back" class="button"/>
      </div>
    </div>
  </fieldset>
</h:form>
```

Before the conversation ends, the confirm() method saves the booking object into the database and reduces the hotel room inventory from the database to reflect the booking. In fact, the two database operations must be performed in an atomic transaction to ensure database integrity. That is the topic for Chapter 9, *Transactions*.

```
public class HotelBookingAction
    implements HotelBooking, Serializable {

  @End
  public String confirm()
          throws InventoryException {
    if (booking==null || hotel==null)
      return "main";

    em.persist(booking);
    hotel.reduceInventory();

    if (bookingList!=null)
      bookingList.refresh();

    return "confirmed";
  }
  // ... ...
}
```

> **Reduce Database Round-trips**
>
> In a complex application, you might need to perform multiple database operations in a conversation. We recommend that you cache all database updates in in-memory objects in the conversation and then synchronize them to the database at the end of the conversation in the `@End` tagged method. That helps reduce database round-trips and preserve database integrity (see Chapter 9, *Transactions*, for more details).

The `clear()` method, on the other hand, is called when the user wants to end the conversation without booking anything. It clears up the conversation context and redirects back to the `main.xhtml` page.

```
public class HotelBookingAction
    implements HotelBooking, Serializable {

  @End
  public String clear() {
    hotels = null;
    hotel = null;
    return "main";
  }
  // ... ...
}
```

> **Use the Back Button to Back Into an Ended Conversation**
>
> After you complete a conversation by calling the `@End` method, you can still use the Back button to view any page in the ended conversation. But if you click on any link or button on the page, you are redirected to the `main.xhtml` page because a valid conversation context no longer exists for that page.

In a Seam application, the conversational state is tied to the business logic. That is, all possible methods to exit the conversation should be tagged with `@End`. Thus, it is unlikely that a user would exit a conversation without calling an @End method. But what if the user abandons the current conversation and loads a new site/conversation with a manual HTTP GET request (see the next section on HTTP GET)? Or what if we simply make a coding error and forget to tag an exiting method with @End? Well, in those cases, the current conversation times out when a preset conversation timeout is reached or the current HTTP session times out.

You can set the global conversation timeout in the components.xml configuration file (see Appendix B, *Using Example Applications as Templates*). The unit is milliseconds.

```
<components ...>

  ... ...

  <core:manager conversation-timeout="120000"/>

</components>
```

Alternatively, you can specify a timeout for each individual conversation in the pages.xml configuration file (see Chapter 8, *Workspaces and Concurrent Conversations*, and Chapter 19, *Stateful Pageflows*).

Based on discussions earlier in this chapter, the abandoned conversation does pose a potential risk for memory leak. But it is not nearly as error prone as manually managing the HTTP session. In addition, the Seam user can actually go back to the abandoned conversation later and pick up where she left off using the conversation switcher (see Chapter 8, *Workspaces and Concurrent Conversations*) or simply using the browser's Back button.

7.2.5. Links and Buttons

So far, our conversation has been driven by a series of button clicks (i.e., regular HTTP POST operations). That is because Seam uses hidden form fields in those POST requests to maintain the conversation context for the user. If the user clicks on a regular link in the middle of a conversation, the browser issues a simple HTTP GET request to get the page, and the current conversation context is lost; Seam then simply starts a new conversation following the link (see Chapter 8, *Workspaces and Concurrent Conversations*, for multiple concurrent conversations for the same user session). But sometimes we want to use hyperlinks to navigate inside a conversation. For instance, we might want to allow the user to right-click on the link and open the subsequent pages in a separate browser tab or window.

An obvious solution is to use the `<commandLink>` component instead of `<commandButton>` in JSF. However, the JSF `<commandLink>` is not really a regular link. When you click on it, JSF internally uses JavaScript to post the request back to the server. That breaks the normal right-click behavior of links. To fix this problem with JSF links, Seam provides its own conversation-aware link component: `<s:link>`. See Chapter 3, *Recommended JSF Enhancements*, for more on how to install and use Seam UI tags.

The `<outputLink>` Component

The JSF `<outputLink>` component renders a regular link in the browser. However, it is not very useful in a Seam conversation because you cannot attach event-handler methods to an `<outputLink>`.

In the following example, we declare the `<s:>` namespace for the Seam tags.

```
<html xmlns="http://www.w3.org/1999/xhtml"
      xmlns:h="http://java.sun.com/jsf/html"
      xmlns:f="http://java.sun.com/jsf/core"
      xmlns:s="http://jboss.com/products/seam/taglib">
```

With the namespace declared, it is easy to use the `<s:link>` tag to build links in your conversation. You can specify an event-handler method for the link or give a direct JSF view ID as the link destination. The rendered link maintains the conversational context and behaves like a regular HTML link.

```
<s:link view-id="/login.xhtml" value="Login"/>
<s:link action="#{login.logout}" value="Logout"/>
```

The `<s:link>` component does more than just provide HTML links for navigation inside conversations. You can actually control the conversation from the links. For instance, if you click on the following link, Seam leaves the current conversation when the `main.xhtml` page is loaded, just as a regular HTTP GET request would do. The propagation attribute can take other parameters, such as `begin` and `end`, to force the beginning or ending of the current conversation.

```
<s:link view-id="/main.xhtml" propagation="none"/>
```

> **Bookmarks**
>
> Another implication of using HTTP POST is that it is difficult to bookmark pages from POST result pages. But in fact, it is fairly easy to build bookmarkable pages in Seam applications (see Chapter 12, *Bookmarkable Web Pages*).

Now, the `<s:link>` component actually has richer conversation-management capabilities than the plain JSF `<commandButton>`, which simply propagates the conversation context between pages. What if you want to exit, begin, or end a conversation context from a button click? You need the Seam `<s:conversationPropagation>` tag. The following example shows a button that exits the current conversation context.

```
<h:commandButton action="main" value="Abandon session">
  <s:conversationPropagation type="none"/>
</h:commandButton>
```

7.3. New Frontiers

Now you've seen how the Seam conversation component simplifies stateful application development. But Seam goes well beyond simplifying the development of traditional web applications.

The fully encapsulated conversation components enable us to tie the user experience and the application's transactional behavior with conversations. That has opened new frontiers in web application development. Seam makes it possible to develop advanced web applications that are either too complex or even impossible in older web frameworks. We cover those new scenarios in Chapter 8, *Workspaces and Concurrent Conversations*, and Chapter 9, *Transactions*.

Workspaces and Concurrent Conversations

As we discussed in the previous chapter, you can have multiple conversations in an HTTP session. It's easy to see how a user can have several consecutive conversations in a session. For instance, in the Hotel Booking example, you can book several hotels in a row, with each booking in its own conversation. But what makes Seam truly unique is its support for multiple concurrent conversations in a session. The concurrent conversations can each run in a separate browser window or tab. That gives rise to the concept of a workspace. In this chapter, we discuss what a Seam workspace is and how to work with workspaces in your web application. Again, we use the Hotel Booking example application in the booking source project.

8.1. What Is a Workspace?

A workspace is actually a common concept in desktop applications. For instance, in a word processor or spreadsheet program, each document is a workspace. In an IDE, each project is a workspace. You can make a change in one workspace without affecting other workspaces. In general, a workspace is a set of self-contained application contexts.

However, most of today's web applications do not support workspaces. The reason is that most web applications manage all their application contexts in HTTP sessions. An HTTP session does not have the granularity to differentiate between browser windows. To best understand this, let's revisit the Seam Hotel Booking application. Let's open two browser tabs and select different hotels to book in each of those tabs. For instance, imagine that you first select the Marriott San Francisco hotel in tab #1. Then you select the Ritz Carlton Atlanta hotel in tab #2. Now, go back to tab #1 and click on the Book Hotel button. The question is, which hotel will be booked? You can see the process in Figure 8.1., "Step 1: Load the Marriott San Francisco hotel in tab #1." and Figure 8.2., "Step #2: Load the Ritz Carlton Atlanta hotel in tab #2."

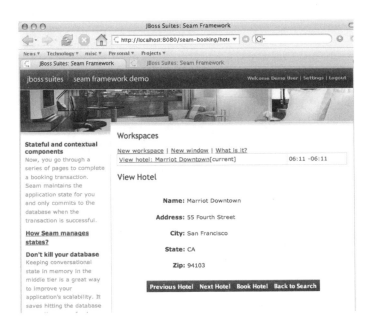

Figure 8.1. Step 1: Load the Marriott San Francisco hotel in tab #1.

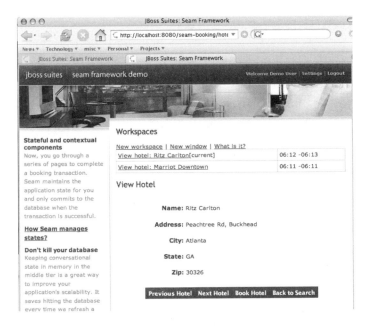

Figure 8.2. Step #2: Load the Ritz Carlton Atlanta hotel in tab #2.

If the application were based on an older-generation web framework and saved states in the HTTP session, you would end up booking the Ritz Carlton Atlanta hotel. The reason is that the Ritz hotel in tab #2 was recently put into the HTTP session, and the button action in either tab #1 or tab #2 would perform the booking operation on that hotel. An HTTP session-based web application does not properly support multiple browser windows/tabs. Those workspaces interfere with each other via the shared application state.

Seam, on the other hand, was designed from the ground up to support stateful application contexts. Seam web applications automatically support workspaces by default. So in our Seam Hotel Booking example, the Book Hotel button in each browser tab works as expected—the button in tab #1 always books the Marriott hotel, and the button in tab #2 always books the Ritz hotel, no matter what order they're invoked in. The conversation in each window is completely independent, although all conversations are tied to the same user. The best way to understand workspace is to try it yourself. You can open several browser windows (or tabs) and load the `hotel.xhtml` page in each of them. You can then book hotels in parallel in all windows.

Figure 8.3. Step #3: Switch to tab #1 and click on the Book Hotel button. The application books the Marriott San Francisco hotel. This is a common-sense result, but only Seam, with its support for multiple workspaces, can deliver.

```
        <f:convertDateTime type="time"
                           pattern="hh:mm"/>
      </h:outputText>
    </h:column>
</h:dataTable>
```

The #{entry} object iterates through conversations in the #{conversationsList} compon-ent. The #{entry.select} property is a built-in JSF action for loading the conversation in an #{entry} in the current window. Similarly, the #{entry.destroy} JSF action destroys an ex-isting conversation. What's interesting is the #{entry.description} property, which con-tains a string description of the current page in the conversation. How does Seam figure out the "description" of a page? That requires another XML file.

The WEB-INF/pages.xml file in the app.war archive file (it is the resources/WEB- INF/ pages.xml file in the source code bundle) specifies the page descriptions. This pages.xml file can also be used to replace the WEB-INF/navigation.xml file for jBPM-based page flow con-figuration (see Chapter 19, *Stateful Pageflows*, for more details). You can also learn more about pages.xml in Chapter 12, *Bookmarkable Web Pages*. The following is the content of the pages.xml file in the Seam Hotel Booking example.

```
<pages>
  <page view-id="/main.xhtml" timeout="3000">
    Search hotels: #{hotelBooking.searchString}
  </page>
  <page view-id="/hotel.xhtml" timeout="3000">
    View hotel: #{hotel.name}
  </page>
  <page view-id="/book.xhtml" timeout="6000">
    Book hotel: #{hotel.name}
  </page>
  <page view-id="/confirm.xhtml" timeout="6000">
    Confirm: #{booking.description}
  </page>
</pages>
```

We can reference Seam components by name in the pages.xml file. Each web page in the conversation also has a timeout value; if a workspace is idle for too long, the conversation automatically expires.

The conversation switcher shown earlier displays conversations in a table. Of course, you can customize how the table looks. But what if you want a switcher in a drop-down menu? The drop-down menu takes less space on a web page than a table, especially if you have many workspaces. However, the #{conversationList} component is a DataModel and cannot be used in a JSF menu. So Seam provides a special conversation list to use in a drop-down menu, as follows. It has a similar structure as the data table.

```
<h:selectOneMenu
      value="#{switcher.conversationIdOrOutcome}">
  <f:selectItems value="#{switcher.selectItems}"/>
</h:selectOneMenu>
<h:commandButton action="#{switcher.select}"
                 value="Switch"/>
<h:commandButton action="#{switcher.destroy}"
                 value="Destroy"/>
```

8.3. Carry a Conversation Across Workspaces

As we discussed earlier, Seam creates a new workspace for each HTTP GET request. By definition, the new workspace has its own fresh conversation. So what if we want to do an HTTP GET and still preserve the same conversation context? For instance, you might have a pop-up browser window that shares the same workspace/conversation as the current main window. That's where the Seam conversation ID comes to help.

If you look at the URLs of the Seam Hotel Booking example application, every page URL is appended with a cid URL parameter. This cid stays constant within a conversation. If the conversation is long running, the URL has an additional clr=true parameter. For instance, a URL in the booking application could look like the this: http://localhost:8080/booking/hotel.seam?cid=10&clr=true.

To GET a page without disrupting the current conversation, you can append the same cid and clr name/value pairs in your HTTP GET URL.

Appending the cid value in URL can be risky business. What if you pass in a wrong value for the cid parameter? Will the application just throw an error? Well, you can also configure the components.xml file to set a default page to forward to when the URL has an unavailable cid value.

```
<components ...>

  ... ...

  <core:pages
      no-conversation-view-id="/main.xhtml"/>

</components>
```

Of course, manually entering the `cid` and `clr` parameters is still not desirable. So to go back to the original question of opening the same workspace in a new window, you need to dynamically render a link with the right parameters already in place. The following example shows you how to build such a link. The Seam tags nested in `<h:outputLink>` generate the right `cid` and `clr` parameters to the link.

```
<h:outputLink value="main.seam" target="_blank">
  <s:conversationId/>
  <s:conversationPropagation
      propagation="join"/>
  <h:outputText value="Open New Tab"/>
</h:outputLink>
```

Use the `<s:link>` Tag

You can use the Seam `<s:link>` tag discussed in Section 7.2.5., "Links and Buttons", to open new browser windows/tabs within the same conversation.

8.4. Managing the Conversation ID

In the previous section, we mentioned that each Seam conversation has a unique ID (i.e., the `cid` HTTP parameter). By default, Seam automatically increases the ID value by one for each new conversation. The default setting is good enough for most applications, but it can be improved for applications that have many workspaces. The numeric number is not very informative, and it is hard to remember which workspace is in what state by looking at the ID numbers. Furthermore, if you have many workspaces in tabs, you might open two different workspaces to perform the same task, and that can get confusing very quickly.

To solve these problems, Seam provides a mechanism for customizing the conversation IDs. All you need is to pass a parameter in the `@Begin` annotation for the long-running conversation. For instance, the following example generates conversation IDs based on the hotel you select to start a conversation. This is obviously more informative than a simple numeric number.

```
@Begin(id="hotel#{hotel.id}")
public String selectHotel() {
  ...
}
```

If you open two workspaces for the same hotel, Seam automatically detects the same conversation ID and redirects the second workspace to the current state of the existing workspace without executing the `@Begin` method. This helps users avoid workspace confusion.

In addition to the conversation ID values, Seam enables you to customize the `cid` and `clr` HTTP parameters. Those HTTP parameter names are configured in the `components.xml` file. The following shows our configuration in the Hotel Booking example to use the `cid` and `clr` names as HTTP parameters.

```
<components ...>

  ... ...

  <core:manager conversation-timeout="120000"
              concurrent-request-timeout="500"
              conversation-id-parameter="cid"
    conversation-is-long-running-parameter="clr"/>

</components>
```

If you don't configure those, Seam uses the verbose `conversationId` and `conversation-IsLongRunning` names by default.

Workspaces and conversations are key concepts in Seam, setting Seam apart from previous generations of stateless web frameworks. It's easy to develop multiworkspace web applications via the rich set of Seam annotations and UI tags. However, web pages in a Seam conversation are typically not bookmarkable because they are tied together by HTTP POST requests with a lot of hidden field data. In the next chapter, we discuss how to build bookmarkable RESTful URLs into your Seam application.

9

Transactions

Transactions are an essential feature for database-driven web applications. In each conversation, we typically need to update multiple database tables. If an error occurs in the database operation (e.g., a database server crashes), the application needs to inform the user, and all the updates this conversation has written into the database must be rolled back to avoid partially updated records (i.e., corrupted records). In other words, all database updates in the conversation must happen inside an atomic operation. Transactions enable you to do exactly that.

In a Seam application, we typically assemble and modify database entity objects throughout a conversation. At the end of the conversation, we commit all those entity objects into the database. For instance, in the Hotel Booking example (the `booking` project in the source code bundle), the `HotelBookingAction.confirm()` method at the end of the conversation (i.e., the method with the `@End` annotation) uses a single transaction to save the `booking` object in the database and then deduct the hotel room inventory from the database.

```
public class HotelBookingAction
    implements HotelBooking, Serializable {

  @End
  public String confirm()
          throws InventoryException {
    if (booking==null || hotel==null)
      return "main";

    em.persist(booking);
    hotel.reduceInventory();

    if (bookingList!=null)
      bookingList.refresh();

    return "confirmed";
  }
  // ... ...
}
```

If anything goes wrong, the entire transaction fails and the database remains unchanged. The user then receives an error message instead of a confirmation number.

9.1. Managing a Transaction

Transactions are enabled by default for all EJB3 session bean methods in a Seam application, so you don't need to do anything special to put the `confirm()` method under a transaction. Seam starts the transaction manager when an event-handler thread starts (e.g., when the `confirm()` method is invoked). The transaction manager commits all the updates to the database at the end of the thread. Because the transaction manager tracks the thread, it manages the event-handler method and all the nested method calls from inside the event handler.

If any database operation in the `confirm()` method fails and throws a `RuntimeException`, the transaction manager rolls back all database operations. For instance, if the hotel inventory-reduction operation fails due to a database connection error, the booking saving operation, which already happened, would be cancelled as well. The database is returned to the state before the conversation. Seam displays an error message instead of the confirmation number to the user (see Figure 9.1., "The RuntimeException Error Page"). We discuss how to display a custom error page for the `RuntimeException` in Section 14.4., "Use pages.xml for System Exceptions". If you do not set up the custom error page, the server just displays the error stack trace in JBoss's standard error page.

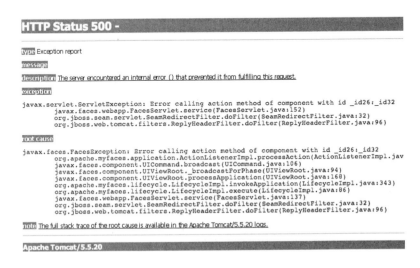

Figure 9.1. The RuntimeException Error Page

The stack trace displayed in Figure 9.1., "The RuntimeException Error Page", does not show the root cause of RuntimeException because the root exception is being wrapped around and rethrown from the JSF and Seam runtime. That has made debugging harder—you have to look in the server log file to see the complete stack trace of the exception. Custom error pages specifically tailored to each exception would definitely improve the application usability here (Section 14.4., "Use pages.xml for System Exceptions").

For a Seam POJO (Section 2.4.1., "Seam POJO Components"), its methods are also managed by the transaction manager by default, assuming that you configured the Transaction-alSeamPhaseListener in faces-config.xml (see Chapter 24, *Seam Without EJB3*). If you do not have the right listener configured, you can still configure any POJO method to be transactional using the @Transactional annotation.

Seam Managed Transaction for Non-EJB3 POJOs

Unlike the EJB3 transaction manager, which starts a transaction when a session bean method is called, the Seam managed transaction manager starts the transaction when a web request comes in. In fact, the Seam transaction manager uses two transactions per request. The first spans the beginning of the update model values phase until the end of the invoke application phase; the second spans the render response phase.

Transaction Attributes

In EJB3 session beans, you can set the transaction attribute for any method using the @TransactionAttribute annotation. For instance, you can start a new transaction in the middle of a call stack or exclude any particular method from the current transaction. Refer to the EJB3 documentation for more.

In Seam POJOs, method-level transaction demarcation is not available.

9.2. Forcing a Transaction Rollback

In a Java application, a `RuntimeException` or an unchecked exception indicates an unexpected runtime error (e.g., a network problem or database crash). By default, the transaction is automatically rolled back only when an unchecked exception is thrown.

However, that is not enough. Transactions are much more useful if we can tell the transaction manager to roll it back when certain conditions occur in the application. Seam provides two easy ways to forcefully roll back a transaction: exceptions and method return values.

9.2.1. Rolling Back Transactions via Checked Exceptions

You can also choose to roll back the transaction when a certain checked exception is thrown. For instance, you could throw checked exceptions to indicate a logic error in the application (e.g., the reserved hotel is not available). The trick is to tag the check exception class with the `@ApplicationException(rollback=true)` annotation. The following is the code for the `InventoryException`, which is used to indicate that the hotel has no available room.

```
@ApplicationException(rollback=true)
public class InventoryException
                        extends Exception {

    public InventoryException () { }

}
```

The `Hotel.reduceInventory()` method could throw this exception.

```
@Entity
@Name("hotel")
public class Hotel implements Serializable {

  // ... ...

  public void reduceInventory ()
        throws InventoryException {

    if (inventory > 0) {
      inventory--;
      return;
```

```
    } else {
      throw new InventoryException ();
    }
  }
}
```

> **Inventory Reduction**
>
> In a real-world hotel booking application, we would reduce the
> hotel room inventory by the booking dates and room type. In this
> example, we simply reduce the available number of rooms for the
> booked hotel. That is, of course, oversimplified. But then, the Seam
> Hotel Booking example is meant only as an example. For instance,
> we do not even have a daily rate for each hotel and do not calculate
> a total bill amount at the end of the conversation.

When an `InventoryException` is thrown from `Hotel.reduceInventory()` in the `Hotel-BookingAction.confirm()` method, the booking saving operation is rolled back when the method aborts. Seam then displays an error message page to the user. Again, in Section 14.3., "Annotate Exceptions", we discuss how to display a custom error page for this particular exception.

9.2.2. Rolling Back Transactions via Return Values

If certain conditions in your application are not as serious as an exception, but you still want to roll back the transaction (e.g., rolling back is part of the business logic), you can use the `@Rollback` annotation on any transactional method.

For instance, the following annotation indicates that the transaction on the `confirm()` method needs to be rolled back if the method returns the string `failure` or `not-valid`. After the transaction is rolled back, JSF displays the navigation target page associated with the return string value, which could well be your error page.

```
@Rollback(ifOutcome={"failure", "not-valid"})
public String confirm () {
  ... ...
}
```

In this case, you do not need to configure a custom error page for the transaction failure because one of your "rollback" outcomes could be associated with a navigation rule to display an error message.

9.3. Atomic Conversation (Web Transaction)

The Seam/EJB3 transaction is tied to a Java thread. It can manage operations only within a method call stack. It flushes all updates to the database at the end of each call stack. That behavior has two problems in a web conversation:

First, it can be inefficient to make multiple round-trips to the database in a conversation when all the updates are closely related.

Second, when a certain operation in the conversation fails, you must manually roll back the already-committed transactions in the conversation to restore the database to its state prior to the conversation.

A much better way is for the application to hold all database updates in memory and flush them all at once at the end of the conversation. If an error occurs in any step in the conversation, the conversation just fails without affecting the database. From the database point of view, the entire conversation either succeeds or fails—hence, atomic conversation. The atomic conversation behavior is also known as a web transaction. Seam makes it easy to implement atomic conversations. In the following sections, we discuss two approaches. The first is for Seam POJOs, and the second is for EJB3 session beans.

9.3.1. Manual Flush of the Persistence Context

If you use a Seam-managed `EntityManager` (i.e., an EntityManager injected via `@In`, see Chapter 24, *Seam Without EJB3*), you can specify the transactional behavior for a conversation in the `@Begin` annotation. Setting the `flushMode` attribute to MANUAL stops the transaction manager from flushing any updates to the database at the end of each transaction. The database updates are cached in the `EntityManager` during the entire conversation. Then, in the `@End` method, you call `EntityManager.flush()` to send the updates to the database all at once. The following is an example Seam POJO to show how this is done.

```
public class HotelBookingPojo Serializable {

  // ... ...
```

```
@In (create=true)
private EntityManager em;

@Begin(join=true, flushMode=MANUAL)
public String find() {
  // ... ...
}

public String bookHotel()
        throws InventoryException {
  // ... ...
  hotel.reduceInventory ();
}

@End
public String confirm() {
  // ... ...
  em.persist (booking);
  em.flush();
}
}
```

EntityManager Flush and Database Query Results

In some applications, you might update the database first and then query it in the same conversation. If we manually flush the Entity-Manager at the end of the conversation, as described in this section, the query result does not reflect the update in the middle of the conversation. Be sure to keep this in mind.

This approach requires the underlying JPA provider to be Hibernate. So it works in any JBoss environment but might not work in other Java EE 5.0 application servers.

9.3.2. One Transaction per Conversation

Another alternative is to disable the transaction manager on all methods except for the @End method. Because this approach requires method-level transaction demarcation, it can be used only on EJB3 session bean components with an EJB3-managed EntityManager (i.e., an EntityManager injected via @PersistenceContext).

This method is not as outrageous as it might sound. The transaction manager is not flushing anything to the database before the end of the conversation, so there is nothing to "roll back" if an error occurs. At the `@End` method, the data is automatically flushed to the database in a properly managed transaction. This is done by declaring all nontransactional methods in a conversation with the `@TransactionAttribute` annotation. Consider this example:

```
public class HotelBookingAction
  implements HotelBooking, Serializable {

  // ... ...

  @PersistenceContext (type=EXTENDED)
  private EntityManager em;

  @Begin(join=true)
  @TransactionAttribute(
    TransactionAttributeType.NOT_SUPPORTED)
  public String find() {
    // ... ...
  }

  @TransactionAttribute(
    TransactionAttributeType.NOT_SUPPORTED)
  public String bookHotel()
          throws InventoryException {
    // ... ...
    hotel.reduceInventory ();
  }

  @End
  @TransactionAttribute(
    TransactionAttributeType.REQUIRED)
  public String confirm() {
    // ... ...
    em.persist (booking);
  }
}
```

Because this approach uses only EJB3 standard annotations, it works in all EJB3-compliant application servers.

III

Integrating Web and Data Components

Seam makes life easier for web developers by acting as the "glue" between the web UI and the back-end data model. It provides annotations to streamline the communication between the UI and model, and, hence, reduces redundant information in the application source code. As a side effect, Seam fixes some of the most nagging problems in JSF development. In this part, we introduce those powerful Seam UI tags, annotations, and ready-to-use components. We show how to enhance the JSF validator infrastructure with Hibernate validators, how to expose data collections directly as JSF data tables, how to build bookmarkable URLs, how to manage custom error pages and debug pages, and how to write simple CRUD database applications with ready-made Seam components.

10

Validating Input Data

A key value proposition of Seam is to unify EJB3 and JSF component models. Through the unified components, we can use EJB3 entity beans to back data fields in JSF forms and then use EJB3 session beans as JSF UI event handlers. But Seam does much more than that. Seam enables us to develop data components that have UI-related "behaviors." For instance, the entity beans can have validators that behave like JSF validators.

In this chapter, we cover the Seam enhanced end-to-end validators that take advantage of Hibernate validator annotations on entity beans as well as Seam UI tags (see Section 3.2., "Seam JSF Enhancements"). We refactor the statful Hello World example to show how to use this Seam feature. The new application is in the `integration` directory in the source code bundle. We use the `integration` application in the next two chapters as well.

> **AJAX Validators**
>
> In this chapter, we cover only the "standard" method of validation via a form submission. In Part IV, "AJAX Support", we discuss how to use AJAX-based validators. But the Seam annotations and tags discussed in this chapter are highly relevant for later AJAX-based validators.

10.1. Form-Validation Basics

Form data validation is a task that almost every web application must implement. As an example, the `integration` application has four data fields on the `hello.xhtml` page, and all of them need to be validated before the `person` object can be saved into the database. For instance, the name must conform to a "Firstname Lastname" pattern with no nonalphabetical characters, the age must be between 3 and 100, the email address must contain an @ and only other legitimate email characters, and the comment must be shorter than 250 characters. If the validation fails, the page redisplays with all the data you already entered and the problem fields highlighted with images and error messages. Figure 10.1., "The web form before submission", and Figure 10.2., "Validation errors in the web form", show what happens when you try to submit a web form with invalid data.

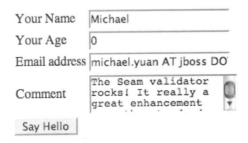

Figure 10.1. The web form before submission

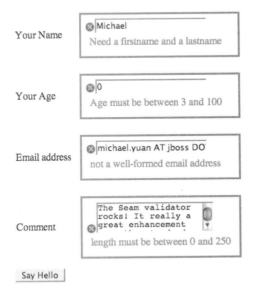

Figure 10.2. Validation errors in the web form

> **Validating on the Server**
>
> The built-in form-validation mechanism in Seam validates the user input data on the server side. You should always validate your data on the server side because a malicious user can tamper with any client-side validation mechanism, such as JavaScripts in the browser.

Form validation may sound easy, but in reality, it can be a nuisance to implement. The web application must manage the validation conditions, handle multiple round-trips between the browser and server, and partially update the entry form for alerts. It could easily take several hundred lines of code to implement the previous validation in previous-generation web frameworks. In Seam, on the other hand, all it takes is a couple of annotations and JSF tags.

> **Validation in the Seam Hotel Booking Example**
>
> In the Seam Hotel Booking example application, the `register.xhtml` form is backed by the User entity bean and is validated by Hibernate validators. So you can use that for an example as well.

10.2. Validation Annotations on the Entity Bean

Because all JSF forms in Seam are backed by EJB3 entity beans, the first thing we do is annotate the validation constraints directly on the entity bean fields. The following is what the `Person` entity bean looks like in the example project.

```
public class Person implements Serializable {

  ... ...

  @NotNull
  @Pattern(regex="^[a-zA-Z.-]+ [a-zA-Z.-]+",
      message="Need a firstname and a lastname")

  public String getName() { return name; }
  public void setName(String name) {
    this.name = name;
```

```
    }

    // @Min(value=3) @Max(value=100)
    @NotNull
    @Range(min=3, max=100,
        message="Age must be between 3 and 100")
    public int getAge() { return age; }
    public void setAge(int age) { this.age = age; }

    // @Pattern(regex="^[\w.-]+@[\w.-]+\.[a-zA-Z]{2,4}$")
    @NotNull
    @Email
    public String getEmail() { return email; }
    public void setEmail(String email) {
      this.email = email;
    }

    @Length(max=250)
    public String getComment() { return comment; }
    public void setComment(String comment) {
      this.comment = comment;
    }
}
```

Do Not Repeat Yourself

Seam validator annotations are specified on entity bean properties. They are enforced all the way from the JSF form to the database fields. You need to specify the validation condition only once in the entire application. No duplicated configuration is necessary for the presentation and database layers.

Those validation annotations have self-explanatory names. Each data property can have multiple annotations. Each annotation can take a `message` attribute, which holds the error message to display on the web form if this validation condition fails. If the `message` attribute is missing, a default error message is used for the annotated field. The `@Pattern` annotation can match the input field to an arbitrary regular expression. The following is a list of validation annotations supported out of the box in Seam.

- `@Length(max=,min=)` applies to a `String` property to check whether the string length is in the range.

- `@Max(value=)` applies to a numeric (or a string representation of a numeric value) property to check that the property value is less than the specified max value.

- `@Min(value=)` applies to a numeric (or a string representation of a numeric value) property to check that the property value is greater than the specified `min` value.

- `@NotNull` applies to any property to check that the property is not `null`.

- `@Past` applies to a `Date` or `Calendar` property to check whether the date is in the past.

- `@Future` applies to a `Date` or `Calendar` property to check whether the date is in the future.

- `@Pattern(regex="regexp", flag=)` applies to a `String` property to check whether the string matches the regular expression. The `flag` attribute specifies how the matching should be done (e.g., whether to ignore cases).

- `@Range(max=,min=)` applies to a numeric (or a string representation of a numeric value) property to check that the property value is inside the given range.

- `@Size(max=,min=)` applies to a collection or array property to check whether the number of elements in the property is inside the given range.

- `@Email` applies to a `String` property to check whether the string conforms to the email address format.

- `@Valid` applies to any property. It performs validation recursively on the associated object. If the object is a Collection or an array, the elements are validated recursively. If the object is a `Map`, the value elements are validated recursively.

If you need custom validation conditions in your applications, you can also implement your own validator annotations. Refer to the documentation for more details.

> **Hibernate Validators**
>
> Seam validator annotations are the same thing as Hibernate validator annotations. The error messages can easily be internationalized (see the Hibernate annotations documentation). The EJB3 entity bean implementation in JBoss is based on the Hibernate framework. Seam links the validators on the entity bean to UI elements on the JSF form.

10.3. Triggering the Validation Action

By default, the entity bean validation process is triggered by database operations. The entity bean objects are validated right before they are saved into the back-end database. When the `EntityManager` tries to save an invalid entity object, Seam throws a `RuntimeException`, which could lead to an error page or a generic HTTP 500 error (see Chapter 14, *Failing Gracefully*).

However, for web form validation, we want the validation to happen immediately after the form is submitted, before even the event-handler method is invoked or any database operation occurs. If the validation fails, we want to display an error page on the form, with all input data still in the fields, instead of being redirected to a special error page. In this section, we discuss how to trigger Hibernate validator actions from a form submission; in Section 10.4., "Display Error Messages on the Web Form", we discuss how to display the error messages.

To trigger validator actions from a form submission, you need to insert the Seam `<s:validate/>` tag inside the input data field elements. When the form is submitted, Seam validates tagged data fields using the corresponding validator on the backing entity bean object. If the validation fails, Seam redisplays the form with error messages (see Section 10.4., "Display Error Messages on the Web Form"). The following listing shows an example for the `integration` example project.

```
<h:form>

    ... ...

    <h:inputText value="#{person.name}">
      <s:validate/>
    </h:inputText>

    ... ...

    <h:inputText value="#{person.age}">
      <s:validate/>
    </h:inputText>

    ... ...

    <h:inputText value="#{person.email}">
      <s:validate/>
    </h:inputText>

    ... ...
```

```
   <h:inputTextarea
           value="#{person.comment}">
     <s:validate/>
   </h:inputTextarea>

<h:commandButton type="submit" value="Say Hello"
                 action="#{manager.sayHello}"/>
</h:form>
```

Using Seam UI tags

As we discussed in Chapter 3, *Recommended JSF Enhancements*, you need to bundle the `jboss-seam-ui.jar` file in your `app.war` file's `WEB-INF/lib` directory to use the Seam UI tags.

The `<s:validate/>` tag enables you to specify each input field to be validated. But in most cases, we want to validate all fields in a form, and the `<s:validate/>` tags become too verbose. To do that, we can enclose multiple fields in a `<s:validateAll/>` tag. For instance, the following code is equivalent to the previous listing:

```
<h:form>

    ... ...

<s:validateAll>
    <h:inputText value="#{person.name}"/>

    ... ...

    <h:inputText value="#{person.age}"/>

    ... ...

    <h:inputText value="#{person.email}"/>

    ... ...

    <h:inputTextarea
            value="#{person.comment}"/>
</s:validateAll>
```

```
<h:commandButton type="submit" value="Say Hello"
              action="#{manager.sayHello}"/>
</h:form>
```

Validation in the UI Event Handler

Alternatively, you can skip the Seam validation tags and specify the validation action on the session bean that handles the form submission button. With this approach, you do not need the `jboss-seam-ui.jar` file if you do not have other Seam UI tags in the application. But for most applications, we strongly recommend that you use validator tags.

To trigger validation in a Seam session bean, you need two annotations. The `@Valid` annotation validates the `person` object injected from the JSF web form. The `@IfInvalid(outcome=REDISPLAY)` annotation tells the Say Hello button's event handler to redisplay the current page with error messages if the injected `person` object is invalid.

```
public class ManagerAction implements Manager {

  @In @Out @Valid
  private Person person;

  ... ...

  @IfInvalid(outcome=REDISPLAY)
  public String sayHello () {
    em.persist (person);
    find ();
    return "fans";
  }

  ... ...
}
```

10.4. Display Error Messages on the Web Form

As we discussed earlier, when the validation fails, we want to redisplay the form with the input data intact and error messages for each invalid field. You can do this in two ways: with the standard JSF error display or with the enhanced Seam decorator approach. The Seam decorator is slightly more complex but offers much richer UI features.

Because the `<s:validate/>` tag incorporates the Hibernate validator as a JSF validator for the form, we can use the standard JSF mechanism to display the error message for each invalid input field. This is done by adding a JSF message element for each input field. Those message elements render the error messages in case of a validation failure. Make sure that the `for` attribute on the message tag matches the input field's `id` tag.

```
<s:validateAll>
  <h:inputText id="name"
          value="#{person.name}"/>
  <h:message for="name" />

  ... ...

</s:validateAll>
```

However, the problem with the standard JSF validation messages is that they are not very flexible. Although you can assign CSS classes to customize the look of the error message itself, you cannot alter the appearance of the input field that contains the invalid input. For instance, in plain JSF, you cannot add an image in front of the invalid field, and you cannot change the size, font, color, or background of the invalid field. The Seam decorator enables you to do all those, and it gets rid of the `id`/`for` nuisance.

To use a Seam decorator, you first define how the decorator behaves using special named JSF facets. The `beforeInvalidField` facet defines what to display in front of the invalid field; the `afterInvalidField` facet defines what to display after the invalid field, and the `<s:messge>` tag shows the error message for the input field; and the `aroundInvalidField` facet defines a span or div element that encloses the invalid field and the error message. You also can use the `aroundField` facet (not shown in the example here) to decorate the appearance of valid (or initial) input fields.

```
<f:facet name="beforeInvalidField">
  <h:graphicImage styleClass="errorImg"
                  value="error.png"/>
</f:facet>
<f:facet name="afterInvalidField">
  <s:message/>
</f:facet>
<f:facet name="aroundInvalidField">
  <s:span styleClass="error"/>
</f:facet>
```

Then you can just enclose each input field in a pair of `<s:decorate>` tags. The result is shown in Figure 10.2., "Validation errors in the web form".

```
... Set up the facets ...

<s:validateAll>

    ... ...

    <s:decorate>
      <h:inputText value="#{person.name}"/>
    </s:decorate>

    ... ...

    <s:decorate>
      <h:inputText value="#{person.age}"/>
    </s:decorate>

    ... ...

    <s:decorate>
      <h:inputText value="#{person.email}"/>
    </s:decorate>

    ... ...

    <s:decorate>
      <h:inputTextarea id="comment"
                       value="#{person.comment}"/>
    </s:decorate>

    ... ...

</s:validateAll>
```

There is no more messing around with the `id` and `for` attributes as we did with the JSF message tags because the `<s:message>` tag "knows" which input field it is associated with through the parent `<s:decorate>` tag.

You can also customize the Seam decorator on a per-input-field basis. For instance, if the `name` input field needs a different highlight, we can custom it as follows:

```
<s:decorate>
  <f:facet name="beforeInvalidField">
    <h:graphicImage src="anotherError.gif"/>
  </f:facet>
  <f:facet name="afterInvalidField">
    <s:message styleClass="anotherError"/>
  </f:facet>
  <f:facet name="aroundInvalidField">
    <s:span styleClass="error"/>
  </f:facet>

  <h:inputText value="#{person.name}"/>
</s:decorate>
```

The Seam `<s:validate>` and `<s:decorate>` tags greatly simplify form validation in the web tier. We highly recommend that you take advantage of them.

10.5. Use JSF Custom Validators

As we discussed, a great benefit of the Seam validator is to minimize repeated configurations in both the presentation and database layers. But in some cases, validation is needed only in the presentation layer. For instance, we might want to make sure that the user enters a valid credit card number for the transaction, and the credit card number might not even get saved in the database when the transaction is finished. For those purposes, you can also use plain JSF validators in Seam applications.

JSF provides only a couple simple validators out of the box. But third-party JSF component libraries provide plenty of custom validators. For instance, the following example shows the use of the Apache Tomahawk validator for credit card numbers. Refer to the Tomahawk documentation for how to install the component library.

```
<h:outputText value="Credit Card Number" />
<s:decorate>
```

```
  <h:inputText id="creditCard" required="true"
        value="#{customer.creditCard}">
    <t:validateCreditCard />
  </h:inputText>
</s:decorate>
```

You can easily use the `<s:decorate>` tag to enhance the error message display for any JSF custom validators as well.

Clickable Data Tables

Besides the validated entity objects, another example of Seam behavioral data components is the clickable data table. A regular JSF data table displays a list of data objects, with each table row showing the contents of an object. A clickable data table has additional "action" columns in the table. Each action column contains buttons (or links) that enable you to operate on the entity data object corresponding to each row.

For instance, the `fans.xhtml` page in the `integration` example application shows an example of the clickable data table (see Figure 11.1., "Clickable data table in the fans.xhtml page"). The table displays all persons in the database, with each row representing a person. Each row also contains a clickable button that enables the user to delete the person represented by the row. In a general clickable data table, you can have multiple action buttons/links for each row.

The Seam Fans

The following persons have said "hello" to JBoss Seam:

Name	Age	Email	Comment		
Michael Yuan	31	michael.yuan@jboss.com	Very cool!	Delete	Edit
John Doe	25	john.doe@mail.com	I like it!	Delete	Edit
Joan Roe	28	joan.roe@oracle.com	Better than Oracle!	Delete	Edit

Go to hello page

Figure 11.1. Clickable data table in the `fans.xhtml` page

In the Hotel Booking example application (the booking project), the main.xhtml page displays a clickable data table containing all previous reservations that you booked and provides buttons to delete any of those reservations (see Figure 11.2., "Clickable data table in the main.xhtml page in the Hotel Booking example").

Current Hotel Bookings

Name	Address	City, State	Check in date	Check out date	Confirmation number	Action
Conrad Miami	1395 Brickell Ave	Miami, FL	Apr 11, 2006	Apr 12, 2006	3	Cancel
W Hotel	Lexington Ave, Manhattan	NY, NY	Apr 11, 2006	Apr 12, 2006	2	Cancel
Marriott Courtyard	Tower Place, Buckhead	Atlanta, GA	Apr 11, 2006	Apr 12, 2006	1	Cancel

Figure 11.2. Clickable data table in the main.xhtml page in the Hotel Booking example

For clarity and simplicity, we use the integration example to illustrate the implementation of a clickable data table in this chapter.

11.1. Implement a Clickable Data Table

In plain JSF, clickable tables are difficult to implement because there is no clean way to associate the row ID with the event handlers for the action buttons in that row. Seam, however, provides two very simple ways to implement those highly useful clickable tables.

11.1.1. Display the Data Table

The JSF page to display the clickable data table is simple. You just need a regular JSF <h:dataTable> UI element. The <h:dataTable> element iterates over a Java List typed component with the @DataModel annotation. The following listing shows the code in the integration example. The @DataModel turns the fans component into a JSF DataModel object, and it already implies the @Out annotation.

```java
public class ManagerAction implements Manager {

    ... ...

    @DataModel
    private List <Person> fans;

    @DataModelSelection
    private Person selectedFan;

    @Factory("fans")
    public void findFans () {
        fans = em.createQuery("select p from Person p")
                                    .getResultList();
    }

    ... ...
}
```

Each property in the Person bean is presented in a column of the table. The Delete buttons occupy their own column and all have the same event-handler method: #{manager.delete} method. We explain how the #{manager.delete} method works in the next two sections.

```html
<h:dataTable value="#{fans}" var="fan">
  <h:column>
    #{fan.name}
  </h:column>
  <h:column>
    #{fan.age}
  </h:column>
  <h:column>
    #{fan.email}
  </h:column>
  <h:column>
    #{fan.comment}
  </h:column>
  <h:column>
    <h:commandButton value="Delete"
                     action="#{manager.delete}"/>
  </h:column>
</h:dataTable>
```

In this example, we showed the Delete button in `<commandButton>`. Of course, we can render an action link for each row in a clickable table with the JSF `<commandLink>` or the Seam `<s:link>` component—those link components can take Seam event-handler methods in the `action` attribute. The Seam `<s:link>` is recommended here because it supports normal browser behavior such as the right-click pop-up menu (see Section 7.2.5., "Links and Buttons" for more details).

But still, since all rows have the same button event handler, how does the `#{manager.delete}` method know which `Person` object to operate on? You can either inject the selected object to the `#{manager}` component or use Seam extended EL to reference the selected object.

11.1.2. Inject Selected Object into Event Handler

We define a `selectedFan` field in the `ManagerAction` class and annotate it with the `@DataModelSelection` annotation. When you click on a button (or link) in any row in the clickable table, Seam injects the `Person` object represented by that row into the `selectedFan` field before invoking the event-handler method. At last, we implement the event handler for the Delete button on each row. The event handler merges the injected `Person` object into the current persistence context and deletes it from the database.

```java
public class ManagerAction implements Manager {

  ... ...

  @DataModel
  private List <Person> fans;

  @DataModelSelection
  private Person selectedFan;

  ... ...

  public String delete () {
    Person toDelete = em.merge (selectedFan);
    em.remove( toDelete );
    findFans ();
    return null;
  }

}
```

The merge is needed because the `ManagerAction` component has the default conversation scope: the component and its persistence context are destroyed when the data table is completely rendered. So when the user clicks on the data table, a new `ManagerAction` component is constructed for the new conversation. The `selectedFan` object is out of the new persistence context and, hence, needs to be merged.

> **Merge Data Objects into Persistence Context**
>
> If we manage data objects in a long-running conversation, there is less need to merge the persistence context from time to time.

11.1.3. Use Extended EL in Data Table

The injection via `@DataModelSelection` decouples the presentation from the event handler. It is the standard "JSF way" of doing things. However, with the Seam extended EL (see Section 3.2.2., "Seam JSF EL Enhancement"), there is a simpler alternative. You can directly reference the object in the selected row.

```
<h:dataTable value="#{fans}" var="fan">
  <h:column>
    #{fan.name}
  </h:column>
  ... ...
  <h:column>
    <h:commandButton value="Delete"
             action="#{manager.delete(fan)}"/>
  </h:column>
</h:dataTable>
```

In the `ManagerAction` class, you need a `delete()` method that takes the `Person` argument.

```
public class ManagerAction implements Manager {

  ... ...

  @DataModel
  private List <Person> fans;

  ... ...
```

```
public String delete (Person selectedFan) {
  Person toDelete = em.merge (selectedFan);
  em.remove( toDelete );
  findFans ();
  return null;
}

}
```

The clickable data table is an excellent example of the tight integration between data and UI components in Seam applications.

11.2. Seam Data-Binding Framework

The @DataModel and @DataModelSelection annotations are just concrete use cases of the Seam data-binding framework, which provides a generic mechanism for turning any data objects into JSF UI components and capturing the user input on the component. For instance, the @DataModel annotation simply turns a Map or Set into a JSF DataModel component, and the @DataModelSelection annotation passes in any selection the user made on the DataModel.

The generic data-binding framework enables third-party developers to extend Seam and write custom annotations to give UI behaviors to arbitrary data model objects. For instance, one might write an annotation to expose an image as a map widget on the web page and capture the user selection as a location on the map. The data-binding framework opens the door for some extremely interesting use cases from the community in the future.

The data-binding framework is an advanced topic because it requires knowledge of the internal workings of Seam and JSF. This is a little beyond the scope of this book; in this section, we just give a brief overview of different components in the framework and leave interested readers to investigate the Seam source code yourselves.

The DataBinder and DataSelector interfaces in the org.jboss.seam.databinding package define the methods you have to implement for your own data binding classes. The DataModelBinder and DataModelSelector classes in the same package provide example implementations. Then, in the @DataModel and @DataModelSelection annotations, we simply pass the task to those implementation classes.

```
@Target({FIELD, METHOD})
@Retention(RUNTIME)
@Documented
@DataBinderClass(DataModelBinder.class)
public @interface DataModel {
   String value() default "";
   ScopeType scope() default ScopeType.UNSPECIFIED;
}

@Target({FIELD, METHOD})
@Retention(RUNTIME)
@Documented
@DataSelectorClass(DataModelSelector.class)
public @interface DataModelSelection {
   String value() default "";
}
```

For more details on how the `DataModelBinder` and `DataModelSelector` classes are implemented, refer to the Seam source code.

12

Bookmarkable Web Pages

One of the loudest criticisms of JSF (and other component-based web frameworks) is its reliance on HTTP POST requests. JSF uses HTTP POST to match user actions (e.g., button clicks) with UI event-handler methods on the server side (i.e., in Seam stateful session beans). It also uses hidden fields in the HTTP POST requests to keep track of the user's conversational state.

In an HTTP POST request, the URL does not contain the complete query information about the request. It is impossible to bookmark a web page dynamically generated from an HTTP POST. However, in many web applications, it is highly desirable to have bookmarkable web pages (a.k.a. RESTful URLs—REST stands for Representational State Transfer). For instance, for an e-commerce web site, you probably want to display information via URLs such as `http://mysite.com/product.seam?pid=123`; for a content site, you probably want to display articles via URLs such as `http://mysite.com/article.seam?aid=123`. The chief benefit of the bookmarkable URLs is that they can be saved for later access and emailed/messaged (i.e., they can be bookmarks).

In plain JSF, bookmarkable pages are somewhat difficult to construct: When the page is loaded from an HTTP GET, it is cumbersome to pass request parameters to backing beans and then automatically start bean method to process the parameters and load page data. However, with Seam, the barrier is easy to overcome. In this chapter, we discuss two approaches: using Seam page parameters and using request parameter injection with component lifecycle methods.

The example application is in the `integration` project in the source code bundle. It works like this: After people enter their names and messages in the `hello.seam` page, you can load any individual's personal details and comments via the `http://localhost:8080/integration/person.seam?pid=n` URL, where n is the unique ID of that individual. You can then make changes to any of the details and submit them back to the database (see Figure 12.1., "The bookmarkable individual person information edit page in the integration example project").

Edit Michael Yuan

Your name: | Michael Yuan

Your age: | 31

Email: | michael.yuan@jboss

Comment: | Very cool!

Update

Figure 12.1. The bookmarkable individual person information edit page in the integration example project

> **When to Use Bookmarkable URLs**
>
> We believe that bookmarkable URLs and POST URLs both have their places. For instance, you probably do not want the user to bookmark a temporary page inside a conversation (e.g., the credit card payment submission page). In that case, a nonbookmarkable POST page is more appropriate.

12.1. Using Page Parameters

The easiest way to pass HTTP GET request parameters to back-end business components is to use Seam page parameters. Each Seam web page can have zero to several page parameters, which are HTTP request parameters bound to properties on back-end components.

Seam page parameters are defined in the `pages.xml` file in the `app.war/WEB-INF/` directory. You have already seen this file in Section 8.2., "Workspace Switcher", where we used it to store the description of each web page for the conversation list. In the following example, when the `person.xhtml` page is loaded, the HTTP GET request parameter `pid` is converted to a `Long` value and bound to the `#{manager.pid}` property. Notice that we can use JSF EL and the converter here, although the `pages.xml` file is not a JSF web page; it is the power of Seam's expanded use of JSF EL.

```
<pages>

  <page view-id="/person.xhtml">
    <param name="pid" value="#{manager.pid}"
           converterId="javax.faces.Long"/>
  </page>

</pages>
```

So when you load a URL such as `person.seam?pid=3`, Seam automatically invokes the `ManagerAction.setPid(3)` method. In the setter method, we initialize the `person` object and outject it.

```java
@Stateful
@Name("manager")
public class ManagerAction implements Manager {

  @In (required=false) @Out (required=false)
  private Person person;

  @PersistenceContext (type=EXTENDED)
  private EntityManager em;

  Long pid;

  public void setPid (Long pid) {
    this.pid = pid;

    if (pid != null) {
      person = (Person) em.find(Person.class, pid);
    } else {
      person = new Person ();
    }
  }

  public Long getPid () {
    return pid;
  }

  ... ...
}
```

> **The Bijection Values Are Not Required**
>
> The `@In` and `@Out` annotations on the `person` field have the `required=false` attribute. When the `ManagerAction.setPid()` method is called, the `person` component does not have a valid value. In fact, we construct the `person` object in the setter and then outject it.
>
> Of course, by setting `@In(required=false)`, Seam could also inject a `null` value for `person` when you invoke any event-handler method in the `ManagerAction` component. If any of the event-handler methods does not provide a valid `person` object to outject (e.g., the `ManagerAction.delete()` method), you must set the `@Out(required=false)` as well.

Using similar techniques, you can have multiple page parameters binding to the same or different back-end components on the same page. The `person.xhtml` page displays the editing form with the outjected `person` component.

```
<s:validateAll>

<table>
  <tr>
    <td>Your name:</td>
    <td>
      <s:decorate>
        <h:inputText value="#{person.name}"/>
      </s:decorate>
    </td>
  </tr>

  <tr>
    <td>Your age:</td>
    <td>
      <s:decorate>
        <h:inputText value="#{person.age}"/>
      </s:decorate>
    </td>
  </tr>

  <tr>
    <td>Email:</td>
    <td>
      <s:decorate>
        <h:inputText value="#{person.email}"/>
```

```
      </s:decorate>
    </td>
  </tr>

  <tr>
    <td>Comment:</td>
    <td>
      <s:decorate>
        <h:inputTextarea value="#{person.comment}"/>
      </s:decorate>
    </td>
  </tr>

</table>

</s:validateAll>

<h:commandButton type="submit" value="Update"
                 action="#{manager.update}"/>
```

When you click on the Update button, the `person` object corresponding to the `pid` is updated. Many readers might find this puzzling: When we first loaded the `person.xhtml` page via HTTP GET, we explicitly gave the `pid` parameter. Why don't we need to explicitly pass the `pid` in an HTTP POST request associated with the Update button submission (e.g., as a hidden field in the form or as a `f:param` parameter for the Update button)? After all, the `person` and `manager` components are both in the default conversation scope (Section 7.1., "The Default Conversation Scope"); they have to be constructed anew when the form is submitted. So how does JSF know which `person` you want to update? Well, as it turns out, the page parameter has a PAGE scope (Section 5.5., "High Granularity Component Lifecycle"). When you submit the page, it always submits the same `pid` parameter from which the page is originally loaded. This is a very useful and convenient feature.

Page Action

When the page is loaded, the page parameter automatically triggers the setter method on the back-end property it binds to. Seam takes this concept one step further: You can trigger any back-end bean method at page load time in the `pages.xml` file. That is called page action. If the page action method is annotated with `@Begin`, the HTTP GET request for the page starts the long-running conversation. Furthermore, you can specify page actions that are executed only

---

> when a JSF EL condition is met. Here are two examples of page action:
>
> ```
> <pages>
>   <page view-id="/foo.xhtml">
>     <action execute="#{barBean.startConv}"/>
>   </page>
>
>   <page view-id="/register.xhtml">
>     <action if="#{validation.failed}"
>            execute="#{register.invalid}"/>
>   </page>
>
>   ... ...
>
> </pages>
> ```
>
> You can check out Section 19.1., "Stateful Navigation Rules in pages.xml", for more on how to use the `pages.xml` file.

The Seam page parameter is an elegant solution for bookmarkable pages. You will see its application again in Chapter 13, *The Seam CRUD Application Framework*.

12.2. The Java-Centric Approach

The page parameter is not the only solution for bookmarkable pages. For one thing, a lot of developers dislike putting application logic in XML files. The `pages.xml` file can also get too verbose in some cases. For instance, you might have the same HTTP request parameter on multiple pages (e.g., `editperson.seam?pid=x`, `showperson.seam?pid=y` etc.) or have multiple HTTP request parameters for the same page. In either case, you then must repeat very similar page parameter definition in the `pages.xml` file.

Furthermore, the page parameter does not work correctly if the page is loaded from a servlet, which is the case for some third party JSF component libraries. Those libraries use their own special servlets to do more processing/rendering of the page. For an example, see Section 15.3., "Use ICEfaces with Seam".

To resolve those issues, Seam provides a mechanism for processing HTTP request parameters in a "pure Java" way. This is more involved than the page parameter approach, but the benefit is that at more points you can add your own custom logic. In this section, we show you how.

12.2.1. Obtaining Query Parameters in an HTTP GET Request

Our first challenge is to pass the HTTP GET query parameter to the business component that provides contents and supports actions for the page. Seam provides a `@RequestParameter` annotation to make this happen. The `@RequestParameter` annotation is applied to the `String` variable in a Seam component. When the component is accessed at runtime, the current HTTP request parameter matching the variable name is automatically injected into the variable. For instance, we could have the following code in the `ManagerAction` stateful session bean to support URLs such as `person.seam?pid=3`. Notice that the HTTP request parameter is a `String` object, but the injected value is a `Long` type. Seam converts the `String` to a `Long` during injection. Of course, you can inject a `String` value and convert it yourself.

```
@Stateful
@Name("manager")
public class ManagerAction implements Manager {

  @RequestParameter
  Long pid;

  // ... ...
}
```

Whenever a method (e.g., a UI event handler, a property accessor, or a component lifecycle method) inside the `ManagerAction` class is accessed, Seam first injects the request parameter `pid` into the field variable with the same name. If your request parameter and field variable have different names, you must use the `value` argument in the annotation. For instance, the following code injects the `pid` request parameter into the `personId` field variable.

```
@RequestParameter (value="pid")
Long personId;
```

12.2.2. Load Data for the Page

Getting the request query parameter is only the first step. When the `person.seam?pid=3` page is loaded, it has to also trigger Seam to actually retrieve the person's information from the database. For instance, the `person.xhtml` page simply displays data from the `person` component. So how do we instantiate the `person` component with the `pid` parameter at the HTTP GET?

12.2.2.1. The @Factory Method

As we discussed in Section 6.1.4., "Factory Methods", we can use a factory method to initialize any Seam component. The factory method for the `person` component is located in the `ManagerAction` bean. Seam calls `ManagerAction.findPerson()` when it instantiates the `person` component. The factory method uses the injected `pid` to retrieve the `Person` object from the database.

```
@Stateful
@Name("manager")
public class ManagerAction implements Manager {

  @In (required=false) @Out (required=false)
  private Person person;

  @PersistenceContext (type=EXTENDED)
  private EntityManager em;

  @RequestParameter
  Long pid;

  ... ...

  @Factory("person")
  public void findPerson () {
    if (pid != null) {
      person = (Person) em.find(Person.class, pid);
    } else {
      person = new Person ();
    }
  }

}
```

In summary, the whole process works like this: When the user loads the `person.seam?pid=3`
URL, the `person.xhtml` page is processed and Seam finds it necessary to instantiate the
`person` component to display data on the page. Seam injects the `pid` value into the
`ManagerAction` object and then calls the `ManagerAction.findPerson()` factory method to
build and outject the `person` component. The page is then displayed with the `person`
component.

12.2.2.2. The @Create Method

The `person` component can be constructed with a factory method. But what if the page data
comes from a business component? For instance, the page could display data from
`#{manager.person}` instead of `#{person}`. In this case, we need to initialize the `person` property in the `manager` component when Seam instantiates the `manager` component. According to
Section 6.1.3., "Stateful Component Lifecycle", we can do it via the `@Create` lifecycle method in the `ManagerAction` class.

```
@Stateful
@Name("manager")
public class ManagerAction implements Manager {

  @RequestParameter
  Long pid;

  // No bijection annotations
  private Person person;

  @PersistenceContext(type=EXTENDED)
  private EntityManager em;

  public Person getPerson () {return person;}
  public void setPerson (Person person) {
    this.person = person;
  }

  @Create
  public String findPerson() {
    if (pid != null) {
      person = (Person) em.find(Person.class, pid);
    } else {
      person = new Person ();
    }
  }

  // ... ...
}
```

Event-Handler Methods

The @Factory and @Create methods can also be used as UI event-handler methods in regular JSF HTTP POST operations. They also can use the injected HTTP request parameter if the POST request has such parameters (see Section 12.2.3., "Further Processing from the Bookmarked Page").

12.2.3. Further Processing from the Bookmarked Page

Without the PAGE scoped page parameter, we must include the HTTP request parameter in all subsequent requests. For instance, the person.xhtml page loads the manager and person components only in the default conversation scope (see Section 7.1., "The Default Conversation Scope"), so the components expire when the page is fully rendered. When the user clicks on the Say Hello button to edit the person's information, a new set of manager and person components must be constructed for the new conversation. Thus, the JSF POST for the Say Hello button submission must also include the pid parameter. The pid is injected into the ManagerAction class, which uses it to build the person component before the event-handler method ManagerAction.sayHello() is invoked. To do that, we use a hidden field in the form.

```
<h:form>

<input type="hidden" name="pid"
       value="#{person.id}"/>

<s:validateAll>
  ... ...
</s:validateAll>

<h:commandButton type="submit" value="Update"
                 action="#{manager.update}"/>
</h:form>
```

If you annotate the @Factory or @Create methods with the @Begin annotation, you can start a long-running conversation from a bookmarked page. For instance, in an e-commerce web site, you can start a shopping cart conversation when the user loads a bookmarked product

---

page with a `productId`. The REST-loaded `product` component stays available throughout the conversation until the user checks out or aborts the shopping session. There is no need to load the `product` component again from the `productId` as long as the conversation stays valid.

The Hidden Field Hack

The hidden field in the web form is really a hack. We do not recommend it because it could confuse code maintainers in the future. If you need a hidden field to make your RESTful page work, you are probably better off injecting the page parameter via the `pages.xml` file instead of using the `@RequestParameter`. But in Section 15.3., "Use ICEfaces with Seam", we will see that this hack is sometimes necessary with third party JSF component libraries.

Seam provides great REST support for JSF applications. This is one of the most compelling reasons to use Seam with JSF.

13

The Seam CRUD Application Framework

Without Seam, a plain JSF application has at least four layers: the UI page, the backing beans for the page data and event handlers, the session beans for business and data access logic, and the entity beans for the data model. Seam now has eliminated the artificial gap between JSF backing beans and EJB3 session beans. But there's more. Seam comes with a built-in framework for Create, Retrieve, Update, and Delete (CRUD) data operations. With this framework, we can make JSF applications even simpler by reusing much of the standard event-handler methods. For small projects, we can even completely eliminate the need for session beans. Too good to be true? Well, read on ...

The Seam CRUD application framework essentially provides prepackaged Data Access Objects (DAOs). Let's start this chapter with a brief introduction to DAOs.

13.1. Data Access Objects (DAOs)

One of the most useful design patterns in enterprise Java is the Data Access Object (DAO) pattern. The DAOs typically support CRUD operations on the ORM entity objects. In Seam applications, the DAO is an EJB3 session bean or a Seam POJO component holding reference to a managed `EntityManager` object.

In many small database-driven applications, the CRUD data access logic is the business logic. The web UI simply provides the user access to the database. In a JSF CRUD application, the web pages reference DAOs directly to operate on the data. For those applications, the back-end programming primarily consists of coding the DAOs. For instance, in the series of Hello World examples we have seen so far in this book, the `ManagerAction` session bean primarily functions as a DAO for the `Person` entity bean.

In large enterprise applications, the benefit of the DAO pattern is that it abstracts out the data access logic from the business logic. The business components contain only the domain specific "business logic" and no data access-specific API calls (e.g., no `EntityManager` references). Hence, the business components are more portable and lightweight, in that they are less attached to the underlying frameworks. That is certainly a good thing, from an architectural point of view.

On the other hand, DAOs are highly repetitive. The DAOs for each entity class are largely the same. They are ideal for code reuse. Seam provides an application framework with built-in generic DAO components. You can develop simple CRUD web applications in Seam without writing a single line of Java "business logic" code. Don't believe me? Well, read on and we show you how. The example application in this chapter is in the `crud` project in the book's source code bundle. In terms of functions, the `crud` example is roughly equivalent to the `integration` example used in the previous chapters.

13.2. Seam CRUD DAOs Are POJOs

Because the DAO is responsible for only data access and does not need any other EJB3 container services, we should be able to use Seam POJOs instead of EJB3 session beans (see Section 2.4.1., "Seam POJO Components"). The benefit of Seam POJOs is that they are simpler than EJB3 session beans and can deploy in older J2EE 1.4 application servers, but they do need a little extra configuration (see Chapter 24, *Seam Without EJB3*). If you use Seam Gen (Chapter 4, *Rapid Application Development Tools*) to generate your configuration files, the POJO settings are enabled by default. If you write your own configuration files from the Hello World examples, you need to pay attention to a couple places. The idea here is to bootstrap a Seam-managed `EntityManager` for the DAO POJOs because the POJOs cannot directly use the EJB3-managed `EntityManager`.

First, in the `faces-config.xml` file in `app.war/WEB-INF`, you need to use the `TransactionalSeamPhaseListener` instead of the standard `SeamPhaseListener` used in typical Seam EJB3 applications. The `TransactionalSeamPhaseListener` provides a Seam-managed transaction manager for the `EntityManager`.

```
<faces-config>

  <lifecycle>
    <phase-listener>
org.jboss.seam.jsf.TransactionalSeamPhaseListener
    </phase-listener>
  </lifecycle>

  ... ...

</faces-config>
```

In the `persistence.xml` file in `app.jar/META-INF`, you need to register the persistence context unit under a JNDI name unique to your application.

```
<persistence>
  <persistence-unit name="helloworld">
    ... ...
    <properties>
      ... ...
      <property
    name="jboss.entity.manager.factory.jndi.name"
    value="java:/crudEntityManagerFactory"/>
    </properties>
  </persistence-unit>
</persistence>
```

Finally, in the `components.xml` file in `app.war/WEB-INF`, you need to define the Seam-managed `EntityManager` component so that it can be injected into other Seam POJO components.

```
<components ...>

  ... ...

  <core:managed-persistence-context name="em"
      persistence-unit-jndi-name=
          "java:/crudEntityManagerFactory"/>

  ... ...

</components>
```

That's it for the `EntityManager` configuration. The Seam DAO components themselves are also defined in the `components.xml` file. Let's check out how they work next.

13.3. The Declarative Seam DAO Component

A useful feature of Seam DAO components is that they can be declaratively instantiated in the Seam `components.xml` file, so you do not even need to write any data access code. Let's look at an example for the `Person` entity bean adopted from previous examples. Because the DAO now manages the entity bean, you no longer need the `@Name` annotation on the entity bean.

```
@Entity
public class Person implements Serializable {

  private long id;
  private String name;
  private int age;
  private String email;
  private String comment;

  ... Getter and Setter Methods ...
}
```

To instantiate a DAO component for the `Person` entity bean, you simply need an `entity-home` element in `components.xml`. The DAO component can be referenced in JSF pages or injected into other Seam components via the Seam name `personDao`. The `#{em}` references the Seam-managed `EntityManager` we defined in the previous section. The DAO uses this `EntityManager` to manage the `Person` object.

```
<components ...
xmlns:fwk="http://jboss.com/products/seam/framework"
         ...>

  ... ...

  <fwk:entity-home name="personDao"
               entity-class="Person"
               entity-manager="#{em}"/>

  ... ...

</components>
```

You can now reference the `Person` instance that `personDao` manages via `#{personDao.instance}`. The following is an example JSF page that uses the DAO to add a new `Person` object to the database.

```
<s:validateAll>
<table>
```

```
<tr>
  <td>Your name:</td>
  <td>
    <s:decorate>
      <h:inputText
        value="#{personDao.instance.name}"/>
    </s:decorate>
  </td>
</tr>

... ...

</table>
</s:validateAll>

<h:commandButton type="submit" value="Say Hello"
                 action="#{personDao.persist}"/>
```

The #{personDao.persist} method returns the String value "persisted" after the object is successfully saved in the database. You can then define navigation rules for "persisted" to decide which page JSF should display next, etc. Besides the persist() method, the DAO component supports remove() and update() methods, which return the String values "removed" and "updated", respectively.

13.3.1. Use Simpler Names for the Entity Object

Using #{personDao.instance} to reference the managed Person instance in the DAO is not as elegant as using #{person}, as we did for the previous example. Fortunately, the component factory in Seam makes it very easy to map #{personDao.instance} to #{person}. Just add the factory element in the components.xml file as follows:

```
<components ...
xmlns:fwk="http://jboss.com/products/seam/framework"
          ...>

  ... ...

  <factory name="person"
           value="#{personDao.instance}"/>
  <fwk:entity-home name="personDao"
                   entity-class="Person"
                   entity-manager="#{em}"/>
```

```
... ...
</components>
```

You can now use #{person} to back the data fields on the page and #{personDao} to back the actions on the #{person} data.

```
<s:validateAll>
<table>

  <tr>
    <td>Your name:</td>
    <td>
      <s:decorate>
        <h:inputText
           value="#{person.name}"/>
      </s:decorate>
    </td>
  </tr>

  ... ...

</table>
</s:validateAll>

<h:commandButton type="submit" value="Say Hello"
                 action="#{personDao.persist}"/>
```

13.3.2. Retrieving and Displaying an Entity Object

A CRUD application typically uses HTTP GET request parameters to retrieve entity objects for a page. The DAO must receive the HTTP request parameter, query the database, and make the retrieved entity object available for the page. In Chapter 12, *Bookmarkable Web Pages*, we discussed how to bind the HTTP request parameter to back-end components. In the Seam DAO objects, all you need is to bind the HTTP request parameter to the DAO's id property.

For instance, in the crud example application, we want to load individual persons via URLs such as person.seam?pid=3. You can use the following element in the app.war/WEB-INF/pages.xml file to accomplish this.

```
<pages>

  <page view-id="/person.xhtml">
    <param name="pid" value="#{personDao.id}"
           converterId="javax.faces.Long"/>
  </page>

</pages>
```

Now when you load the `person.seam?pid=3` URL, the DAO automatically retrieves the `Person` object with an ID equal to 3. You can then reference the entity object via the JSF EL expression `#{person}`.

13.3.3. Initializing a New Entity Instance

When a new DAO is created, the DAO instantiates its managed entity object. If the `id` property in the DAO is not set, it just creates a new entity object using the entity bean's default constructor. You can initialize the newly created entity object in the `entity-home` component. The `new-instance` property allows Seam to inject an existing entity object, which is also created in the `components.xml` as a component, into the DAO. The following is an example. Notice that the property values in the `newPerson` component can also be JSF EL expressions.

```
<fwk:entity-home name="personDao"
                 entity-class="Person"
                 entity-manager="#{em}"
                 new-instance="#{newPerson}"/>

<component name="newPerson" class="Person">
  <property name="age">25</property>
</component>
```

13.3.4. Success Messages

As we discussed in Section 7.1.1., "Display JSF Messages", Seam enhances the JSF messaging system to display success messages after an operation. In the `entity-home` component, you can customize the success messages for the CRUD operations. You can now simply use the `<h:message>` components on any page to display the messages. This is a great time saver in simple CRUD applications.

```
<fwk:entity-home name="personDao"
                 entity-class="Person"
                 entity-manager="#{em}">
  <fwk:created-message>
    New person #{person.name} created
  </fwk:created-message>
  <fwk:deleted-message>
    Person #{person.name} deleted
  </fwk:deleted-message>
  <fwk:updated-message>
    Person #{person.name} updated
  </fwk:updated-message>
</fwk:entity-home>
```

> **Handling Failures**
>
> Obviously, the success messages are not sent to the JSF messaging
> system when the CRUD operation fails. In this case, we can redirect
> to a custom error page (see Chapter 14, *Failing Gracefully*).

13.4. Queries

Data querying is a key feature in database-driven applications. The Seam application framework provides query components in addition to the basic CRUD DAO components. You can
use the query component to declare queries in `components.xml` without writing a line of Java
code.

The declarative approach to data queries helps us manage all queries in a central location and
allows the Java code to reuse queries. It is a proven approach similar to the `NamedQuery` in
Hibernate or Java Persistence API.

For instance, the following element defines a Seam query component named `fans`. When the
query is executed, it retrieves all `Person` objects from the database.

```
<components ...>

  ... ...
```

```
<fwk:entity-query name="fans"
      entity-manager="#{em}"
      ejbql="select p from Person p"/>

</components>
```

On a JSF web page, you can execute the query and reference its result list via `#{fans.resultList}`.

```
<h:dataTable value="#{fans.resultList}" var="fan">
  <h:column>
    <f:facet name="header">Name</f:facet>
    #{fan.name}
  </h:column>
  <h:column>
    <f:facet name="header">Age</f:facet>
    #{fan.age}
  </h:column>
  <h:column>
    <f:facet name="header">Email</f:facet>
    #{fan.email}
  </h:column>
  <h:column>
    <f:facet name="header">Comment</f:facet>
    #{fan.comment}
  </h:column>
  <h:column>
    <a href="person.seam?pid=#{fan.id}">Edit</a>
  </h:column>
</h:dataTable>
```

You can use the WHERE clause to constrain the query results in the `ejbql` property. However, you cannot use parameterized query constraints because no Java code explicitly calls the `Query.setParameter()` method at runtime. To use dynamic queries, you must declaratively bind user input to the query. We discuss that technique in the next section.

13.4.1. Dynamic Queries

Static database queries are useful. But in real-world applications, most queries are dynamically constructed from user input. For instance, the user might search for all persons under age 35 who have a `redhat.com` email address.

Dynamic querying binds user input values (search criteria) to placeholders in the constraint clause of the query. The query API in the `EntityManager` enables you to place parameters (i.e., the placeholders) in the query string and then use the `setParameter()` method to set the parameter value at runtime before the query is executed. The Seam query component enables you to do similar things.

The Seam query component is defined in `components.xml`, so we can declaratively bind the user input to query constraints. You do so by using the JSF EL to capture user input in `components.xml`. For instance, let's assume that you have a `#{search}` component that backs the input fields on the search query page. The age constraint in the query is bound to `#{search.age}`, and the email constraint is bound to `#{search.email}`. The following is the query example in the `components.xml` file.

```
<fwk:entity-query name="fans"
                  entity-manager="#{em}"
                  ejbql="select p from Person p"
                  order="name">
  <fwk:restrictions>
    <value>age < #{search.age}</value>
    <value>
lower(email) like lower('%' + #{search.email})
    </value>
  </fwk:restrictions>
</fwk:entity-query>
```

Although it is possible to bind any JSF EL expression to the query constraint, the most common pattern is to use an example entity component to capture the user input. It provides a more structured way to manage the data fields. In the following example, notice that you can use the `order` property to order the query results.

```
<component name="examplePerson" class="Person"/>

<fwk:entity-query name="fans"
                  entity-manager="#{em}"
                  ejbql="select p from Person p"
                  order="name">
  <fwk:restrictions>
    <value>age < #{examplePerson.age}</value>
    <value>
lower(email) like lower('%'+#{examplePerson.email})
    </value>
  </fwk:restrictions>
</fwk:entity-query>
```

The web page for the query form and results list follows. Notice that the form submission button for the page is not bound to any back-end event-handler method; it simply submits the user input search criteria to the #{search} component. When JSF renders the #{fans} component later in the page, Seam invokes the query with the parameters in the #{search} component, as shown earlier.

```
<h:form>
Search filters:<br/>
Max age:
<h:inputText value="#{examplePerson.age}"/>
Email domain:
<h:inputText value="#{examplePerson.email}"/>
<h:commandButton value="Search" action="/search.xhtml"/>
</h:form>

<h:dataTable value="#{fans.resultList}" var="fan">
  <h:column>
    <f:facet name="header">Name</f:facet>
    #{fan.name}
  </h:column>
  <h:column>
    <f:facet name="header">Age</f:facet>
    #{fan.age}
  </h:column>
  <h:column>
    <f:facet name="header">Email</f:facet>
    #{fan.email}
  </h:column>
  <h:column>
    <f:facet name="header">Comment</f:facet>
    #{fan.comment}
  </h:column>
  <h:column>
    <a href="person.seam?pid=#{fan.id}">Edit</a>
  </h:column>
</h:dataTable>
```

13.4.2. Displaying Multipage Query Results

If your query has a long list of results, you usually want to display those results across multiple pages with links to navigate between pages. The Seam query component has built-in support for paged data tables. First, you specify how many result objects you want to display on each page via the max-results property.

```
<fwk:entity-query name="fans"
        entity-manager="#{em}"
        ejbql="select p from Person p"
        order="name"
        max-results="20"/>
```

Then on the JSF page, you use the `firstResult` HTTP request parameter to control which part of the result set to display. The `firstResult` parameter is automatically injected into the query component (i.e., `fans`) when the page loads, and no more coding is needed. For instance, the URL `fans.seam?firstResult=30` for the following page displays query result objects numbered 30 to 49.

```
<h:dataTable value="#{fans.resultList}" var="fan">
  <h:column>
    <f:facet name="header">Name</f:facet>
    #{fan.name}
  </h:column>

  ... ...
</h:dataTable>
```

The `entity-query` component also provides built-in support for pagination links. That makes it easy to add Next/Prev/First/Last links on the data result page.

```
<h:dataTable value="#{fans.resultList}" var="fan">
  <h:column>
    <f:facet name="header">Name</f:facet>
    #{fan.name}
  </h:column>

  ... ...
</h:dataTable>

<a href="fans.seam?firstResult=0">First Page</a>
<a href=
"fans.seam?firstResult=#{fans.previousFirstResult}">
  Previous Page
</a>
<a href=
"fans.seam?firstResult=#{fans.nextFirstResult}">
  Next Page
```

```
</a>
<a href=
"fans.seam?firstResult=#{fans.lastFirstResult}">
  Last Page
</a>
```

The static HTML pagination links appear even if the query result is only one page; for multiple-page results, they appear regardless of whether the user is already on the first/last page. A better approach is to use the Seam `<s:link>` component to render the links (see Section 3.2.1., "Seam UI Tags"). This way, you can control when the pagination links are rendered. Consider this example:

```
<h:dataTable value="#{fans.resultList}" var="fan">
  <h:column>
    <f:facet name="header">Name</f:facet>
    #{fan.name}
  </h:column>

  ... ...
</h:dataTable>

<s:link view="/fans.xhtml"
        rendered="#{fans.previousExists}"
        value="First Page">
  <f:param name="firstResult" value="0"/>
</s:link>

<s:link view="/fans.xhtml"
        rendered="#{fans.previousExists}"
        value="Previous Page">
  <f:param name="firstResult"
           value="#{fans.previousFirstResult}"/>
</s:link>

<s:link view="/fans.xhtml"
        rendered="#{fans.nextExists}"
        value="Next Page">
  <f:param name="firstResult"
           value="#{fans.nextFirstResult}"/>
</s:link>

<s:link view="/fans.xhtml"
        rendered="#{fans.nextExists}"
        value="Last Page">
  <f:param name="firstResult"
           value="#{fans.lastFirstResult}"/>
</s:link>
```

With the Seam CRUD framework, you can write an entire database application declaratively. But if you are not comfortable with coding in XML, you can also extend the Seam POJO classes behind the `entity-home` and `entity-query` components to accomplish the same. Refer to the Seam reference documentation for more details.

14

Failing Gracefully

Like input validation, error handling is a very important aspect of web applications, but it is hard to get done right. Without proper error handling, uncaught exceptions in the application (e.g., a RuntimeException or a transaction-related exception) would propagate out of the web framework and cause a generic "Internal Server Error" (HTTP error code 500). The user would see a page full of technical jargon and a partial stack trace of the exception itself (see Figure 14.1., "An uncaught exception from the Seam event handler method"). That is certainly unprofessional. Instead, we should try to fail gracefully and display a nice custom error page for the user.

HTTP Status 500 -

type Exception report

message

description The server encountered an internal error () that prevented it from fulfilling this request.

exception

```
javax.servlet.ServletException: Error calling action method of component with id _id26:_id32
        javax.faces.webapp.FacesServlet.service(FacesServlet.java:152)
        org.jboss.seam.servlet.SeamRedirectFilter.doFilter(SeamRedirectFilter.java:32)
        org.jboss.web.tomcat.filters.ReplyHeaderFilter.doFilter(ReplyHeaderFilter.java:96)
```

root cause

```
javax.faces.FacesException: Error calling action method of component with id _id26:_id32
        org.apache.myfaces.application.ActionListenerImpl.processAction(ActionListenerImpl.jav
        javax.faces.component.UICommand.broadcast(UICommand.java:106)
        javax.faces.component.UIViewRoot._broadcastForPhase(UIViewRoot.java:94)
        javax.faces.component.UIViewRoot.processApplication(UIViewRoot.java:168)
        org.apache.myfaces.lifecycle.LifecycleImpl.invokeApplication(LifecycleImpl.java:343)
        org.apache.myfaces.lifecycle.LifecycleImpl.execute(LifecycleImpl.java:86)
        javax.faces.webapp.FacesServlet.service(FacesServlet.java:137)
        org.jboss.seam.servlet.SeamRedirectFilter.doFilter(SeamRedirectFilter.java:32)
        org.jboss.web.tomcat.filters.ReplyHeaderFilter.doFilter(ReplyHeaderFilter.java:96)
```

note The full stack trace of the root cause is available in the Apache Tomcat/5.5.20 logs.

Apache Tomcat/5.5.20

Figure 14.1. An uncaught exception from the Seam event handler method

With the tight integration between the business components and presentation components, Seam makes it easy to "convert" any business-layer exception to a custom error page. In this chapter, we go back to the `booking` example discussed in Chapter 7, *Conversations*, to Chapter 9, *Transactions*, and show how errors are handled from the transactions.

Before we discuss the Seam approach, we present a quick overview on the "standard" error-handling mechanism in Java EE and why it is insufficient.

14.1. Why Not Standard Servlet Error Pages?

Java EE (the servlet specification) uses a standard mechanism for handling servlet or JSP exceptions. Using the error-page element in `web.xml`, you can redirect to a custom error page upon any exception or HTTP error code. The following is an example that redirects to the `/error.html` page when an uncaught error is thrown from the application or to the `/notFound.html` page when an HTTP 404 error is encountered.

```
<web-app>

  ... ...

  <error-page>
    <exception-type>
       java.lang.Throwable
    </exception-type>
    <location>/error.html</location>
  </error-page>

  <error-page>
    <error-code>
       404
    </error-code>
    <location>/notFound.html</location>
  </error-page>

</web-app>
```

However, a problem with this approach is that the JSF servlet wraps around the exception from the business layer and throws a generic `ServletException` instead, before the server captures the exceptions and redirects to the error page. So in the `exception-type` attribute, you cannot accurately specify the actual exception in the business layer. Some people would just capture a very generic `java.lang.Throwable` and redirect to a generic error page. That is not satisfactory because you would probably want to display different error messages for different error causes and present remedy action choices to the user.

In the JSP world, a workaround exists: You can simply redirect to a JSP error page. From that page, you can access the JSP built-in variable: `exception`. Then you can programmatically drill down to the root cause of the exception and display the appropriate message. Unfortunately, the `exception` variable does not work properly in JSF-rendered JSP pages or Facelets XHTML pages.

Seam provides a much better solution and enables you to integrate the error page directly into your existing JSF view. Better yet, Seam enables you to declare whether the exception should end the current conversation, if it were thrown from inside a long-running conversation.

14.2. Set Up the Exception Filter

Seam uses a servlet filter to capture uncaught exceptions and then render the appropriate custom error page (or error code). Make sure that the following elements are present in your `app.war/WEB-INF/web.xml` file (see Section 3.3., "Add Facelets and Seam UI Support"):

```
<web-app ...>

  ... ...

  <filter>
    <filter-name>Seam Filter</filter-name>
    <filter-class>
      org.jboss.seam.web.SeamFilter
    </filter-class>
  </filter>

  <filter-mapping>
    <filter-name>Seam Filter</filter-name>
    <url-pattern>/*</url-pattern>
  </filter-mapping>

</web-app>
```

With the Seam filter properly set up, you can now specify custom error pages for exceptions via one of the following two ways: For application-defined exceptions, you can use annotations, and for system or framework exceptions, you can use the `pages.xml` file. We discuss both approaches in this chapter.

14.3. Annotate Exceptions

If your application throws its own exceptions, you can use three annotations to tell Seam what to do when the annotated exception is uncaught.

The @Redirect annotation instructs Seam to display the error page specified in the viewId attribute when this exception is thrown. The end attribute specifies whether this exception ends the current long-running conversation; by default, the conversation does not end. The following example was taken from the Hotel Booking sample application (see Chapter 9, *Transactions*). This exception is thrown when the requested hotel is not available. It rolls back the database transaction but does not end the conversation, to enable the user to use the browser Back button to go back and select another hotel to book.

```
@ApplicationException(rollback=true)
@Redirect(viewId="/inventoryError.xhtml")
public class InventoryException
                    extends Exception {

    public InventoryException () { }

}
```

The error page inventoryError.xhtml is just a regular JSF view page (Figure 14.2., "The error page showing unavailable room inventory"). Notice that it still has access to the conversation scoped components (i.e., #{hotel}) and the user can use the browser Back button to book another hotel in the same conversation.

```
<ui:composition ... ...
        template="template.xhtml">

  <ui:define name="content">
    <div class="section">
      <h1>Insufficient Inventory</h1>
      <p>The <b>#{hotel.name}</b> hotel
      in #{hotel.city} does not have any room left.
      Please use your browser's BACK button to
      go back and book another hotel!</p>
    </div>
  </ui:define>

  ... ...

</ui:composition>
```

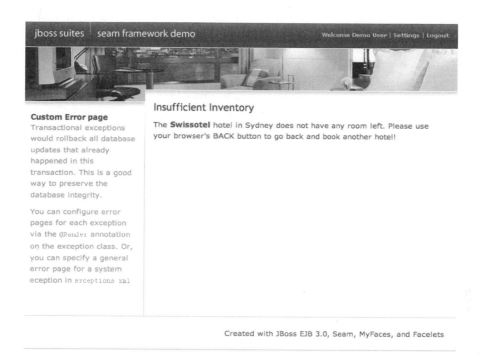

Figure 14.2. The error page showing unavailable room inventory

> **No Stack Trace**
>
> Notice that we do not display the exception stack trace in the custom error page here. You should never display the stack trace on a product web site. If you are debugging the application and want to see the stack trace, you can enable Seam debugging (Section 3.3., "Add Facelets and Seam UI Support") and go to /debug.seam.

The @HttpError annotation causes Seam to send an HTTP error code back to the browser when the annotated exception propagates out of the Seam runtime. The message attribute takes the HTTP message to be sent to the browser, and the end attribute specifies whether the current long-running conversation should end here.

```
@HttpError(errorCode=404, end=true)
public class SomeException extends Exception {
  ...
}
```

14.4. Use pages.xml for System Exceptions

The annotation approach applies only to application-defined exceptions. Of course, that is inadequate because many runtime errors are system- or framework-level exceptions. For instance, when a database connection occurs, the application throws a RuntimeException, which is not defined by the application and, hence, cannot be annotated.

In a Seam application, you can configure how to deal with system or framework exceptions via the pages.xml file we discussed earlier in the book (e.g., see Section 12.1., "Using Page Parameters"). This file should be packaged in the app.war file's WEB-INF directory together with web.xml, components.xml, etc. Similar to the annotations, we can redirect to a custom JSF page, send HTTP error code, and end the current long-running conversation when such exceptions are thrown.

The following pages.xml is from the Hotel Booking sample application. It configures custom error pages for the RuntimeException and other system exceptions. When Seam redirects to an error page, it sends along a JSF message that can be displayed via <h:messages/> UI element on the error page.

```xml
<pages>

  ... Page actions and parameters ...

  <exception
      class="javax.persistence.EntityNotFoundException">
    <http-error error-code="404"/>
  </exception>

  <exception
      class="javax.persistence.PersistenceException">
    <end-conversation/>
    <redirect view-id="/generalError.xhtml">
      <message>Database access failed</message>
    </redirect>
  </exception>

  <exception class="java.lang.RuntimeException">
    <redirect view-id="/generalError.xhtml">
      <message>Unexpected failure</message>
    </redirect>
  </exception>

</pages>
```

When a `RuntimeException` is thrown from the application, Seam redirects to the /
generalError.xhtml page with the JSF error message, but without ending the current long-
running conversation. The generalError.xhtml page is as follows; Figure 14.3., "The gen-
eralError.xhtml page for RuntimeException" shows it in a browser.

```
<ui:composition ...>

<ui:define name="content">
<div class="section">
<h1>General</h1>
<p>The following general error has occurred</p>

<p><h:messages/></p>

<p>Please come back and try again! Thanks.</p>
</div>
</ui:define>

<ui:define name="sidebar">
<h1>Custom Error page</h1>
... ...
</ui:define>

</ui:composition>
```

Figure 14.3. The `generalError.xhtml` page for `RuntimeException`

> **Error Message with @Redirect**
>
> The `@Redirect` annotation can also take a `message` attribute to send a JSF message to the error page it redirects to.

> **Use Error Page with Seam Security**
>
> It is easy to redirect to a custom login page when an un-authenticated user tries to access a restricted web page protected by the Seam security framework (see Chapter 20, *Rule-Based Security Framework*). You just need to capture and redirect the `org.jboss.seam.security.NotLoggedInException`.

14.5. Debug Information Page

The custom error pages are nice for production systems. However, when we develop the application, we do not know when and what kinds of errors might come up. Seam and Facelets provide generic mechanisms to capture any error during development and redirect to the debug information page so that you can accurately pinpoint the error source.

14.5.1. The Facelets Debug Page

To enable the Facelets debug page, you need to set Facelets in `development` mode in the `app.war/WEB-INF/web.xml` file, as follows:

```
<web-app ...>
  ... ...

  <context-param>
    <param-name>facelets.DEVELOPMENT</param-name>
    <param-value>true</param-value>
  </context-param>
</web-app>
```

If an error occurs when Facelets renders a page, Facelets displays a professional-looking error page with accurate debugging information pinpointing the line number in the Facelets XHTML file (see Figure 14.4., "The Facelets debug page"). The source file line number is useful because the standard JSF stack trace gives you the useless line numbers on the servlet compiled from the view page.

An Error Occurred:

Error Parsing /hello.xhtml: Error Traced[line: 25] The element type "p" must be terminated by the matching end-tag "</p>".

- Stack Trace

```
com.sun.facelets.FaceletException: Error Parsing /hello.xhtml: Error Traced[line: 25] The element type "p" must be
    at com.sun.facelets.compiler.SAXCompiler.doCompile(SAXCompiler.java:228)
    at com.sun.facelets.compiler.Compiler.compile(Compiler.java:104)
    at com.sun.facelets.impl.DefaultFaceletFactory.createFacelet(DefaultFaceletFactory.java:192)
    at com.sun.facelets.impl.DefaultFaceletFactory.getFacelet(DefaultFaceletFactory.java:141)
    at com.sun.facelets.impl.DefaultFaceletFactory.getFacelet(DefaultFaceletFactory.java:93)
    at com.sun.facelets.FaceletViewHandler.buildView(FaceletViewHandler.java:483)
    at com.sun.facelets.FaceletViewHandler.renderView(FaceletViewHandler.java:533)
    at org.apache.myfaces.lifecycle.LifecycleImpl.render(LifecycleImpl.java:384)
    at javax.faces.webapp.FacesServlet.service(FacesServlet.java:138)
    at org.apache.catalina.core.ApplicationFilterChain.internalDoFilter(ApplicationFilterChain.java:252)
    at org.apache.catalina.core.ApplicationFilterChain.doFilter(ApplicationFilterChain.java:173)
    at org.jboss.seam.servlet.SeamExceptionFilter.doFilter(SeamExceptionFilter.java:46)
    at org.apache.catalina.core.ApplicationFilterChain.internalDoFilter(ApplicationFilterChain.java:202)
    at org.apache.catalina.core.ApplicationFilterChain.doFilter(ApplicationFilterChain.java:173)
    at org.jboss.seam.servlet.SeamRedirectFilter.doFilter(SeamRedirectFilter.java:32)
    at org.apache.catalina.core.ApplicationFilterChain.internalDoFilter(ApplicationFilterChain.java:202)
    at org.apache.catalina.core.ApplicationFilterChain.doFilter(ApplicationFilterChain.java:173)
    at org.apache.catalina.core.StandardWrapperValve.invoke(StandardWrapperValve.java:213)
    at org.apache.catalina.core.StandardContextValve.invoke(StandardContextValve.java:178)
    at org.apache.catalina.core.StandardHostValve.invoke(StandardHostValve.java:126)
    at org.apache.catalina.valves.ErrorReportValve.invoke(ErrorReportValve.java:105)
    at org.apache.catalina.core.StandardEngineValve.invoke(StandardEngineValve.java:107)
    at org.apache.catalina.connector.CoyoteAdapter.service(CoyoteAdapter.java:148)
    at org.apache.coyote.http11.Http11Processor.process(Http11Processor.java:869)
    at org.apache.coyote.http11.Http11BaseProtocol$Http11ConnectionHandler.processConnection(Http11BaseProtoco
    at org.apache.tomcat.util.net.PoolTcpEndpoint.processSocket(PoolTcpEndpoint.java:527)
    at org.apache.tomcat.util.net.LeaderFollowerWorkerThread.runIt(LeaderFollowerWorkerThread.java:80)
    at org.apache.tomcat.util.threads.ThreadPool$ControlRunnable.run(ThreadPool.java:684)
    at java.lang.Thread.run(Thread.java:613)
```

+ Component Tree

+ Scoped Variables

Dec 4, 2006 2:39:57 PM - Generated by Facelets

Figure 14.4. The Facelets debug page

The debug page also gives information about the current internal state of the JSF rendering engine. For instance, you can view the complete JSF component tree associated with the current page. You can actually launch the debug page as a pop-up from any Facelets page; you just need to put the `<ui:debug hotkey="d"/>` element in your Facelets page. At runtime, the user presses the Ctrl+Shift+d hot key combination to launch the debug pop-up. You can choose any hot key besides the d shown here. Of course, if there is no error at this moment, the debug page shows only the component tree and scoped variables, without the stack trace.

14.5.2. The Seam Debug Page

If an error occurs outside the JSF Facelets page-rendering operation (e.g., an error from the UI event-handler method), the Facelets debug page will not catch it. We can use the Seam debug page for this type of error.

To use the Seam debug page, you need the following instructions in Section 3.3., "Add Facelets and Seam UI Support" to bundle the `jboss-seam-debug.jar` and set up the Seam Exception Filter. Then in the `app.war/WEB-INF/components.xml` file, you must enable debugging on the `core:init` component.

```
<components ...>

  <core:init
    jndi-pattern="booking/#{ejbName}/local"
    debug="true"/>

  ... ...

</components>
```

Now any uncaught error will be redirected to the `/debug.seam` page, which displays the context information as well as the stack trace (Figure 14.5., "An uncaught exception without a custom error page is redirected to /debug.seam").

- Session Context

bookingList

bookings

facelets.ui.DebugOutput

localeSelector

loggedIn

org.jboss.seam.core.conversationEntries

resourceBundle

user

+ Application Context

- Exception

Exception during INVOKE_APPLICATION(5): java.lang.RuntimeException: Simulated DB error

```
org.jboss.ejb3.tx.Ejb3TxPolicy.handleExceptionInOurTx(Ejb3TxPolicy.java:69)
org.jboss.aspects.tx.TxPolicy.invokeInOurTx(TxPolicy.java:83)
org.jboss.aspects.tx.TxInterceptor$Required.invoke(TxInterceptor.java:197)
org.jboss.aop.joinpoint.MethodInvocation.invokeNext(MethodInvocation.java:101)
org.jboss.aspects.tx.TxPropagationInterceptor.invoke(TxPropagationInterceptor.java:7
org.jboss.aop.joinpoint.MethodInvocation.invokeNext(MethodInvocation.java:101)
org.jboss.ejb3.stateful.StatefulInstanceInterceptor.invoke(StatefulInstanceIntercept
org.jboss.aop.joinpoint.MethodInvocation.invokeNext(MethodInvocation.java:101)
org.jboss.aspects.security.AuthenticationInterceptor.invoke(AuthenticationIntercepto
org.jboss.ejb3.security.Ejb3AuthenticationInterceptor.invoke(Ejb3AuthenticationInter
org.jboss.aop.joinpoint.MethodInvocation.invokeNext(MethodInvocation.java:101)
org.jboss.ejb3.ENCPropagationInterceptor.invoke(ENCPropagationInterceptor.java:47)
org.jboss.aop.joinpoint.MethodInvocation.invokeNext(MethodInvocation.java:101)
org.jboss.ejb3.asynchronous.AsynchronousInterceptor.invoke(AsynchronousInterceptor.j
org.jboss.aop.joinpoint.MethodInvocation.invokeNext(MethodInvocation.java:101)
org.jboss.ejb3.stateful.StatefulContainer.localInvoke(StatefulContainer.java:203)
org.jboss.ejb3.stateful.StatefulLocalProxy.invoke(StatefulLocalProxy.java:98)
$Proxy111.confirm(Unknown Source)
org.jboss.seam.example.booking.HotelBooking$$FastClassByCGLIB$$c83b792d.invoke(<gene
net.sf.cglib.proxy.MethodProxy.invoke(MethodProxy.java:149)
org.jboss.seam.intercept.RootInvocationContext.proceed(RootInvocationContext.java:45
org.jboss.seam.intercept.ClientSideInterceptor$1.proceed(ClientSideInterceptor.java:
org.jboss.seam.intercept.SeamInvocationContext.proceed(SeamInvocationContext.java:55
org.jboss.seam.interceptors.RemoveInterceptor.removeIfNecessary(RemoveInterceptor.ja
sun.reflect.GeneratedMethodAccessor105.invoke(Unknown Source)
sun.reflect.DelegatingMethodAccessorImpl.invoke(DelegatingMethodAccessorImpl.java:25
java.lang.reflect.Method.invoke(Method.java:585)
org.jboss.seam.util.Reflections.invoke(Reflections.java:18)
```

Figure 14.5. An uncaught exception without a custom error page is redirected to /debug.seam

Again, the Seam /debug.seam page works even if there is no error. You can load that page at any time to look at the current Seam runtime context information.

Seam integrates exceptions in the business layer right into custom error pages in the presentation layer. This is yet another benefit of the unified component approach Seam uses. You have no more excuse for ugly error pages!

IV

AJAX Support

Leveraging JavaServer Faces (JSF), Seam offers excellent support for cutting-edge web technologies. In this part, we discuss several different ways to make your web pages more dynamic, more responsive, and more user friendly using the AJAX (Asynchronous JavaScript and XML) technology. You can easily add AJAX features in Seam applications and access Seam back-end components using a specialized asynchronous JavaScript library.

15

Custom and AJAX UI Components

Asynchronous JavaScript and XML (AJAX) is a rich web UI approach pioneered by Google. The term itself was coined by Jesse James Garret of Adaptive Path in 2005. The idea is to use JavaScript to retrieve dynamic content from the server and then update related UI components in the web page without refreshing the entire page. For instance, on a Google Maps (`http://maps.google.com/`) web page, you can use the mouse to move and zoom the map without page reload. The map display page captures the user's mouse events via JavaScript and then makes AJAX calls back to the server to retrieve new maps to display based on the mouse event. The user simply sees that the map gets updated as she moves the mouse. Another well-known AJAX example is Google Suggest (`http://www.google.com/webhp?complete=1&hl=en`). The search box in Google Suggest makes an AJAX call to the server whenever you type something in the box. The server returns a list of suggested search phrases based on the current content in the box, and the page displays the selectable list as a pop-up window underneath the box. This instant search-and-update action happens in real time as the user types, so it feels like the smart text field is "guessing" the user's intention all the time.

AJAX allows a web page to become a rich application by itself. From the user perspective, AJAX web pages are responsive and intuitive to use. In fact, most Web 2.0 sites today have some AJAX elements. The AJAX UI is essentially a dynamic UI rendered by network-aware JavaScript in the browser.

So what are the challenges to use AJAX with JSF and Seam web applications? After all, JSF and Seam enable you to use arbitrary HTML tags and JavaScripts on the web page. You can certainly use any JavaScript library to build whatever web UI you want. Well, the real challenge is how to integrate those JavaScript-rendered UI with back-end business components. For instance, you might be able to use an off-the-shelf JavaScript library to render a rich-text editor on the web page, but how do you bind the user input text in the editor box to a back-end component (e.g., a string property on a Seam EJB3 entity bean)? The JavaScript-rendered dynamic UI is not a JSF component, and it does not interpret the JSF EL (i.e., the `#{obj.property}` notation) for backing bean references.

A naive approach is to write a special HTTP servlet to handle AJAX requests from the JavaScripts. The servlet can then interact with objects in the `FacesContext` or `HttpSession` to save the user input or generate AJAX response to the JavaScript. However, the problem with this approach is that it includes a lot of manual coding on both the client-side JavaScript and the server-side Java Servlet. The AJAX servlet developer must be very careful with the states of the server-side objects. This is obviously not the ideal solution. Is there an easier, simpler way to support AJAX in JSF and Seam applications?

Fortunately, as a cutting-edge web framework, JSF and Seam provide several elegant ways to integrate AJAX support in your web applications. In this book, we primarily cover the following three approaches:

- The first approach is to reuse AJAX-enabled JSF UI components. The benefits of this approach are simplicity and power: You do not need to write a single line of JavaScript or AJAX servlet code, yet the component itself knows how to render JavaScript and AJAX visual effects; the JavaScript and back-end communication mechanism are encapsulated in the component itself. AJAX services are implemented in Seam back-end components bound to the UI component. We cover this approach later in this chapter.

- The second approach is to use a generic AJAX component library for JSF, such as the Ajax4jsf library. The benefit is that it enables you to add AJAX functionality to any existing JSF component. Again, it does not require any JavaScript or AJAX servlet code, but it cannot render visual effects beyond rerendering certain JSF components. Because all the Ajax requests happen within the JSF component lifecycle, the back-end value binding just works without any additional code. We cover this approach in Chapter 16, *Enabling AJAX for Existing Components*.

- The last approach is to use the Seam Remoting JavaScript library to access back-end Seam components directly when a page event happens. You can access the back-end components via JSF EL in the JavaScript calls. This approach works with any third-party JavaScript library and provides the most flexibility. We cover this approach in Chapter 17, *Direct JavaScript Integration*.

Let's begin with the first approach in this chapter. We use the open-source ICEfaces JSF component library to illustrate how to use AJAX components in Seam applications. The example application for this chapter is the `ajax` project in the book's source code bundle. This is an AJAX-ified version of the `integration` example we discussed earlier in the book.

What Is ICEfaces?

ICEfaces is an AJAX-enabled JSF component library from ICEsoft Technologies. It became an open-source product in November 2006. ICEsoft provides commercial support for ICEfaces users. Visit the ICEfaces web site (`http://www.icefaces.org/`) for more details on the product and support options. The ICEfaces component showcase web site (`http://component-showcase.icefaces.org/`) has a live demo for all AJAX components in the ICEfaces library; we highly recommend it.

ICEfaces and Seam teams are committed to making the two frameworks work together. However, at the time of writing, both teams are still working on some integration issues. They are expected to be fully resolved by Q2 2007. Between now and then, use caution when using ICEfaces on production-ready Seam applications. Also send feedback to the teams via the discussion forums on Seam and ICEfaces web sites.

15.1. Partial Form Submission Example

The first AJAX example we showcase here is partial submission of a web form. It allows the application to validate the input fields immediately after the user enters data. The user does not need to click on the Submit button to see the validation errors (see the `integration` example in Chapter 10, *Validating Input Data*, for non-AJAX validation). Figure 15.1., "The partial submission text field in action", shows the validation error for the email field. The error highlight is displayed immediately after the user moves the cursor out of the email input field.

Integration Demo for IceFaces

Your name: Michael Yuan

Your age: 31

Email: myuan AT redhat.c
          not a well-formed email address

Comment:

Say Hello

Figure 15.1. The partial submission text field in action

A Common AJAX Use Case

Partial form submission is a basic AJAX use case. We cover this use case again later in this book, in Section 16.1., "AJAX Validator Example" and Section 17.1., "AJAX Name Validation Example (Reloaded)".

Implementing the partial form submission in ICEfaces is easy. You can just replace the standard JSF `<h:inputText>` component with the ICEfaces `<ice:inputText>` component. Set the `partialSubmit` attribute on the `<ice:inputText>` component to `true` to enable form validation after the user moves the cursor out of this field.

```
<html xmlns="http://www.w3.org/1999/xhtml"
      xmlns:ui="http://java.sun.com/jsf/facelets"
      xmlns:h="http://java.sun.com/jsf/html"
      xmlns:f="http://java.sun.com/jsf/core"
xmlns:s="http://jboss.com/products/seam/taglib"
xmlns:ice="http://www.icesoft.com/icefaces/component">

  <head>
    <link href="style.css" rel="stylesheet"
                            type="text/css"/>
    <link rel='stylesheet' type='text/css'
                href='./xmlhttp/css/xp/xp.css'/>
  </head>

  <body>

    ... ...

    <h:form>

      ... ...

      <tr>
        <td>Email:</td>
        <td>
          <s:decorate>
            <ice:inputText value="#{person.email}"
                           partialSubmit="true"/>
          </s:decorate>
        </td>
      </tr>

    </h:form>

  </body>
</html>
```

Make sure that you declare the `ice` namespace in the `html` element. ICEfaces provides the additional CSS style sheet to style the forms.

The ICEfaces form also automatically detects the connection to the server. If the connection is lost (e.g., the server becomes unavailable or the network is disconnected), it grays out all the controls on the form and displays a message in the browser (Figure 15.2., "Auto-detect server connection").

Figure 15.2. Auto-detect server connection

15.2. Auto-complete Text Input Example

The second AJAX example we showcase in the `ajax` example is an auto-complete text-input field similar to the one in Google Suggest.

The text-input field for the person name (on the `hello.xhtml` page) can automatically suggest a list of popular names based on your partial input. For instance, if you type in the string `"an"`, names `"Michael Yuan"` and `"Norman Richards"` are suggested because they both contain `"an"`. The JavaScript associated with the text box captures every keystroke in the box, makes AJAX calls to retrieve autocompletion suggestions, and then displays those suggestions. Figure 15.3., "The AJAX autocompletion text field in action", shows how the autocompletion text field guesses a list of popular names based on the user's partial input.

Figure 15.3. The AJAX autocompletion text field in action

The autocompletion text field requires some complex interaction between the browser and the server. But with the well-encapsulated ICEfaces component, you do not need to worry about any of those; you simply drop the `<ice:selectInputText>` component into your web page as if it is a regular text-input field. The following listing shows how the `<ice:selectInputText>` component works. The nested `<f:selectItems>` component provides a list of suggestions from #{manager.nameHints}. The valueChangeListener attribute specifies that the #{manager.updateNameHints} method is invoked every time the user types in the field. The #{manager.updateNameHints} method updates the #{manager.nameHints} list for a new set of suggestions based on the current input in the field. The rows attribute specifies the maximum number of suggestions.

```
<html xmlns="http://www.w3.org/1999/xhtml"
      xmlns:ui="http://java.sun.com/jsf/facelets"
      xmlns:h="http://java.sun.com/jsf/html"
```

```
      xmlns:f="http://java.sun.com/jsf/core"
xmlns:s="http://jboss.com/products/seam/taglib"
xmlns:ice="http://www.icesoft.com/icefaces/component">

  ... ...

  <tr>
    <td>Your name:</td>
    <td>
      <ice:selectInputText rows="10"
                 value="#{person.name}"
                 valueChangeListener=
                   "#{manager.updateNameHints}">
        <f:selectItems value="#{manager.nameHints}"/>
      </ice:selectInputText>
    </td>
  </tr>

</html>
```

The next listing shows the two bean methods to support the `<ice:selectInputText>` component. These are quite self-explanatory.

```
@Stateful
@Name("manager")
public class ManagerAction implements Manager {

  String [] popularNames = new String [] {
      "Gavin King", "Thomas Heute", "Michael Yuan",
      ... ...
  };

  // Suggestions for the input text field
  ArrayList <SelectItem> nameHints;
  public List getNameHints () {
    return nameHints;
  }

  // Update the suggestions when the user changes
  // value in the input text field
  public void updateNameHints (ValueChangeEvent e) {
    String prefix = (String) e.getNewValue ();
    int maxMatches =
      ((SelectInputText) e.getComponent()).getRows();

    nameHints = new ArrayList <SelectItem> ();

    int totalNum = 0;
```

```
    if (prefix.length() > 0) {
      for (int i=0; i<popularNames.length; i++) {
        if (popularNames[i].toLowerCase()
              .indexOf(prefix.toLowerCase())!=-1
            && totalNum < maxMatches) {

          nameHints.add(
              new SelectItem (i, popularNames[i]));
          totalNum++;
        }
      }
    } else {
      for (int i=0; i<maxMatches &&
              i<popularNames.length; i++) {
        nameHints.add(
              new SelectItem (i, popularNames[i]));
        }
      }
    }

    ... ...
}
```

That's it! Within minutes, we have an AJAX-enabled example application, and we have not written a single line of JavaScript or DHTML code.

15.3. Use ICEfaces with Seam

To use ICEfaces with Seam, you need to bundle ICEfaces JAR files in the application and configure ICEfaces servlets and filters. The ICEfaces JARs should be included in the `app.jar` archive, as follows. Because ICEfaces provides a replacement for the standard Facelets library, you should remove the `jsf-facelets.jar` from the `app.war/WEB-INF/lib` directory.

```
mywebapp.ear
|+ app.war
   |+ web pages
   |+ WEB-INF
      |+ web.xml
      |+ faces-config.xml
      |+ other config files
      |+ lib
         |+ jboss-seam-ui.jar
         |+ jboss-seam-debug.jar
|+ app.jar
```

```
   |+ Component classes
   |+ commons-fileupload.jar
   |+ icefaces.jar
   |+ icefaces-comps.jar
   |+ icefaces-facelets.jar
|+ el-api.jar
|+ el-ri.jar
|+ jboss-seam.jar
|+ META-INF
   |+ application.xml
   |+ other config files
```

> **Why Not Bundle ICEfaces JARs in `app.war`?**
>
> ICEfaces is a web component framework, so why don't we bundle
> its JAR files in the `app.war/WEB-INF/lib` directory? We don't
> because we might need to access the ICEfaces components from
> within Seam methods in `app.jar`. See the
> `#{manager.updateNameHints}` method in the previous example.
>
> Of course, if you are building a WAR deployment of a Seam POJO
> application (see Chapter 24, *Seam Without EJB3*), you should
> bundle all library JARs in the `WEB-INF/lib` directory of the WAR
> archive.

Next, replace the `SeamFaceletViewHandler` in `faces-config.xml` with an ICEfaces custom
view handler.

```
<faces-config>

  ... ...

  <!-- Facelets support -->
  <application>
    <view-handler>
com.icesoft.faces.facelets.D2DSeamFaceletViewHandler
    </view-handler>
  </application>

</faces-config>
```

Then, in the `web.xml` file, remove the Seam view handler for Facelets. Add two ICEfaces servlets in the `web.xml` file to handle non-JSF AJAX requests.

```
<web-app ...>

  ... ...

  <context-param>
    <param-name>
      com.icesoft.faces.actionURLSuffix
    </param-name>
    <param-value>.seam</param-value>
  </context-param>

  ... ...

  <servlet>
    <servlet-name>Persistent Servlet</servlet-name>
    <servlet-class>
com.icesoft.faces.webapp.xmlhttp.PersistentFacesServlet
    </servlet-class>
    <load-on-startup>1</load-on-startup>
  </servlet>

  <servlet-mapping>
    <servlet-name>Persistent Servlet</servlet-name>
    <url-pattern>*.seam</url-pattern>
  </servlet-mapping>

  <servlet-mapping>
    <servlet-name>Persistent Servlet</servlet-name>
    <url-pattern>/xmlhttp/*</url-pattern>
  </servlet-mapping>

  <servlet>
    <servlet-name>Blocking Servlet</servlet-name>
    <servlet-class>
com.icesoft.faces.webapp.xmlhttp.BlockingServlet
    </servlet-class>
    <load-on-startup>1</load-on-startup>
  </servlet>

  <servlet-mapping>
    <servlet-name>Blocking Servlet</servlet-name>
    <url-pattern>/block/*</url-pattern>
  </servlet-mapping>

</web-app>
```

> **Seam Page Parameters in ICEfaces**
>
> In Section 12.1., "Using Page Parameters", we discussed Seam page parameters for RESTful URLs. However, with ICEfaces, the page parameters in the `pages.xml` file do not always work. For instance, in the `ajax` example, when the user submits the `person.xhtml` page, the page is submitted to the ICEfaces block servlet; the `pid` parameter defined for `person.xhtml` would be lost in the submission. For this reason, we use the `@RequestParameter` approach discussed in Section 12.2., "The Java-Centric Approach", to manage RESTful pages in ICEfaces applications.

15.4. Other JSF Component Libraries

By standardizing the web component architecture in Java EE, JSF has fostered a common marketplace for component libraries. Besides ICEfaces, more than a dozen commercial and open-source vendors are competing in this marketplace, providing a decent selection of high-quality JSF components for web developers. Following is the partial list of some of the well-known third-party JSF component packages. JSF community web sites, such as `jsfcentral.com` and `java.net`, maintain updated lists of component vendors.

* Exadel (see `http://www.exadel.com/`) is a Java development tool vendor. Its main product is an Eclipse-based IDE for JSF. The IDE bundles proprietary AJAX-based JSF components, which you can drag and drop in the IDE UI designer to assemble JSF applications.

* The Apache MyFaces Tomahawk project (`http://myfaces.apache.org/tomahawk/`) develops rich web UI components such as advanced data tables, tabbed panels, calendars, and color pickers, etc., as well as input data validators beyond the standard ones. Tomahawk components are all released under the Apache open-source license.

* Oracle Application Development Framework (ADF) Faces is one of the first commercial JSF component suites. It provides more than 80 UI components, including alternatives to all standard components. The ADF components have a great look-and-feel, and they can all be skinned to different themes. ADF components are also high performance because

each component is rendered via partial page updates (AJAX style, without page reload). Oracle has denoted the ADF Faces source code to the open-source Trinidad project (`http://incubator.apache.org/adffaces/`) in the Apache foundation.

- The Woodstock project (see `https://woodstock.dev.java.net/`) is an open-source project to develop AJAX-based enterprise-ready JSF web UI components. It already has more than a dozen components available.

- The Sun blueprint catalog (see `https://bpcatalog.dev.java.net/`) provides AJAX-enabled JSF components under the BSD license. Those components are primarily provided for educational purposes.

- The ILOG JView JSF components (see `http://www.ilog.com/products/jviews/`) render professional-looking business charts from data models. This is one of the leading business data visualization products.

- Otrix (see `http://www.otrix.com/`) provides commercial AJAX JSF components for trees, menus, data grids, etc.

Most JSF component libraries include both UI components as well as validator components. As we discussed in Chapter 10, *Validating Input Data*, custom JSF validators are useful when corresponding Seam validators are not available. The following example shows how to use the credit card validator component in the Apache Tomahawk library:

```
Credit Card Number:
<h:inputText id="creditCard" required="true"
        value="#{customer.creditCard}">
  <t:validateCreditCard />

</h:inputText>
* <h:message for="creditCard"
            styleClass="error"/>
```

Custom JSF component libraries help Seam applications stay at the cutting edge of web presentation technologies. As developers, we should leverage them to build better applications.

16

Enabling AJAX for Existing Components

In the previous chapter, we showed how easy it is to use repackaged AJAX JSF components. However, developing those components is not a trivial exercise; it requires not only JavaScript/AJAX skills, but also deep knowledge of how JSF works. In most cases, it is not cost-effective to write your own AJAX JSF components unless you plan to reuse them extensively. Most developers are limited to the components third-party vendors already offer.

But what if the existing components do not do exactly what you want? What if the available components are simply too expensive? Those situations occur often in real-world enterprise applications. We need an AJAX solution that is not only easy to use, but also flexible enough to address different customization requirements. In this chapter, we introduce Ajax4jsf, which provides flexible and customizable AJAX support for JSF components. This is the second AJAX approach discussed at the beginning of Chapter 15, *Custom and AJAX UI Components*.

Ajax4jsf is an open-source JSF component library developed by Exadel as the basis of Exadel's own proprietary AJAX JSF components. The unique feature that sets Ajax4jsf apart from other AJAX JSF frameworks is that Ajax4jsf adds AJAX functionalities to any existing JSF component. In fact, it can turn any JSF operation already in your application into an AJAX operation and then display the result via a partial page update (i.e., no page reload). If you want to learn more about Ajax4jsf, visit its web site at `https://ajax4jsf.dev.java.net/`.

Ajax4jsf works by submitting JSF requests via AJAX and then rerendering specific elements on the page based on the updated state of the back-end components. To demonstrate how it works, we use a revised Hello World example again. The sample code is available in the `ajax4jsf` project. The project uses the Facelets + Seam + Ajax4jsf stack of technologies.

16.1. AJAX Validator Example

One of the simplest and most useful examples for showcasing the capability of Ajax4jsf is AJAX validation on input fields. In Chapter 10, *Validating Input Data*, you saw how Hibernate validator annotations and Seam JSF tags work together to validate form inputs according to database constraints and display nice-looking error messages. However, the error messages are displayed only after you submit the form. AJAX can greatly improve the validation workflow: The JavaScript on the web page could send the user input in each field back to the server for validation immediately after the field loses focus; if the validation fails, the error message is immediately displayed without the page being submitted.

However, it is very difficult to add AJAX support into the Seam JSF validation process through "regular" AJAX techniques. The Seam JSF validation process is almost completely declarative, and no "hook" exists for the client-side JavaScript to trigger the server-side validation functions or access the validation messages. Ajax4jsf solves this problem by integrating AJAX support right into existing JSF components and the standard JSF lifecycle.

The following is an example of an AJAX-validated input field (see Figure 16.1., "AJAX validation of input field"). The `<s:validate/>` tag indicates that this input field should be validated by the `@NotNull` `@Email` Hibernate validator on `Person.getEmail()`, and the `<s:decorate>` tag highlights the input field with images, background, and border when a validation error occurs. See Chapter 10, *Validating Input Data*, for more on how those tags work. What's important here is the `<a4j:support>` tag, which we discuss shortly.

```
Please enter your Email:<br/>
<a4j:outputPanel id="emailInput">
  <s:decorate>
    <h:inputText value="#{person.email}" size="15">
      <s:validate/>
      <a4j:support event="onblur"
                   reRender="emailInput"/>
    </h:inputText>
  </s:decorate>
</a4j:outputPanel>
```

Seam Hello World

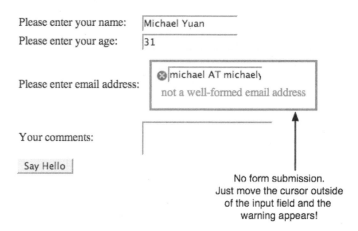

Figure 16.1. AJAX validation of input field

Compared with the non-AJAX version of <h:inputText, the AJAX-enabled JSF component encloses a <a4j:support element. That's it! The event attribute specifies the JavaScript event upon which the AJAX call is invoked. In this case, whenever the input text field loses focus (i.e., onblur), Ajax4jsf submits the text in the field to the component's back-end binding property (i.e., the #{person.email} property) via a JSF POST operation. The AJAX submission goes through the regular Seam JSF validation process. After the AJAX request is processed, Ajax4jsf rerenders the component with the emailInput ID, which is the entire decorated input component itself. If any error occurs, it shows up in the rerendering (see Figure 16.1., "AJAX validation of input field"). We need an <a4j:outputPanel> element here to give the entire decorated input field a JSF ID.

Of course, using the reRender attribute, you can rerender any component on the page upon completing the AJAX call. You can even rerender multiple components: Just assign multiple component IDs separated by commas to the reRender attribute. The rerendered components reflect the new state of the server-side components after the AJAX call.

> **The <a4j:outputPanel> Component**
>
> Why do we need the <a4j:outputPanel> element here? Can't we just use <s:decorate id="emailInput">? Well, the problem is that the <s:decorate> element is not rendered when there is no error

(i.e., when the form is first loaded). So no `emailInput` HTML element exists for the Ajax4jsf JavaScript to rerender without a page refresh.

The `<a4j:outputPanel id="emailInput">` element guarantees that the HTML element with the proper JSF ID will be in the page. This is very useful in wrapping page elements (e.g., a piece of free XHTML text in a Facelets page) that do not have proper JSF IDs. You can enclose multiple JSF components and other XHTML text in the `<a4j:outputPanel>` element, and they will all be rerendered together after the AJAX call is completed. Indeed, we recommend that you use the `<a4j:outputPanel>` element to wrap all your Ajax4jsf `reRender` components.

In the previous example, the `a4j:support` component rerenders a JSF component after the AJAX call returns. You can also tell the browser to execute arbitrary JavaScript upon the completion of the AJAX response. Just add the JavaScript function call to the `oncomplete` attribute of the `a4j:support` tag. Consider this example:

```
<h:inputText value="#{person.email}" size="15">
    <s:validate/>
    <a4j:support event="onblur"
                 reRender="emailInput"
                 oncomplete="alertUser()"/>
</h:inputText>
```

16.2. Programmatic AJAX

The validator example is nice and simple, but it does not really involve any programming because everything is declarative. For most innovative AJAX applications, however, we want to execute our own application-specific code in the AJAX interaction.

For instance, in the following example, we use an AJAX call to check whether a new person's name is already in the database as soon as the user types something in the input field (see Figure 16.2., "AJAX interaction with custom logic"). The database query here is the custom logic that is not easily handled by any existing validation framework. This feature is often implemented to support an on-time username/email availability check on site registration forms.

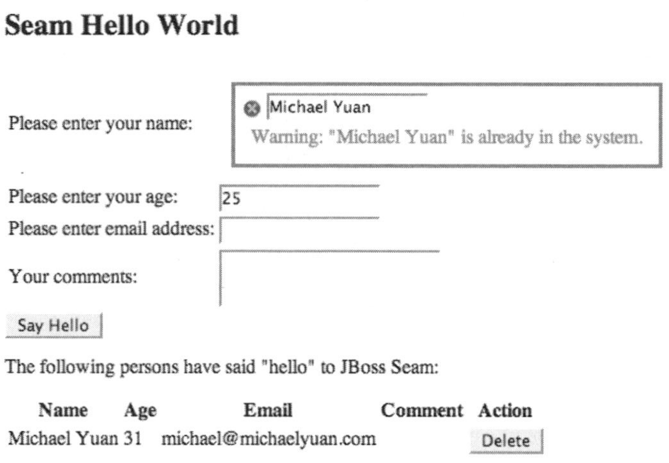

Seam Hello World

Please enter your name:

❌ Michael Yuan

Warning: "Michael Yuan" is already in the system.

Please enter your age: 25

Please enter email address:

Your comments:

Say Hello

The following persons have said "hello" to JBoss Seam:

Name	Age	Email	Comment	Action
Michael Yuan	31	michael@michaelyuan.com		Delete

Figure 16.2. AJAX interaction with custom logic

In Ajax4jsf, the custom code (i.e., to check the database in this example) is executed in JSF backing component methods. Those methods are invoked in the standard JSF lifecycle when an Ajax4jsf request is submitted. We use them to control what is displayed in the AJAX rer-endered component after the call is completed. Now let's check out how it works.

The JSF component for the name input field follows:

```
Please enter your name:
... ...
<h:inputText value="#{manager.name}" size="15">
  <a4j:support event="onblur"
             reRender="nameInput"/>
</h:inputText>
```

Again, the a4j:support element indicates that whenever the input text field loses focus (i.e., onblur), Ajax4jsf submits the value of this component to its back-end binding property (i.e., the #{manager.name} property). When the AJAX request is processed, Ajax4jsf rerenders the component with the nameInput ID. The following is the nameInput component. The #{manager.nameErrorMsg} backing bean property controls the display of the nameInput component. If the property is not an empty string, the component highlights the text field with an error icon and message. So in the AJAX interaction, we need to add code to alter the #{manager.nameErrorMsg} value at the back end before the AJAX call returns.

```
<a4j:outputPanel id="nameInput">
  <f:subview
      rendered="#{!empty(manager.nameErrorMsg)}">
    <f:verbatim><div class="error"></f:verbatim>
    <h:graphicImage styleClass="errorImg"
                            value="error.png"/>
  </f:subview>

  <h:inputText value="#{manager.name}" size="15">
    <a4j:support event="onblur"
              reRender="nameInput"/>
  </h:inputText>

  <f:subview
      rendered="#{!empty(manager.nameErrorMsg)}">
    <h:outputText styleClass="errorMsg"
                value="#{manager.nameErrorMsg}"/>
    <f:verbatim></div></f:verbatim>
  </f:subview>
</a4j:outputPanel>
```

At the `onblur` event, the AJAX request causes JSF to invoke the `setName()` method on the manager component to bind the component value. The `setName()` method contains the custom logic for this AJAX interaction: It checks whether the name is already available in the database. If the name already exists, the `setName()` method sets the `nameErrorMsg` property, which is then displayed when the `nameErrorMsg` component is rerendered when the AJAX call is returned asynchronously.

```
@Stateful
@Name("manager")
public class ManagerAction implements Manager {

  ... ...

  String name;
  public void setName (String name) {

    this.name = name;

    List <Person> existing = em.createQuery(
        "select p from Person p where name=:name")
        .setParameter("name", name)
        .getResultList();

    if (existing.size() != 0) {
```

```
       nameErrorMsg = "Warning: \"" + name +
           "\" is already in the system.";
    } else {
       nameErrorMsg = "";
    }
    return;
  }
  public String getName () {
    return name;
  }

  String nameErrorMsg;
  public void setNameErrorMsg (String nameErrorMsg) {
    this.nameErrorMsg = nameErrorMsg;
  }
  public String getNameErrorMsg () {
    return nameErrorMsg;
  }

}
```

16.3. AJAX Buttons

Ajax4jsf can turn any JSF `commandButon` or `commandLink` operation into an AJAX operation. The AJAX buttons or links submit the form via a JavaScript call and rerender specified components on the page based on new back-end state after the server-side JSF event-handler method for the button is invoked.

To demonstrate this feature, let's AJAX-enable the delete buttons in the data table for `fans`. When you click on any of those buttons, the current fan is removed from the database and the `dataTable` component is rerendered to reflect the change. But the page update is done in AJAX fashion: No page reload occurs. That is especially useful when you have a very long `dataTable`. A whole page refresh would have lost the current scrollbar position, and you would have had to scroll from the top again (see Figure 16.3., "AJAX deletion of a table row").

The Seam Greeters

The following persons have said "hello" to JBoss Seam:

Name	Age	Email	Comment	Action
Michael Yuan	31	michael@michaelyuan.com		Delete
John Doe	25	john@redhat.com		Delete
Jane Roe	28	jane@redhat.com	Hello Seam!	Delete
Bill Gates	40	bill@microsoft.com	I love Seam!	Delete

Delete a row without a page refresh

The Seam Greeters

The following persons have said "hello" to JBoss Seam:

Name	Age	Email	Comment	Action
Michael Yuan	31	michael@michaelyuan.com		Delete
John Doe	25	john@redhat.com		Delete
Jane Roe	28	jane@redhat.com	Hello Seam!	Delete

Figure 16.3. AJAX deletion of a table row

To use an AJAX submission button, you just need to replace the `h:commandButton` (or `h:commandLink`) with `a4j:commandButton` (or `a4j:commandLink`). As is the case with the `a4j:support` component, the `a4j` components take a `reRender` property to specify which components are to be updated when the AJAX call returns. So here is our new AJAX `dataTable`:

```
<h:form>
<h:dataTable id="fans"
             value="#{fans}" var="fan">
  <h:column>
    <f:facet name="header">
```

```
      <h:outputText value="Name" />
    </f:facet>
    <h:outputText value="#{fan.name}"/>
  </h:column>

  ... ...

  <h:column>
    <f:facet name="header">
      <h:outputText value="Action" />
    </f:facet>
    <a4j:commandButton type="submit"
                       value="Delete"
                       reRender="fans"
                       action="#{manager.delete}"/>
  </h:column>
</h:dataTable>
</h:form>
```

That's it; you have no more back-end code to write. When a user clicks on the Delete button, the back-end component sees only a standard JSF form submission. It goes through the standard JSF lifecycle. The Ajax4jsf framework automatically takes care of the AJAX plumbing.

Via the `onclick` and `oncomplete` attributes, you can specify arbitrary JavaScript functions to be executed before the AJAX call is made and after the AJAX call is completed. In the following example, we change the cursor shape to a "waiting" symbol when we start the AJAX call and restore it when the AJAX response is received and the components are updated.

```
<a4j:commandButton type="submit"
                   value="Delete"
                   reRender="fans"
                   onclick="showWaitCursor()"
                   oncomplete="restoreCursor()"
                   action="#{manager.delete}"/>
```

16.4. AJAX Containers

In standard JSF, a button click submits the entire form to the server and then triggers the event-handler method. The full-form submission is often not necessary in AJAX requests. We sometimes need to submit only one or two related input components to the back end for the

AJAX call to function correctly. Submitting the entire form would be a waste of bandwidth in this case. Ajax4jsf provides a special tag `a4j:region` to limit the part of the form you want to submit. Only components included in the `<a4j:region>...</a4j:region>` element are submitted when a user clicks on an AJAX button inside the region. So the `a4j:region` component is also known as an AJAX container because it contains the AJAX activity in parts of the page. Other AJAX container tags include `a4j:form` and `a4j:page`. Refer to the Ajax4jsf documentation for their use.

The AJAX container tags take an optional `ajaxListener` property, which points to a back-end method that is to be invoked whenever an AJAX event happens on any component in the region. So we can trigger back-end event-handler methods directly from a JSF input component, without manually clicking on a button.

16.5. Other Goodies

Besides AJAX input components and AJAX buttons/links, the Ajax4jsf library provides some other important tags/components to facilitate AJAX development.

The `a4j:poll` component periodically polls the server and rerenders specified components based on the current state of the server. For instance, you might want a progress bar display for a long-running server process: The page would periodically poll the server to partially update a progress bar based on the server process's current progress.

The `a4j:mediaOutput` component enables us to use a server-side method to paint an image and then display it in the browser. The server-side `paint()` method can use any of the Java SE 2D and Swing drawing APIs. That enables us to render dynamic custom graphics in the browser. This is great for simple visual effects associated with AJAX calls (e.g., the progress bar mentioned earlier would be a good fit).

The `a4j:include` component can include an external JSF page in the current page. The included page can update itself and navigate from one page to another without affecting its host page. Think of it as an embedded HTML frame without the hassles associated with frames. That enables us to write in-page AJAX wizards.

The `a4j:status` and `a4j:log` components display AJAX interactions between the client and server in real time. These are very useful for debugging purposes.

The Ajax4jsf library has more cool components. Refer to its documentation for more details.

16.6. Configuring Ajax4jsf

In this section, we discuss how to configure Ajax4jsf to work with Seam and Facelets (see Section 3.1., "An Introduction to Facelets"). Note that some problems have been observed when Ajax4jsf is used with Seam + JSP (without Facelets), so we highly recommend Facelets here.

To configure Ajax4jsf, you must add an Ajax4jsf filter in your web.xml file (in app.war/WEB-INF/).

```
<web-app>

    <!-- Ajax4jsf setup -->
    <filter>
      <display-name>Ajax4jsf Filter</display-name>
      <filter-name>ajax4jsf</filter-name>
      <filter-class>
        org.ajax4jsf.Filter
      </filter-class>
    </filter>
    <filter-mapping>
      <filter-name>ajax4jsf</filter-name>
      <servlet-name>Faces Servlet</servlet-name>
      <dispatcher>REQUEST</dispatcher>
      <dispatcher>FORWARD</dispatcher>
      <dispatcher>INCLUDE</dispatcher>
    </filter-mapping>
    <context-param>
      <param-name>
        org.ajax4jsf.VIEW_HANDLERS
      </param-name>
      <param-value>
org.jboss.seam.ui.facelet.SeamFaceletViewHandler
      </param-value>
    </context-param>

</web-app>
```

Notice that the Ajax4jsf filter loads the Facelets view handler, to avoid a potential conflict between Facelets and Ajax4jsf. You no longer need the Facelets view handler definition in the faces-config.xml file (in app.war/WEB-INF/). Let's comment it out here:

```
<faces-config>

  <lifecycle>
    <phase-listener>
      org.jboss.seam.jsf.SeamPhaseListener
    </phase-listener>
  </lifecycle>

  <!-- Facelets support.
       DO NOT use it with ajax4jsf,
       which loads SeamFaceletViewHandler
       in web.xml
  <application>
    <view-handler>
org.jboss.seam.ui.facelet.SeamFaceletViewHandler
    </view-handler>
  </application>
  -->

</faces-config>
```

Next, in each web page that uses Ajax4jsf components, you must declare the a4j XML namespace.

```
<html xmlns="http://www.w3.org/1999/xhtml"
  xmlns:ui="http://java.sun.com/jsf/facelets"
  xmlns:h="http://java.sun.com/jsf/html"
  xmlns:f="http://java.sun.com/jsf/core"
  xmlns:a4j="https://ajax4jsf.dev.java.net/ajax">

    ... ...
</html>
```

Finally, you must package the Ajax4jsf library JAR files in the application. The ajax4jsf.jar is the main Ajax4jsf component library, and the oscache-xxx.jar is a dependent library that Ajax4jsf requires. We put both files in the WAR file (i.e., the app.war). This is the packaging structure for the JAR files in ajax4jsf.ear:

```
ajax4jsf.ear
|+ META-INF
|+ jboss-seam.jar
|+ el-ri.jar
```

```
|+ el-api.jar
|+ app.war
|   |+ WEB-INF
|   |   |+ lib
|   |   |   |+ ajax4jsf.jar
|   |   |   |+ oscache-2.3.2.jar
|   |   |   |+ jboss-seam-ui.jar
|   |   |   |+ jboss-seam-debug.jar
|   |   |   |+ jsf-facelets.jar
|+ app.jar
```

16.7. Pros and Cons

Ajax4jsf turns regular JSF components into AJAX-enabled components. It works with existing JSF applications and requires little change to existing code. Ajax4jsf is easy to learn, easy to understand, and much more versatile than the prepackaged component approach discussed in Chapter 15, *Custom and AJAX UI Components*.

However, Ajax4jsf also has some limitations. Because the AJAX update is based on rerendering JSF components, it is difficult to add fancy JavaScript effects; you must make extensive changes to the components themselves, which, as we discussed, is not an easy task. Sure, you can use the `a4j:mediaOutput` component to render custom graphics, but it is slow to do animations and other visual effects from the server side. Also, because Ajax4jsf uses the same lifecycle as regular JSF, it has to submit all JSF state information in each AJAX call. That results in excessive bandwidth usage and slow response when you use client-side state saving in JSF.

To fully resolve those issues, we must look at solutions that provide tighter integration to JavaScript. That is the topic for the next chapter.

17

Direct JavaScript Integration

So far, we have discussed two approaches for supporting AJAX in Seam applications. Both require zero JavaScript or XML communication code—but they also have some drawbacks.

The componentized AJAX UI approach (see Chapter 15, *Custom and AJAX UI Components*) is easy, but you are limited to what the vendor offers. You face quite a steep learning curve if you want to implement an AJAX-enabled JSF component to render your own custom visual effects or back-end logic. The Ajax4jsf approach (see Chapter 16, *Enabling AJAX for Existing Components*) works well in the JSF context, but it is difficult to implement components with visual effects (e.g., drag-and-drops, fades, pop-ups) beyond the standard HTML widgets already supported in existing JSF components. In addition, it is bandwidth intensive to wrap JSF requests in AJAX calls, especially if you use client-side state saving.

With so many high-quality free JavaScript libraries available, it seems silly not to take advantage of them just because you are limited by JSF component vendors, right? Well, Seam provides a JavaScript remoting framework that enables you to access any Seam back-end component from the JavaScript UI. Thus, you can easily bind user input captured in a JavaScript UI widget to the back end, and use the back-end component to generate AJAX data to alter the web page display dynamically.

In this chapter, we demonstrate how to use the Seam remoting JavaScript library to tie Seam server-side components with HTML/JavaScript UI elements. In the last section, we give concrete examples on how to integrate the popular Dojo JavaScript toolkit into Seam applications.

17.1. AJAX Name Validation Example (Reloaded)

In Chapter 16, *Enabling AJAX for Existing Components*, we showed how to validate a user input name via AJAX in the Seam Hello World example. The user input name is sent to the server as the user fills out the web form, and the name is checked against the database. If the name already exists in the database, a warning message is displayed next to the text input field—all without a page submission. In the first example in this chapter, we reimplement this feature using the Seam remoting approach. The example code in this section is in the `remote` project in the source code bundle. When the application is running, you can access it via the `http://localhost:8080/remote/` URL.

To use Seam remoting, make sure that the `jboss-seam-remoting.jar` file is included in your `app.war/WEB-INF/lib` directory like this:

```
mywebapp.ear
|+ app.war
   |+ web pages
   |+ WEB-INF
      |+ web.xml
      |+ faces-config.xml
      |+ other config files
      |+ lib
         |+ jsf-facelets.jar
         |+ jboss-seam-ui.jar
         |+ jboss-seam-debug.jar
         |+ jboss-seam-remoting.jar
... ...
```

17.1.1. Server-Side Component

First, we need a method in the back-end Seam component to check the input name against the database. We add a `checkName()` in the `ManagerAction` class:

```
@Stateful
@Scope(SESSION)
@Name("manager")
public class ManagerAction implements Manager {

  ... ...

  public boolean checkName (String name) {
    List <Person> existing = em.createQuery(
        "select p from Person p where name=:name")
      .setParameter("name", name)
      .getResultList();

    if (existing.size() != 0) {
      return false;
    } else {
```

```
        return true;
    }
  }
}
```

Now comes the important part: In the session bean interface, you must tag the method with the @WebRemote annotation for it to be accessible through the Seam remoting JavaScript.

```
@Local
public interface Manager {

  ... ...

  @WebRemote
  public boolean checkName (String name);
}
```

The Seam resource servlet handles all AJAX calls from the client side JavaScript to the @WebRemote annotated methods. The AJAX calls are routed via the seam/resource/remoting/* URL. AJAX-related resource files (e.g., dynamically generated JavaScript—see later) are also served via this special URL. In Section 3.3., "Add Facelets and Seam UI Support", we already explained how to configure the resource servlet. You just need to add the following lines in your web.xml file.

```
<servlet>
  <servlet-name>Seam Resource Servlet</servlet-name>
  <servlet-class>
    org.jboss.seam.servlet.ResourceServlet
  </servlet-class>
</servlet>

<servlet-mapping>
  <servlet-name>Seam Resource Servlet</servlet-name>
  <url-pattern>/seam/resource/*</url-pattern>
</servlet-mapping>
```

17.1.2. Triggering a JavaScript Event on the Web Page

With the back-end method ready, let's check out how the AJAX call is triggered on the web page.

```
<h:inputText id="name"
      value="#{person.name}"
      onfocus="hideCheckNameError()"
      onblur="checkName()"
      size="15"/>
<span id="nameError" style="display:none">
  You have already said hello! :)
</span>
<h:message for="name" />
```

The `onblur` property on `h:inputText` indicates the JavaScript method to invoke when the text field loses focus. So when the user finishes the input and clicks outside the field, the `checkName()` JavaScript method is invoked. The JavaScript method takes the input text in the field and then invokes the `ManagerAction.checkName()` method on the server side via an AJAX call. The return value of the AJAX call determines whether the error message in the `<span>` element should be shown. Let's look at how the JavaScript `checkName()` method works next.

Hiding and Showing the `span` Element

The `style="display:none"` property indicates that the `span` element for the error message is not displayed initially. JavaScript can display it if the `ManagerAction.checkName()` method returns `false`. The JavaScript `hideCheckNameError()` method makes sure that the error message is hidden when the text field is activated again. The following are the `hideCheckNameError()` and `show-CheckNameError()` methods for manipulating the `span` element:

```
function showCheckNameError () {
  var e = document.getElementById("nameError");
  if (!(e === null)) {
    e.style.visibility = "inherit";
    e.style.display = "";
  }
```

```
}

function hideCheckNameError () {
  var e = document.getElementById("nameError");
  if (!(e === null)) {
    e.style.visibility = "hidden";
    e.style.display = "none";
  }
}
```

17.1.3. Making an AJAX Call

The heart of the AJAX operation involves making the AJAX call and then getting the result asynchronously. In the page where you need to make AJAX calls, load the `seam/re-source/remoting/resource/remote.js` JavaScript. The Seam resource servlet assembles and then serves this script on the fly. For each Seam component that contains `@WebRemote` annotated methods, Seam generates a custom JavaScript for accessing this component as well. In our example, we load the `interface.js?manager` JavaScript for accessing the Seam back-end component named `manager`.

```
<script type="text/javascript"
  src="seam/resource/remoting/resource/remote.js">
</script>

<script type="text/javascript"
  src="seam/resource/remoting/interface.js?manager">
</script>
```

Now you can get a JavaScript version of the `manager` component via a `Seam.Component.getInstance("manager")` call. The call to the JavaScript `manager.checkName()` method is then translated into an AJAX call to the server-side `manager.checkName()` method. We get the text from the text field and then use the `manager.checkName()` method to check whether it already exists in the server-side database.

```
<script type="text/javascript">
  // Seam.Remoting.setDebug(true);

  // don't display the loading indicator
  Seam.Remoting.displayLoadingMessage = function() {};
  Seam.Remoting.hideLoadingMessage = function() {};

  // Get the "manager" Seam component
  var manager =
      Seam.Component.getInstance("manager");

  // Make the async call with a callback handler
  function checkName () {
    var e = document.getElementById("form:name");
    var inputName = e.value;
    manager.checkName(inputName, checkNameCallback);
  }

  ... ...

</script>
```

Creating a JavaScript Object for an Entity Bean or JavaBean POJO Component

The `Seam.Component.getInstance()` method obtains a singleton stub object for a Seam session bean. You can make AJAX method calls against the session bean. But for Seam entity bean or simple JavaBean components, you need to create corresponding JavaScript objects using the `Seam.Component.newInstance()` method. All the getter and setter methods on the entity bean (JavaBean) are available in the JavaScript object. You can edit the entity objects and then pass them as call arguments in AJAX calls against session bean components.

The JavaScript and server-side `manager.checkName()` methods take the same call arguments. As we mentioned in the previous sidebar, you can even construct entity bean instances in JavaScript and then pass them to a remote AJAX method as a call argument. However, there's one more twist: The JavaScript method takes an additional asynchronous callback handler as a call argument: The `manager.checkName()` call is invoked asynchronously so that the

JavaScript does not block the UI waiting for the response, which could potentially take a long time because the call goes through the network. So instead of waiting for the return value from the remote call, we pass in a JavaScript callback handler, `checkNameCallback`, and let the JavaScript method call `manager.checkName()` return immediately. The `checkNameCallback()` method is invoked with the server-side method's return value when the server method finishes. The callback handler then decides whether to display the error message based on the return value.

```
<script type="text/javascript">

  ... ...

  function checkNameCallback (result) {
    if (result) {
      hideCheckNameError ();
    } else {
      showCheckNameError ();
    }
  }

  ... ...

</script>
```

In an earlier sidebar, we discussed how the `hideCheckNameError()` and `showCheckNameError()` methods hide and display the `span` element for the error message.

So that's it for the simple example. Of course, the server-side name validation is hardly exciting—we already did it with no JavaScript in Chapter 16, *Enabling AJAX for Existing Components*. But it does serve as an example for more complex use cases. In the next section, we look at a more complex example.

The Comment Field

As you probably noticed in the `remote/hello.seam` form, the user comment field is not a regular HTML text area. You click on the text to edit it and then click on the Save button to persist the new comment. That is done with the Dojo inline editing widget. We discuss it in Section 17.3.2., "Input Widgets".

17.2. The AJAX Progress Bar

The Seam AJAX progress bar example is a more sophisticated AJAX example for Seam remoting. We use it to demonstrate how to use AJAX widgets that are completely unrelated to JSF components and how to poll for AJAX content. The source code is in the ProgressBar directory in the source code bundle. After you build it and deploy the progressbar.ear into your JBoss AS, you can access the application at the http://localhost:8080/progressbar/ URL. On the progressbar.seam page, click on the Go button to start the progress bar (Figure 17.1., "The AJAX Progress Bar in Seam"). When the progress bar reaches 100 percent, the server redirects to the complete.seam page.

Figure 17.1. The AJAX Progress Bar in Seam

17.2.1. Seam Components

When you click on the Go button, the progressBarAction.doSomething Seam method is invoked as the event handler.

```
<h:commandButton value="Go!"
    action="#{progressBarAction.doSomething}"/>
```

The `progressBarAction.doSomething` method performs whatever the task that takes a long time to complete and, in the process, updates the `progress` component stored in the session context.

```java
@Stateless
@Name("progressBarAction")
@Interceptors(SeamInterceptor.class)
public class ProgressBarAction implements ProgressBar {

  @In(create = true)
  Progress progress;

  public String doSomething() {
    Random r = new Random(System.currentTimeMillis());
    try {
      for (int i = 0; i < 100;)
      {
        Thread.sleep(r.nextInt(200));
        progress.setPercentComplete(i);
        i++;
      }
    }
    catch (InterruptedException ex) {
    }

    return "complete";
  }

  public Progress getProgress() {
    return progress;
  }
}
```

The `progress` component is just a JavaBean with properties related to the progress bar.

```java
@Name("progress")
@Scope(ScopeType.SESSION)
public class Progress {

  private int percentComplete;

  public int getPercentComplete() {
    return percentComplete;
  }

  public void setPercentComplete(int percentComplete) {
```

```
      this.percentComplete = percentComplete;
   }
}
```

Now we provide a mechanism for the client JavaScript to access the `progress` component via AJAX calls by tagging the `getProgress()` method with the `@WebRemote` annotation.

```
@Local
public interface ProgressBar {
  String doSomething();
  @WebRemote Progress getProgress();
}
```

17.2.2. Accessing Seam Components from JavaScript

Now load the necessary JavaScript for accessing the `progressBarAction` component.

```
<script type="text/javascript"
  src="seam/resource/remoting/resource/remote.js">
</script>

<script type="text/javascript"
  src="seam/resource/remoting/interface.js?progressBarAction">
</script>

<script type="text/javascript">
  //<![CDATA[
    // Seam.Remoting.setDebug(true);

    // don't display the loading indicator
    Seam.Remoting.displayLoadingMessage = function() {};
    Seam.Remoting.hideLoadingMessage = function() {};

    // Get the progressBarAction Seam component
    var progressBarAction =
      Seam.Component.getInstance("progressBarAction");

    ... used the progressBarAction object ...

  // ]]>
</script>
```

You can now invoke the `progressBarAction.getProgress` method with a callback. The current `progress` object is passed to the callback when the server-side AJAX method exists. The `progressCallback()` function uses the `progressBar` object defined in the `slider.js` file to actually draw the updated progress bar. Finally, because we need to obtain the progress periodically to update the progress bar, we wrap the asynchronous `progressBarAction.getProgress()` call in a `setTimeout()` JavaScript function, which calls the wrapped function every time the timeout elapses (i.e., 250 milliseconds, in our case).

```
<script type="text/javascript">
  //<![CDATA[

    ... ...

    // Make the async call with a callback handler
    function getProgress() {
      progressBarAction.getProgress(progressCallback);
    }

    // The callback function for receiving the AJAX response
    // and then update the progress bar
    function progressCallback(progress) {
      progressBar.setPosition(progress.percentComplete);
      if (progress.percentComplete < 100)
        queryProgress();
    }

    // Wrap the async call in timeout so that it is
    // called again and again to update the progress bar
    function queryProgress() {
      setTimeout("getProgress()", 250);
    }

  // ]]>
</script>
```

This JSF snippet ties together the `commandButton` component, the server-side `progressBarAction.doSomething` method, and the `queryProgress()` JavaScript method for AJAX interactions:

```
<h:form onsubmit="queryProgress();return true;">

  <h:commandButton value="Go!"
      action="#{progressBarAction.doSomething}"/>

</h:form>
```

When the user clicks on the Go button, the browsers sends in a request to start the `progress-BarAction.doSomething` method on the back end and, at the same time, starts the `queryProgress()` JavaScript function. While the browser is waiting for the `progressBarAction.doSomething` method to complete, the `queryProgress()` method keeps updating the progress bar via AJAX calls to the `progressBarAction.getProgress()` method.

17.3. Integrating the Dojo Toolkit

Now you have seen how to use Seam remoting to develop vanilla AJAX applications. But in reality, many fancy AJAX web applications use third-party JavaScript libraries to add rich UI widgets and effects. In this section, we examine how to integrate third-party JavaScript libraries into Seam applications. We use the popular Dojo toolkit as an example here. Again, the sample application is in the `remote` source code project.

What Is Dojo?

Dojo is an open-source JavaScript library for rich web applications. AJAX developers use it widely. You can learn more about Dojo from its web site, `http://dojotoolkit.org/`.

Aside from communication and data-modeling utilities, third-party JavaScript libraries typically provide two types of UI widgets: visual effects and enhanced user input controls.

17.3.1. Visual Effects

The first type of widgets are for rich UI effects. They include the visual effects functions such as animation, fade in/out, drag-and-drops, etc., as well as navigation/layout widgets, such as tabs, accordion, trees, etc. The Dojo JavaScript functions retrieve XHTML elements by their IDs or types and then operate on those elements to create the desired visual effects. For those functions and widgets, Seam applications are no different than other HTML web applications. You just need to enclose content segment in Dojo `<div>` tags with the appropriate IDs. That is especially easy with Facelets (see Section 3.1., "An Introduction to Facelets") because Facelets pages are simply XHTML pages with JSF components. To make our point, let's look at two simple Dojo examples. The following listing shows how to create a three-tab panel in Dojo. The contents in the first two tabs are loaded when the page is loaded, and the third tab content is loaded from another page when you click on it.

```
<div id="mainTabContainer"
    dojoType="TabContainer"
    selectedTab="tab1">

  <div id="tab1" dojoType="ContentPane"
                 label="Tab 1">
    <h1>First Tab</h1>
    ... HTML and JSF component tags
       for tab content ...
  </div>

  <div id="tab2" dojoType="ContentPane"
                 label="Tab 2">
    ... More HTML and JSF component tags
       for tab content ...
  </div>

  <a dojoType="LinkPane" href="somepage.seam"
     refreshOnShow="true">Tab 3</a>

  ... ...
</div>
```

Another example is to use Dojo JavaScript functions to fade in and fade out the part of the web page enclosed in the <div> tags.

```
<a href="javascript:void(
    dojo.lfx.html.fadeOut('fade', 300).play())">
Fade out</a> |
<a href="javascript:void(
    dojo.lfx.html.fadeIn('fade', 300).play())">
Fade in</a> |
<a href="javascript:void(
    dojo.html.setOpacity(
       document.getElementById('fade'), 0.5))">
Set opacity = 50%</a>

<div id="fade">
... XHTML and JSF components to be faded in/out
    by the above links ...
</div>
```

As you can see, these examples use nothing specific to Seam. You can enclose any number of Seam JSF components between those `<div>` tags, and the Dojo JavaScript will work just fine.

It gets more complicated when the Dojo JavaScript function needs to directly operate on a JSF component. For most cases, you can just enclose the JSF component in a pair of Dojo `<div>` tags. If that is not possible, you must manually figure out the ID of the rendered JSF component. That is typically pretty easy; you just need to look at the HTML source of the generated page. But those generated IDs do change from one JSF implementation to the next.

17.3.2. Input Widgets

The second type of Dojo widgets are input widgets that replace the standard HTML input fields. For instance, Dojo provides a rich-text editor, an inline text editor, a GUI date/time picker, and many other useful input widgets. Because those widgets are not JSF components, we cannot directly bind their values to a backing bean property. Seam remoting can really help here. Figure 17.2., "Dojo Rich-Text Editor", shows a Dojo rich-text editor in the `hello.xhtml` form. It generates HTML-styled comments.

Seam Hello World

Your Name   Michael Yuan

Your Age   31

Email address   michael@michaelyuan.com

Comment:

[Normal ▾] ⋮≡ ≡ | **B** *I* U̲ S̶ | 🔗

This *is* a̲ s̶t̶y̶l̶e̶d̶ *comment!*

[Say Hello]

The Seam Greeters

The following persons have said "hello" to JBoss Seam:

Name	Age	Email	Comment	Action
Michael Yuan	31	michael@michaelyuan.com	**This** *is* a̲ s̶t̶y̶l̶e̶d̶ *comment!*	[Delete]

Figure 17.2. Dojo Rich-Text Editor

The following is the relevant code for the web page. Most of it is just standard Dojo. When the form submits, the comment in the rich-text editor is not submitted to JSF because the Dojo rich-text widget does not have any JSF back-end value binding. So we invoke the JavaScript function submitComment() to submit the comment separately when the user clicks on the Submit button.

```
<script src="dojo-0.3.1-editor/dojo.js"
        type="text/javascript">
</script>
<script type="text/javascript">
    dojo.require("dojo.widget.Editor");
</script>

... ...

Comment:<br/>
<div id="comment" dojoType="Editor"></div>


<h:commandButton type="submit"
                 value="Say Hello"
                 onclick="submitComment()"
                 action="#{manager.sayHello}"/>
```

The is the code for the submitComment() JavaScript function. Notice that I do not pass in a callback function to the Seam remoting call here because I do not need to process the return value.

```
<script language="javascript">

  ... ...

  // Get the "manager" Seam component
  var manager =
      Seam.Component.getInstance("manager");

  ... ...

  function submitComment () {
    var ed = dojo.widget.byId("comment");
    manager.setComment (ed.getEditorContent());

    //  This works too
    // var eds = dojo.widget.byType("Editor");
    // manager.setComment (
    //            eds[0].getEditorContent());
  }
</script>
```

Of course, as we mentioned earlier, the #{manager.setComment} method must be a Seam @WebRemote method. It simply sets the submitted value to the person component.

```
@Local
public interface Manager {

  ... ...

  @WebRemote
  public void setComment (String comment);
}

... ...
@Name("manager")
public class ManagerAction implements Manager {

  ... ...

  public void setComment (String comment) {
    person.setComment (comment);
  }
}
```

> **An Alternative**
>
> An alternative way to use the Dojo rich-text component is to render it into an HTML textarea instead of a div. The rich text in the textarea is submitted as an HTTP request parameter when the user submits the form. Although you still cannot directly bind a Dojo textarea with a Seam component, you can at least retrieve the HTTP request parameter at the back end via the @RequestParameter injection (see Chapter 12, *Bookmarkable Web Pages*). This is probably easier than the Seam remoting approach, in most cases.

The rich-text editor is simple. Now let's take a look at a more complex example: the Dojo in-line editor on the hello.xhtml form. The idea is that comment appears to be normal text until you click on it; then it becomes an editable text field, where you can change the comment and save it to the back end.

1. Click on the "Hello Seam" text

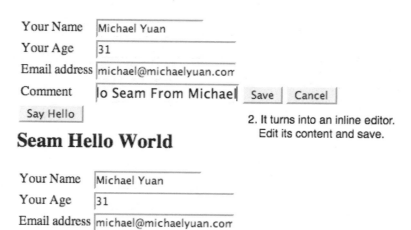

2. It turns into an inline editor.
Edit its content and save.

3. Use "Say Hello" to submit the
rest of the form

The Seam Greeters

The following persons have said "hello" to JBoss Seam:

Name	Age	Email	Comment	Action
Michael Yuan	31	michael@michaelyuan.com	Hello Seam From Michael	Delete

Figure 17.3. Dojo Inline Editor

The JavaScript code is a little more involved here. We give the inline editor widget an `onSave` handler method `submitComment()`, which saves its current content to the back end via Seam remoting. As you can see, even with this widget, a single line of Seam remoting code handles the back-end communication.

```
<script src="dojo-0.3.1-editor/dojo.js"
        type="text/javascript">
</script>
<script type="text/javascript">
    dojo.require("dojo.widget.InlineEditBox");
    dojo.require("dojo.event.*");
</script>

<script language="javascript">
  ... ...

  // Get the "manager" Seam component
  var manager =
      Seam.Component.getInstance("manager");

  function submitComment (newValue, oldValue) {
    manager.setComment (newValue);
  }

  function init () {
    var commentEditor =
              dojo.widget.byId("comment");
    commentEditor.onSave = submitComment;
  }

  dojo.addOnLoad(init);
</script>

... ...

<tr>
  <td>Comment</td>
  <td>
    <div id="comment" dojoType="inlineEditBox">
    Hello Seam
    </div>
  </td>
</tr>
```

Although the examples we gave here are Dojo examples, Seam remoting can work with any third-party JavaScript library. The possibilities are limitless!

V

Business Processes and Rules

Besides data-driven web applications, Seam supports business process-driven web applications via the jBPM business process engine and also supports business rules via the JBoss Rules engine (formerly known as Drools). With several simple annotations, you can attach Seam stateful components to business processes that require actions from multiple users and can survive multiple server reboots. Each user automatically is presented with the tasks the process requires. Business processes and rules are integrated into the very heart of the Seam framework: Seam leverages jBPM workflow to manage the JSF pageflow in a stateful manner, and the Seam security framework makes heavy use of the JBoss Rules engine to manage access security rules. We cover all these important use cases in this part of the book.

18

Managing Business Processes

In previous chapters, we showed that Seam is a great framework for developing stateful web applications. However, all our stateful application examples so far have dealt with only session states that are associated with a single web user, and those sessions have lasted only minutes to hours. In real-world business applications, the application state is often defined in long-running business processes involving multiple tasks and multiple actors. For instance, let's examine a simple use-case scenario: An author edits a document that a manager must approve before sending it to the publisher. This very simple example involves several tasks (writing, approving, sending the manuscript, and publishing) and several actors (author, manager, publisher). To manage the long-running process manually, you must carefully design your web UI, business logic methods, and database schema to work together. You must keep track of many little pieces of information throughout the application. This is tedious and results in hard-to-maintain applications.

Business process frameworks alleviate those problems by capturing all the process information in a single document and then integrating the process into the application code. Those frameworks have become very popular among enterprise developers these days. The JBoss jBPM product is the leading open-source business process framework for Java developers. The remarkable thing about Seam is that it provides a consistent state-management framework for everything from conversation states to jBPM business process states. Seam makes it easy to attach jBPM processes to Seam stateful components (e.g., EJB3 stateful session beans).

This chapter doesn't cover the details of the jBPM framework. Instead, we focus on showing you how to integrate business processes into Seam applications. The sample application for this chapter is the Ticketing project in the source code bundle. If you don't know anything about jBPM, fear not: The first part of this chapter gives you the jBPM basics so you can start writing your business processes. If you are familiar with jBPM basics and vocabulary, you can skip the first section of this chapter.

18.1. jBPM Basics and Vocabulary

The key concepts in a business process are states and tasks. The system generally is at various states waiting for the user actions (i.e., through a series of web pages and event handlers) to accomplish a task associated with the state. When the task is completed, the system moves on to another state, as defined by the process-definition document, waiting for the user to complete another associated task. Figure 18.1., "A simple business process", shows a very simple business process.

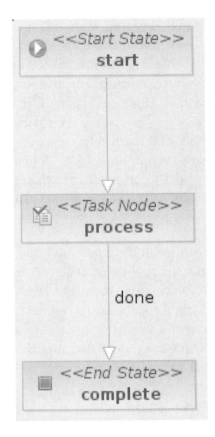

Figure 18.1. A simple business process

In jBPM, a process is defined in a process-definition XML file. Whenever you want to use a process definition, you must create a process instance to hold and save data related to that particular instance. In a sense, the process definition is analogous to a Java class, and the process instance is like a Java object.

You can create a process definition XML file by hand, or you can visually create it using the JBoss Eclipse IDE. Figure 18.2., "Designing a process definition", shows an example order-fulfillment process in the JBoss Eclipse IDE's visual process designer. The process describes how to approve (or reject) an order based on certain conditions. To create a process, you first define each potential application state as a node (either a graphical node element in the designer or an XML element in the actual process-definition file). Then, for each node, you define transition rules to move the system from the current state to another state represented by another node.

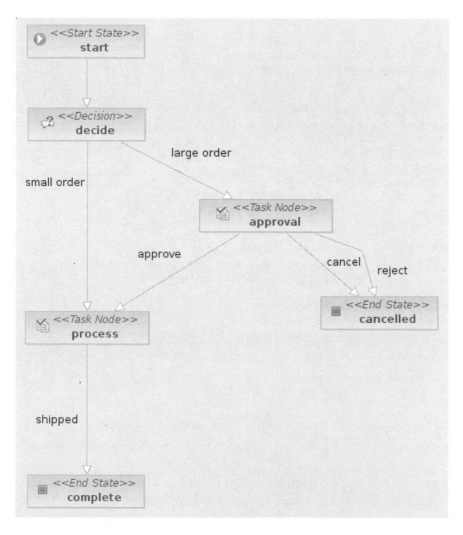

Figure 18.2. Designing a process definition

The JBoss Eclipse IDE generates the following XML file for the process definition shown in Figure 18.2., "Designing a process definition". As you can see, the XML file is intuitive and highly readable. It is not difficult to create it by hand.

```xml
<process-definition name="OrderManagement">

  <start-state name="start">
    <transition to="decide"/>
  </start-state>

  <decision name="decide"
      expression="#{orderApproval.howLargeIsOrder}">
    <transition name="large order" to="approval"/>
    <transition name="small order" to="process"/>
  </decision>

  <task-node name="approval" end-tasks="true">
    <task name="approve" description="Review order">
      <assignment pooled-actors="reviewers"/>
    </task>
    <transition name="cancel"  to="cancelled"/>
    <transition name="approve" to="process"/>
    <transition name="reject"  to="cancelled"/>
  </task-node>

  <task-node name="process">
    <task name="ship" description="Ship order">
      <assignment
        pooled-actors="#{shipperAssignment.pooledActors}"/>
    </task>
    <transition name="shipped" to="complete">
      <action expression="#{afterShipping.log}"/>
    </transition>
  </task-node>

  <end-state name="complete"/>
  <end-state name="cancelled"/>

</process-definition>
```

You can probably guess what this process does. Basically, we defined an initial state and a final state; in the middle, we added a decision node to let the system pick the right way to take in our graph, depending on a Seam expression. We also defined two task nodes and transitions between those nodes and other nodes. If the system is in a task node, it must complete the task first and then transit to another state node, depending on the task outcome. The `assignment` tag lets us pass the process to other actors. Finally, we used `action` to call a method whenever the `shipped` transition is triggered. If you want to learn more about jBPM and its process-definition language, refer to the official jBPM documentation at `http://www.jboss.org/products/jbpm/docs`.

> **Referencing Seam Components in a Process Definition**
>
> You bind Seam components directly to jBPM process-definition documents using the `#{}` notation, much like what we use in JSF pages. The process can reference values from Seam data components to automatically invoke Seam session bean methods as transition actions.

In the next section, for the sake of simplicity and clarity, we provide a new example for a ticketing process commonly found on customer service web sites. The example project is in the `ticketing` directory in the book's source code bundle. It integrates a business process for employees to assign open support tickets to themselves and then answer and close the assigned tickets.

18.2. Application Users and jBPM Actors

As we mentioned, a business process typically involves multiple collaborators. The process definition spells out which tasks can be assigned to whom. The jBPM runtime maintains a list of actors that can be assigned to tasks. For instance, in the `ticketing` example, the `answer` task, which requires the user to reply to a ticket, should be visible (and accessible) only to the `admin` actor.

```
<task-node name="process">
  <task name="answer"
        description="#{ticket.title}">
    <assignment pooled-actors="admin" />
  </task>
  ... ...
</task-node>
```

To integrate a business process into your web application, the first challenge is to map your web users to jBPM actors. Multiple web users can have the same jBPM actor role. For instance, multiple web users (i.e., every employee in the company) can be the admin actor in the ticketing example. So the jBPM actor is similar to a permission group in traditional role-based authorization systems.

The Seam jBPM API makes it easy to assign jBPM actor roles to web users. The login.xhtml page in the ticketing example enables the user to log in either as a user, to raise tickets, or as an admin, to answer tickets. We need to assign different jBPM actors, depending on whether the user clicks on the As User or As Admin buttons to log in. This is the relevant code snippet on the login.xhtml page:

```
<h:inputText value="#{user.username}" />
... ...
<h:commandButton type="submit" value="As User"
                 action="#{login.loginUser}"/>
<h:commandButton type="submit" value="As Admin"
                 action="#{login.loginAdmin}"/>
```

Seam maintains the jBPM actor role for the current user in a built-in component called #{actor}. The application can choose its desired user-authentication mechanism. After the user is authenticated, the application updates the actor component for the actor role of the user who just logged in. Because the actor component is session-scoped, the actor role is maintained as long as the user is logged in. The following is the Seam event-handler method for the Log In as User button in the ticketing example application. When we call #{login.loginUser}, we tell the jBPM actor component that the current user has the user role. The jBPM engine then figures out which tasks or processes should be available for this user.

```
@Stateful
@Name("login")
@Scope(ScopeType.SESSION)
public class LoginAction implements Login {

  @In(create = true)
  private Actor actor;

  @In
  private User user;

  public String loginUser() {
```

```
    // Check user credentials etc.
    actor.setId(user.getUsername());
    actor.getGroupActorIds().add("user");
    return "home";
  }

  // ... ...
}
```

We can also assign multiple actor roles to the user currently logged in. For instance, when the user logs in as `admin` in the `ticketing` example, we tell jBPM that the current user has both the `user` and `admin` roles so that process tasks for both actors become available to the user.

```
public String loginAdmin() {
  // Check user credentials etc.
  actor.setId(user.getUsername());
  actor.getGroupActorIds().add("user");
  actor.getGroupActorIds().add("admin");
  return "home";
}
```

In Section 18.4.3.2., "The pooledTask Component", we discuss how to assign tasks to users with jBPM actor roles.

18.3. Creating a Business Process

Earlier in Chapter 6, *A Simple Stateful Application*, you saw that Seam defines a `Process` scope. The process instance itself clearly defines the lifecycle of this scope. Any state information attached to this process instance survives after the machine reboots. The process instance can be shared among user sessions because you can assign tasks to different users.

In this section, we discuss how to create a business process definition, start it in your application, and create data components associated with the process.

18.3.1. Defining the Process

As an example, let's try to define the business process in the Ticketing example. The system works like this: A user enters questions into a system and waits for the administrators to respond (see Figure 18.3., "The process for the user: log in and create a ticket"); when an administrator logs in, he can assign tasks to himself and reply to the question (see Figure 18.4., "The process for the administrator: log in, assign tickets to self, and reply to the tickets").

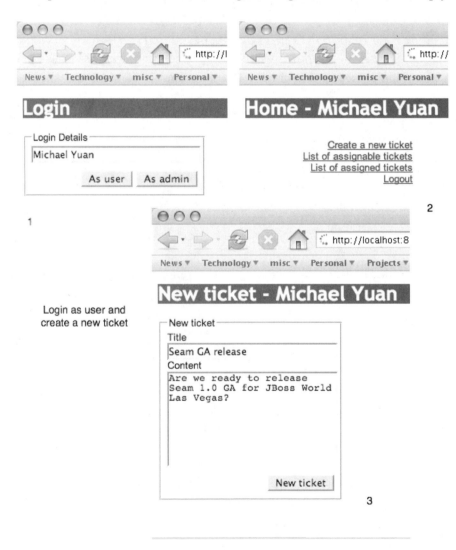

Figure 18.3. The process for the user: log in and create a ticket

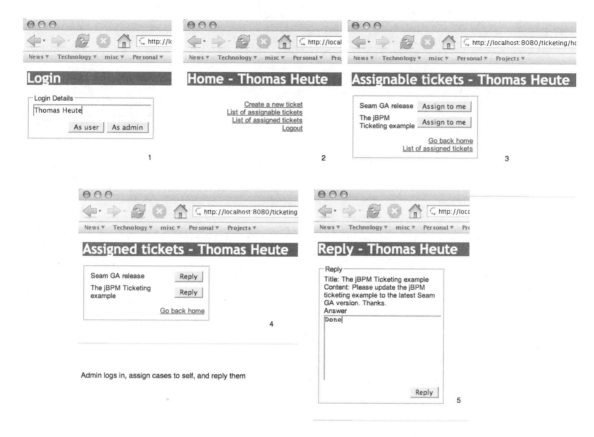

Figure 18.4. The process for the administrator: log in, assign tickets to self, and reply to the tickets

The following is the business process definition in the `ticketProcess.jpdl.xml` file. Immediately after the process starts, it transitions to the `process` node and waits in that state. When an `admin` user logs in, that user must complete the `answer` task to move forward. When the `answer` task is completed, the system transitions to the `complete` node while executing the action method `myLogger.myLog()`. The process ends, and the process instance is destroyed at the `complete` state.

```
<process-definition name="TicketProcess">

  <start-state name="start">
    <transition to="process"/>
  </start-state>
```

```
<task-node name="process">
  <task name="answer" description="#{ticket.title}">
    <assignment pooled-actors="admin" />
  </task>
  <transition name="done" to="complete">
    <action expression="#{myLogger.myLog}" />
  </transition>
</task-node>

<end-state name="complete"/>
</process-definition>
```

18.3.2. Creating a Business Process Instance

A business process must be triggered by a user action. In our example, when the user clicks on the New Ticket button on the web page, the system creates a new business process for that ticket, with the `ticket` object attached in the `Process` scope. The process ends when the administrator replies to the ticket and the system logs the reply. To implement this, we annotated the New Ticket button event-handler method with a `@CreateProcess` annotation. Each process definition has a name that is the unique parameter to pass to the `@CreateProcess` annotation.

```
@Stateless
@Name("ticketSystem")
public class TicketSystemAction
         implements TicketSystem {

  @CreateProcess(definition="TicketProcess")
  public String newTicket() {
    return "home";
  }

  ... ...
}
```

Now whenever the user invokes the `newTicket()` method, a process instance based on the `TicketProcess` process definition is created. One business process instance exists for each new ticket created. The web user can select which business process she wants to work on by passing the `taskId` HTTP request parameter to the web pages (see Section 18.4.2., "Specifying a Task to Work On", for more).

> **What About Stateful Session Beans?**
>
> In this example, we put the business logic in the stateless session bean `TicketSystemAction` and use POJO components for the stateful data associated with the process (see Section 18.3.3., "Binding Data Objects in Process Scope"). We do this for clarity: It enables us to first discuss how to implement the business logic in the business process and then to cover how the state is maintained in the process.
>
> When you understand how the system works, you can easily mesh the two and use business process-scoped stateful session beans to implement both business logic and application state. We leave this as an exercise for the reader.

18.3.3. Binding Data Objects in Process Scope

A business process always has data associated with it. In the `ticketing` example, a `Ticket` object is associated with each process instance. Using `#{ticket}`, you can refer to the `Ticket` object associated with the current process in both the process-definition document and the JSF page. In Section 18.4.3., "Selecting a Task in the UI", we discuss how to select a business process as "current." In this section, we focus on how to bind a data object with a business process instance.

To bind a value to the business process scope, you can directly use `@Out(scope=BUSINESS_PROCESS)` for all primitives and `string`s. If you want to store more complex objects, you must make sure they are serializable. Having POJOs stored as serialized objects in your database is probably not the best way; instead, you can store those objects as entity beans and just store the ID of the bean to the process instance. This example merely shows you that storing serializable objects in the process instance is possible. Another linked problem is that because the object is serialized, you can't retrieve a variable if you have to change the class definition. In a real-world scenario, only the entity bean identifier is linked to the business process, and modifying the entity bean definition usually affects only the database table definition.

> **Do Not Intercept**
>
> The example uses the `Ticket` class as a Seam component annotated with `@Intercept(InterceptionType.NEVER)`. This means that Seam will not intercept this Java bean. As of this writing, interceptable Java beans cannot be bound to a business process because they cannot be unserialized after a server shutdown.

```java
import java.io.Serializable
import org.jboss.seam.*;

@Name("ticket")
@Intercept(InterceptionType.NEVER)
@Scope(ScopeType.BUSINESS_PROCESS)
public class Ticket implements Serializable {

  private String title;
  private String content;
  private String answer;

  public String getContent() {
    return content;
  }
  public void setContent(String content) {
    this.content = content;
  }

  public String getTitle() {
    return title;
  }
  public void setTitle(String title) {
    this.title = title;
  }

  public String getAnswer() {
    return answer;
  }
  public void setAnswer(String answer) {
    this.answer = answer;
  }
}
```

This object can be attached to a business process instance and "lives" with it.

18.4. Managing Tasks

Tasks are central elements in a business process. After a business process is created, it waits for the user to complete the tasks defined in the process. Whenever the user completes a task, the process moves forward and decides which task the user needs to do next. To support business processes in web applications, Seam provides a mechanism for associating web actions (e.g., button clicks) with tasks. In this section, we explain how this works.

18.4.1. Implementing Business Logic for Tasks

The tasks in the jBPM business process definition file are just nodes in the XML file. The process itself does not specify what actions are needed for each task and how the task is completed (i.e., the business logic). It just needs to know when the user starts and completes a task so that the process can move on to the next task node waiting.

In a Seam jBPM application, the business logic for each task is implemented in Java and JSF code. The user starts and completes a task by going through several web pages. Hence, we need to tell the application which web UI event starts a task and which event ends the task. For instance, in the Ticketing example application, the Reply button should start the `answer` task. To do that, we annotate the UI event-handler method of the Reply button (i.e., the `TicketSystemAction.reply()` method) with the `@BeginTask` annotation. In this example, the `reply()` method simply redirects to the reply page. The ticket information on that page is available in the Seam `#{ticket}` component associated with this business process instance (see Section 18.3.3., "Binding Data Objects in Process Scope"). In a stateful session bean, the `@BeginTask` annotated method usually fetches and initiates data for the task.

```
@Stateless
@Name("ticketSystem")
public class TicketSystemAction
          implements TicketSystem {

  ... ...

  @BeginTask
  public String reply() {
    return "reply";
  }

  ... ...
}
```

The #{ticketSystem.reply} method returns reply, which directs JSF to display the reply.xhtml page. A task can take several web pages to complete. Hence, it spans multiple Seam session bean methods. The @BeginTask annotation declares the first method to invoke to start a task. From there, the user can go over multiple pages and session bean methods to complete the task. At the end of the task, the @EndTask annotation declares the last method in the task. In our example, the Answer button event handler sends out the reply, completes the task, and causes the process to move to the next state. If more than one transition from the current task node exists, you must specify which transition to pass by giving the transition name to the @EndTask annotation (@EndTask("approve"), for example).

```
@Stateless
@Name("ticketSystem")
public class TicketSystemAction
          implements TicketSystem {

  ... ...

  @EndTask
  public String sendAnswer() {
    // send the answer to user
    return "home";
  }

  ... ...
}
```

When the task is completed, the process moves to the next task. The web user can then assign the task and work on it until the process completes.

Tasks with Multiple Transitions

The following example, taken from the DVD demo store available within the Seam distribution, shows how to handle multiple transitions in a task node. During the task, the Seam stateful session bean component determines which transition to invoke and then guides the user to click on the appropriate @EndTask method to finish the task.

```
@BeginTask
public String viewTask() {
```

```
        order = (Order) em.createQuery("from Order o " +
          "join fetch o.orderLines " +
          "where o.orderId = :orderId")
            .setParameter("orderId", orderId)
            .getSingleResult();
        return "accept";
    }

    @EndTask(transition="approve")
    public String accept() {
        order.process();
        return "admin";
    }

    @EndTask(transition="reject")
    public String reject() {
        order.cancel();
        return "admin";
    }
```

The transition to trigger is defined in the `@EndTask` annotation, and the returned string is the JSF outcome to display the next view page.

18.4.2. Specifying a Task to Work On

The `@BeginTask` and `@EndTask` annotations do not take parameters. So how does the application know that the `#{ticketSystem.reply()}` method is supposed to start an `answer` task, not some other task defined in the process? Furthermore, because the application has multiple business processes running at the same time, multiple `answer` tasks are waiting in different processes (i.e., different tickets) at any given time. How does the system know which of those `answer` tasks it is supposed to begin in response to a particular Reply button?

The answer here is to use the `taskId` HTTP request parameter. In jBPM, each task in the "waiting" state has a unique ID. If multiple tasks exist in a process, only the one that is currently waiting for user action has a valid ID. You can apply `@BeginTask`, `@EndTask`, or other methods to a task with a specific ID. For instance, the following Reply button applies to the waiting task with ID 123. The `taskId` is conceptually similar to the `conversationId` we discussed in Chapter 8, *Workspaces and Concurrent Conversations*.

```
<h:commandLink action="#{ticketSystem.reply}">
  <h:commandButton value="Reply"/>
  <f:param name="taskId" value="123"/>
</h:commandLink>
```

Using this technique, we can associate any button or link to the task it intends to operate on. Furthermore, we can associate a web page to a specific task or business process. For instance, when you load the `reply.seam?taskId=123` URL, the `#{ticket}` component on the `reply.xhtml` page is already loaded with the business process scoped `#{ticket}` component associated with `taskId` `123`. So the `reply.xhtml` page is really simple.

```
Title: #{ticket.title}
...
Content: #{ticket.content}
...
Answer: <h:inputTextarea value="#{ticket.answer}"/>
...
<h:commandLink action="#{ticketSystem.sendAnswer}">
  <h:commandButton value="Reply"/>
  <f:param name="taskId" value="#{param.taskId}"/>
</h:commandLink>
```

When the user clicks on the Reply button, the current `taskId` for the page is passed on to the `#{ticketSystem.sendAnswer}` method. The `sendAnswer()` method also knows which task it is operating on. As we discussed before, it ends the task and causes the business process to move on.

Of course, in the real world, we do not hard-code the `taskId` (e.g., `123`) into the web pages. Instead, we ask the system to dynamically generate `taskIds` for the tasks available for the currently logged-in user. That is the topic in Section 18.4.3., "Selecting a Task in the UI".

18.4.3. Selecting a Task in the UI

Earlier in Section 18.4.2., "Specifying a Task to Work On", we explained that web actions are associated with jBPM tasks via the `taskId` parameter. Each available task in the waiting state has a `taskId`. But how do users determine the available `taskIds`, and how do they assign tasks to users? They can do that via built-in Seam jBPM components.

> **Business Processes and Conversations**
>
> We can draw an analogy here between business processes and long-running conversations. When a user has multiple long-running conversations, she can choose one to join by switching the browser window or selecting from the #{conversationList}. Business processes are not tied to browser windows. The Seam components in this section are the business process equivalents to #{conversationList}.

18.4.3.1. The `pooledTaskInstanceList` Component

The `pooledTaskInstanceList` component finds all the task instances that can be assigned to the logged-in user. This can be used in a ticketing system, for example, where an admin gets the list of unassigned tasks he can work on. This example code could be used (i.e., the `assignableTickets.xhtml` page):

```
<h:dataTable value="#{pooledTaskInstanceList}"
             var="task">
    <h:column>
        <f:facet name="header">Id</f:facet>
        #{task.id}
    </h:column>
    <h:column>
        <f:facet name="header">
          Description
        </f:facet>
        #{task.description}
    </h:column>
</h:dataTable>
```

As we defined in the process-definition file (see Section 18.3., "Creating a Business Process"), the #{task.description} is the #{ticket.title} in the task's process scope.

18.4.3.2. The `pooledTask` Component

This component is typically used inside a #{pooledTaskInstanceList} data table. It has a unique method of assigning a task to the current logged-in actor. The `id` of the task to assign must be passed as a request parameter so that the action method (i.e., the @BeginTask method) can determine which task it starts for. To use this component, you can write the following code. The #{task.id} comes from the #{pooledTaskInstanceList} iterator (see previous section).

```
<h:commandLink
    action="#{pooledTask.assignToCurrentActor}">
      <h:commandButton value="Assign"/>
      <f:param name="taskId" value="#{task.id}"/>
</h:commandLink>
```

18.4.3.3. The `taskInstanceList` Component

This component's goal is to get all the task instances that have been assigned to the logged-in user. In the Ticketing example, this component is used in the assignedTickets.xhtml page to show a list of processes/tickets already assigned to the user.

```
<h:dataTable value="#{taskInstanceList}"
                              var="task">
    <h:column>
        <f:facet name="header">Id</f:facet>
        #{task.id}
    </h:column>
    <h:column>
        <f:facet name="header">
          Description
        </f:facet>
        #{task.description}
    </h:column>
</h:dataTable>
```

18.4.3.4. The `taskInstanceListByType` Component

This component can be seen as a filtered version of the previous component. Instead of returning the whole list of task instances, this component returns only the task instances of a certain type.

```
<h:dataTable
      value="#{taskInstanceListByType['todo']}"
```

```
        var="task">
    <h:column>
        <f:facet name="header">Id</f:facet>
        #{task.id}
    </h:column>
    <h:column>
        <f:facet name="header">
          Description
        </f:facet>
        #{task.description}
    </h:column>
</h:dataTable>
```

In a nutshell, you can use jBPM to define the process, use Seam stateful session beans to handle the tasks and transitions in the process, and then use Seam built-in components to tie the process actions to UI elements on the JSF page.

18.5. jBPM Libraries and Configuration

To use jBPM components, you must bundle the `jbpm-x.y.z.jar` file in your application JAR file (i.e., the `app.jar` inside the EAR file). We recommend JBPM 3.1.2 or above.

You also must add the following configuration files to the root of your EAR file: `*.jpdl.xml` defines the business processes, `jbpm.cfg.xml` configures the jBPM engine, and `hibernate.cfg.xml` configures the database that stores the process states.

```
ticketing.ear
|+ ticketProcess.jpdl.xml
|+ hibernate.cfg.xml
|+ jbpm.cfg.xml
|+ app.war
|+ app.jar
|   |+ class files
|   |+ jbpm-3.1.2.jar
|   |+ seam.properties
|   |+ META-INF
|+ jboss-seam.jar
|+ el.api.jar
|+ el-ri.jar
|+ META-INF
```

The `jbpm.cfg.xml` file overrides the default attributes in the jBPM engine. Primarily, you must disable the jBPM transaction manager for persistent data because Seam now manages database access.

```xml
<jbpm-configuration>

  <jbpm-context>

    <service name="persistence">
      <factory>
        <bean class=
"org.jbpm.persistence.db.DbPersistenceServiceFactory">
          <field name="isTransactionEnabled">
            <false/>
          </field>
        </bean>
      </factory>
    </service>


  </jbpm-context>

</jbpm-configuration>
```

The jBPM engine stores the process state in a database to make the process long lived—even after the server reboots. The `hibernate.cfg.xml` file configures which database to store jBPM state data and loads jBPM data-mapping files to set up database tables. In this example, we just save the jBPM state data in the embedded HSQL database at `java:/DefaultDS`. Many jBPM mapping files exist; we do not fully list them here. You can refer to the `hibernate.cfg.xml` file in the `ticketing` project to find out more.

```xml
<hibernate-configuration>
  <session-factory>
    <property name="dialect">
      org.hibernate.dialect.HSQLDialect
    </property>
    <property name="connection.datasource">
      java:/DefaultDS
    </property>
    <property name="transaction.factory_class">
org.hibernate.transaction.JTATransactionFactory
    </property>
    <property
      name="transaction.manager_lookup_class">
```

```
org.hibernate.transaction.JBossTransactionManagerLookup
    </property>
    <property
      name="transaction.flush_before_completion">
      true
    </property>
    <property name="cache.provider_class">
      org.hibernate.cache.HashtableCacheProvider
    </property>
    <property name="hbm2ddl.auto">update</property>

    <mapping resource=
      "org/jbpm/db/hibernate.queries.hbm.xml"/>

    <mapping .../>
  </session-factory>
</hibernate-configuration>
```

In addition, you must tell the Seam runtime where to find the `*.jpdl.xml` files. You do this by adding a `core:Jbpm` component in the `components.xml` file.

```
<components>

  ... ...

  <core:Jbpm
    processDefinitions="ticketProcess.jpdl.xml"/>

</components>
```

Overall, Seam greatly simplifies the development of process-driven web applications. Traditional web developers might find the business process concepts a little confusing initially. But when you get past the basic syntax, you will find it extremely easy to use and very powerful. Seam lowers the bar for applying business processes in web applications.

19

Stateful Pageflows

In Chapter 18, *Managing Business Processes*, you saw that Seam does an excellent job of integrating business processes into web applications. The user can create, assign, switch, and end tasks via regular web actions (i.e., button clicks, page loads), and Seam automatically loads all the process-scoped data for the current task. In addition to application-level integration with jBPM, Seam deeply integrates business processes into the framework itself. One of the most useful use cases for jBPM in Seam is to use business processes to manage the pageflows of the web application.

In a standard JSF application, the page-navigation rules are defined in the `navigation.xml` or `faces-config.xml` files. You can reference those rules from links/buttons on web pages to specify which page to display when the link/button is clicked. When an event-handler method is invoked from a link/button, the method returns a literal string value that matches one of the navigation rules to determine which page to display next. That works well in simple applications. However, as web applications grow more complex, many potential outcomes could result from an event-handler method, and multiple navigation rules might point to the same target page. The `navigation.xml` or `faces-config.xml` files could quickly become bloated and hard to debug. Seam provides an alternate way to manage the navigation rules. Instead of relying on the event-handler methods to return the exact literal strings, a Seam application can automatically determine the next page to display based on the actual state of the application. To understand how this works, let's look at an example.

19.1. Stateful Navigation Rules in pages.xml

In Section 8.2., "Workspace Switcher", and Section 12.1., "Using Page Parameters", we discussed the use of the `pages.xml` file, which is an important element in making Seam more "web friendly." You can put page-specific parameters and actions in `pages.xml` and also use it to support navigation rules for each page. The following is an example `pages.xml` file from the Hotel Booking example in the Seam distribution (i.e., the `examples/booking` project).

```
<pages no-conversation-view-id="/main.xhtml">

  <page view-id="/register.xhtml">
    <action if="#{validation.failed}"
            execute="#{register.invalid}"/>

    <navigation>
      <rule if="#{register.registered}">
        <redirect view-id="/home.xhtml"/>
      </rule>
    </navigation>

  </page>
```

This rule indicates that, after the user submits the register.xhtml page, Seam checks whether the #{register.registered} property is true. If so, it displays the home.xhtml page; if not, it redisplays the register.xhtml page. Of course, the #{register.register} method, which is the event-handler method for the Register button, sets the #{register.registered} property. Notice that the user can submit the register.xhtml page through any button/link with any event-handler method—not just the Register button. The application state in the #{register.registered} property solely determines the navigation outcome.

```
  <page view-id="/confirm.xhtml"
        conversation-required="true">

    <description>
      Confirm booking: #{booking.description}
    </description>

    <navigation
        from-action="#{hotelBooking.confirm}">
      <redirect view-id="/main.xhtml"/>
    </navigation>

  </page>
```

When the user submits the confirm.xhtml page and invokes the #{hotelBooking.confirm} method, the next page is main.xhtml, as long as the method is successfully executed (i.e., no exception is thrown). The #{hotelBooking.confirm} method does not need to return any string value.

```
<page view-id="/main.xhtml">

  <action execute="#{login.validateLogin}"/>

  <navigation
      from-action="#{login.validateLogin}">
    <rule if="#{not login.loggedIn}">
      <redirect view-id="/home.xhtml"/>
    </rule>
  </navigation>

  <navigation from-action=
      "#{hotelBooking.selectHotel(hot)}">
    <redirect view-id="/hotel.xhtml"/>
  </navigation>

</page>
```

When the `main.xhtml` page is loaded, Seam first executes the `#{login.validateLogin}` method to check whether the current user is logged in. The `#{login.validateLogin}` method sets the login status in the property `#{login.loggedIn}`. Immediately after the `#{login.validateLogin}` method is executed, Seam checks `#{login.loggedIn}` and redirects to `home.xhtml` if the user is not logged in.

> **A Better Way to Manage Security**
>
> In the example in this chapter, we use a home-grown `#{login}` component to manage security. The Seam security framework provides a much better way to manage security. Refer to Chapter 20, *Rule-Based Security Framework*, for more details.

After the user submits the `main.xhtml` page with the Select Hotel button that invokes the `#{hotelBooking.selectHotel}` method, Seam redirects to the `hotel.xhtml` page if the method is successfully executed.

```
<page view-id="*">

  <navigation from-action="#{login.logout}">
    <redirect view-id="/home.xhtml"/>
  </navigation>
```

```
   <navigation
       from-action="#{hotelBooking.cancel}">
     <redirect view-id="/main.xhtml"/>
   </navigation>

  </page>

  ... ...

</pages>
```

Finally, you can specify navigation rules that apply to multiple pages. The previous rule indicates that if the #{login.logout} method is invoked on any page, Seam redirects to the home.xhtml page after the method is successfully executed.

With navigation rules in pages.xml, event-handler methods do not need to return arbitrary literal strings, and the navigation outcome completely depends on the application's internal state.

Still, how does that have anything to do with business processes? As it turns out, the pages.xml file can take not only navigation rules, but also business process definitions.

19.2. Associating a Business Process with a Web Page

A navigation rule dictates the next page to display. But a business process specifies a flow of web pages following the current page. To best illustrate how a business process works, check out the numberguess example in the book's source code bundle. The application has two processes attached to the numberGuess.xhtml and confirm.xhtml pages, respectively.

```
<pages>
  <page view-id="/numberGuess.xhtml">
    <begin-conversation join="true"
                        pageflow="numberGuess"/>
  </page>
  <page view-id="/confirm.xhtml">
    <begin-conversation nested="true"
                        pageflow="cheat"/>
```

```
    </page>
</pages>
```

The `numberGuess.xhtml` page displays a form for you to guess a random number generated by the application. After you enter a guess, the application tells you whether it is too high or too low and asks you to guess again until you reach the right guess. This is the `numberGuess.xhtml` page:

```
<h:outputText value="Higher!"
      rendered= "#{numberGuess.randomNumber gt
                  numberGuess.currentGuess}"/>
<h:outputText value="Lower!"
      rendered="#{numberGuess.randomNumber lt
                  numberGuess.currentGuess}"/>
<br/>
I'm thinking of a number between
#{numberGuess.smallest} and
#{numberGuess.biggest}. You have
#{numberGuess.remainingGuesses} guesses.
<br/>
Your guess:
<h:inputText value="#{numberGuess.currentGuess}"
             id="guess" required="true">
  <f:validateLongRange
        maximum="#{numberGuess.biggest}"
        minimum="#{numberGuess.smallest}"/>
</h:inputText>

<h:commandButton value="Guess" action="guess"/>
<s:button value="Cheat" view="/confirm.xhtml"/>
<s:button value="Give up" action="giveup"/>
```

The Guess and Give Up buttons map to `guess` and `giveup` transitions in the business process associated with the page. The `giveup` transition is simple: It just redirects to the `giveup.xhtml` page, from which you can click on buttons mapped to `yes` or `no` actions. The `guess` transition is slightly more complex: Seam first executes the `#{numberGuess.guess}` method, which compares the user's guess against the random number and saves the current guess. Then the process goes on to the `evaluateGuess` decision node. The `#{numberGuess.correctGuess}` method compares the current guess with the random number. If the outcome is `true`, the process moves to the `win` node and displays the `win.xhtml` page.

```
<pageflow-definition name="numberGuess">

  <start-page name="displayGuess"
              view-id="/numberGuess.xhtml">
    <redirect/>
    <transition name="guess" to="evaluateGuess">
      <action expression="#{numberGuess.guess}"/>
    </transition>
    <transition name="giveup" to="giveup"/>
  </start-page>

  <decision name="evaluateGuess"
        expression="#{numberGuess.correctGuess}">
    <transition name="true" to="win"/>
    <transition name="false"
        to="evaluateRemainingGuesses"/>
  </decision>

  <decision name="evaluateRemainingGuesses"
            expression="#{numberGuess.lastGuess}">
    <transition name="true" to="lose"/>
    <transition name="false" to="displayGuess"/>
  </decision>


  <page name="giveup" view-id="/giveup.xhtml">
    <redirect/>
    <transition name="yes" to="lose"/>
    <transition name="no" to="displayGuess"/>
  </page>

  <page name="win" view-id="/win.xhtml">
    <redirect/>
    <end-conversation/>
  </page>

  <page name="lose" view-id="/lose.xhtml">
    <redirect/>
    <end-conversation/>
  </page>

</pageflow-definition>
```

The following are the #{numberGuess.guess} and #{numberGuess.correctGuess} methods we discussed earlier. With the support of business processes, those methods need to contain only business logic code — they do not need to couple it with the navigation logic.

```
@Name("numberGuess")
@Scope(ScopeType.CONVERSATION)
public class NumberGuess {

  ... ...

  public void guess() {
    if (currentGuess > randomNumber) {
      biggest = currentGuess - 1;
    }
    if (currentGuess < randomNumber) {
      smallest = currentGuess + 1;
    }
    guessCount ++;
  }

  public boolean isCorrectGuess() {
    return currentGuess == randomNumber;
  }
}
```

If the user loads the `confirm.xhtml` page, the `cheat` process starts. If you click on the button mapped to the `yes` action, the `#{numberGuess.cheated}` is invoked to mark you as a cheater, and the process moves to the `cheat` node to display the `cheat.xhtml` page.

```
<pageflow-definition name="cheat">

  <start-page name="confirm"
              view-id="/confirm.xhtml">
    <transition name="yes" to="cheat">
      <action expression="#{numberGuess.cheated}"/>
    </transition>
    <transition name="no" to="end"/>
  </start-page>

  <page name="cheat" view-id="/cheat.xhtml">
    <redirect/>
    <transition to="end"/>
  </page>

  <page name="end" view-id="/numberGuess.xhtml">
    <redirect/>
    <end-conversation/>
  </page>

</pageflow-definition>
```

The Back Button

When navigating using a stateful pageflow model, you make sure that the application decides what is possible. Think about the transitions: If you passed a transition, you cannot go backward unless you make it possible in your pageflow definition. If a user decides to press the Back button of her browser, it could lead to an inconsistent state. Fortunately, Seam automatically brings the user back to the page that he should be seeing. This enables you to make sure that a user will not twice confirm his $1 million order just because he accidentally pressed the Back button and submitted it again.

19.3. Pageflow and Stateful Conversation

The jBPM pageflow can be tightly integrated with Seam conversations. You can start a long-running conversation when the process (or a node in the process) starts, and end the conversation when a process node is reached. That amounts to declarative management of Seam conversations. No more need exists for the `@Begin` and `@End` annotations when conversations are defined in the `pages.xml` and `*.jpdl.xml` files.

In the previous example, the conversation starts when the `numberGuess.xhtml` page is loaded.

```
<pages>
  <page view-id="/numberGuess.xhtml">
    <begin-conversation join="true"
                        pageflow="numberGuess"/>
  ... ...
</pages>
```

The conversation ends when the `win` or `lose` node in the process is reached.

```
<pageflow-definition name="numberGuess">

  ... ...
```

```
<page name="win" view-id="/win.xhtml">
  <redirect/>
  <end-conversation/>
</page>

<page name="lose" view-id="/lose.xhtml">
  <redirect/>
  <end-conversation/>
</page>

</pageflow-definition>
```

Between the start and end of the conversation, the `#{numberGuess}` component keeps all the application information associated with the conversation (i.e., the application-generated random number, the current guess, the number of remaining guesses, etc.).

19.4. Configuration

To use the jBPM-based pageflows, you must bundle the jBPM library JAR (3.1.2+) and the process-definition files (i.e., the `*.jpdl.xml` files) in your application. This is the structure of the `numberguess.ear` application:

```
numberguess.ear
|+ pagefolow.jpdl.xml
|+ cheat.jpdl.xml
|+ app.war
|+ app.jar
|   |+ class files
|   |+ jbpm-3.1.2.jar
|   |+ seam.properties
|   |+ META-INF
|+ jboss-seam.jar
|+ el.api.jar
|+ el-ri.jar
|+ META-INF
```

Because we do not need to persist the business process state into a database, you do not need to bundle the `hibernate.cfg.xml` and `jbpm.cfg.xml` files in the application. However, you do need to declare the pageflow definition files to Seam via the `core:Jbpm` component in the `components.xml` file.

```
<components ...>

  ... ...

  <core:Jbpm>
    <property name="pageflowDefinitions">
      <value>pageflow.jpdl.xml</value>
      <value>cheat.jpdl.xml</value>
    </property>
  </core:Jbpm>

</components>
```

No Extra Configuration Needed for Rules in `pages.xml`

If you just need to use navigation rules in the `pages.xml` file and do not need full jBPM-based pageflow support, you do not need to install the jBPM library JAR in your application.

20

Rule-Based Security Framework

Business process is closely related to business rules. Seam integrates the JBoss Rules (formerly known as Drools) engine to support sophisticated rules. In fact, Seam itself uses JBoss Rules to implement an innovative security framework for web applications. In this chapter, we introduce the Seam security framework and showcase how business rules are used to manage security.

Managed security is one of those "half-measure solutions" in enterprise Java. The standard Java EE security model works okay for the simplest cases (e.g., to require login to access part of the site). But more often than not, developers struggle against the standard Java EE security schemes and work around it rather than using it.

The Seam security model, on the other hand, is based on rules. You can specify who is permitted to access which page, which UI element, and which bean method. As with everything else in Seam, all Seam security rules are stateful. That means each rule's outcome depends on the current state of the application context. Hence, you can give certain users access to certain application features only when some runtime conditions are met. The Seam security framework offers great power and flexibility for almost every use case a web application encounters.

20.1. Authentication and User Roles

The most important aspect of a security framework is user authentication. Each user must log in with a username and password combo to access restricted parts of the web application.

Each user also has one or several security roles. For instance, on an e-commerce web site, user `johndoe` might have the `visitor` role. He can perform tasks such as changing his own address, checking out the shopping cart, and paying for the purchase. The user `bigshot` might have the `admin` role. He can manage inventories and answer customer support queries.

First, you need to write a login form for the user to enter username and password. In the login form, you should bind the user credentials and actions to the Seam built-in `#{identity}` component as follows:

```
<div>
  Username:
  <h:inputText value="#{identity.username}"/>
</div>

<div>
  Password:
  <h:inputSecret value="#{identity.password}"/>
</div>

<div>
  <h:commandButton value="Login"
                   action="#{identity.login}"/>
</div>
```

The `#{identity}` component is scoped to the HTTP session. Once a user is logged in, she stays logged in until the session expires. The `#{identity.login}` method in turn invokes an "authenticator" method in your session beans or Seam POJOs to perform the actual authentication work. We will discuss how to write and configure the authenticator method shortly. If the login succeeds, the `#{identity.login}` method returns the string value `loggedIn`, which you can use in the navigation rules to determine the next age to display. If the login fails, the `#{identity.login}` method returns `null` to redisplay the login form with an error message.

> **Logout**
>
> The `#{identity.logout}` method provides a simple mechanism for logging out a user from a Seam application. It simply invalidates the current session and causes Seam to reload the current page—to be redirected to the login page if the current page is restricted.

The authentication method, invoked from `#{identity.login}`, checks the username and password combo from the injected `identity`. If it is valid, the method returns `true`; otherwise, the method returns `false`. After the username and password are verified, the authentication method optionally retrieves the security roles for the user and adds those roles to the `identity` component via `identity.addRole()`. The following `login()` method is an example authentication method. It checks the `User` table in the database to authenticate the user and retrieves the user's roles from the same database upon successful authentication.

```java
@Stateless
@Name("authBean")
public class AuthBean implements Auth {
  @In
  Identity identity;

  @PersistenceContext
  EntityManager em;

  public boolean login () {
    try {
      User user = (User) em.createQuery(
            "from User where username = :username "
          + "and password = :password")
        .setParameter("username", username)
        .setParameter("password", password)
        .getSingleResult();

      if (user.getRoles() != null) {
        for (UserRole mr : user.getRoles())
          identity.addRole(mr.getName());
      }
      return true;

    } catch (NoResultException ex) {
      FacesMessages.instance().add(
            "Invalid username/password");
      return false;
    }
  }
  ... ...
}
```

Because you can put any Java code in the authentication method, it is easy to authenticate against a LDAP server or any other data store. For Seam to know that the `login()` method is the authentication method for the application, you must declare it in the `components.xml` file, as follows:

```xml
<components
    xmlns="http://jboss.com/products/seam/components"
    xmlns:security=
          "http://jboss.com/products/seam/security"
    xmlns:core="http://jboss.com/products/seam/core">

  ... ...
```

```
<security:identity authenticate-method=
                   "#{authBean.login}"/>

</components>
```

20.2. Declarative Access Control

Authentication by itself is not very useful; it must be combined with an authorization scheme to grant access to the application based on the user's identity. Seam makes it easy to declare access constraints on web pages, UI components, and Java methods via XML tags, annotations, and JSF EL expressions.

20.2.1. Web Pages

One of the most common access-control scenarios involves displaying certain web pages only when the user is logged in. That can be easily done with the pages.xml file. The following example shows that only logged-in users can access the checkout.xhtml page, as well as any page with the /members/* URL pattern. If the user is not logged in, the login.xhtml page is displayed instead.

```
<pages login-view-id="/login.xhtml">

  ... ...
  <page view-id="/checkout.xhtml" login-required="true"/>
  <page view-id="/members/*" login-required="true"/>

</pages>
```

If you want to redirect the user to the page she originally requested after the login, add the following elements in your components.xml file.

```
<event type="org.jboss.seam.notLoggedIn">
  <action expression="#{redirect.captureCurrentView}"/>
</event>

<event type="org.jboss.seam.postAuthenticate">
  <action expression="#{redirect.returnToCapturedView}"/>
</event>
```

Using simple EL expressions in the `<restrict>` tag, we can also limit access to a page to users with a certain security role. For instance, the following example indicates that the `inventory.xhtml` page is accessible only by logged-in users with the `admin` role.

```
<pages>

  ... ...

  <page view-id="/inventory.xhtml">
    <restrict>#{s:hasRole('admin')}</restrict>
  </page>

</pages>
```

When access is denied for the page, Seam throws the `NotLoggedInException` or the `AuthorizationException`, depending on whether the user is currently logged in. You can use the techniques described in Chapter 14, *Failing Gracefully*, to redirect to custom error pages when those exceptions occur.

20.2.2. UI Components

Besides controlling access to entire web pages, you can use EL expressions to selectively display UI elements on a page to different users. That is done via the `rendered` attribute on JSF components. The login status of the current user is available from the `#{identity.loggedIn}` property. The following listing shows a user information panel on a web page that is displayed only when the user is logged in.

```
<s:div rendered="#{identity.loggedIn}">
  <s:link value="Your Profile"
          action="#{user.edit}"/>
  <s:link value="Previous Orders"
          action="#{user.history}"/>
  <s:link value="Logout"
          action="#{identity.logout}"/>
</s:div>
```

The next example shows a link in the panel that is available only to users with the `admin` role.

```
<s:div rendered="#{identity.loggedIn}">
  <s:link value="Check Inventory"
          action="#{manager.checkInventory}"
          rendered="#{s:hasRole('admin')}"/>
```

```
... ...
</s:div>
```

20.2.3. Method-Level Access Control

Access control on the UI is easy to understand, but it is not sufficient. A clever cracker might be able to get past the UI layer and access methods on Seam components directly. It is important to secure individual Java methods in the application as well. Fortunately, you can easily declare method-level access constraints with Seam annotations and EL expressions. The following example shows a `checkout()` method that is accessible only to logged-in users.

```
@Stateful
@Name("manager")
public class ManagerAction implement Manager {

  public String addToCart () {
    // code
  }

  @Restrict("#{identity.loggedIn}")
  public String checkout () {
    // code
  }
}
```

Similarly, you can tag methods to be accessible only by users with a certain role. The following example shows that the `checkInventory()` method can be executed only by users with the `admin` role.

```
@Stateful
@Name("manager")
public class ManagerAction implement Manager {

  ... ...

  @Restrict("#{s:hasRole('admin')}")
  public String checkInventory () {
    // code
  }
}
```

When access is denied for the method, Seam throws the `NotLoggedInException` or the `AuthorizationException`, depending on whether the user is currently logged in. You can use the techniques described in Chapter 14, *Failing Gracefully*, to redirect to custom error pages when those exceptions occur.

20.3. Rule-Based Access Control

So far, you have seen how the Seam built-in `#{identity}` component is used for authentication and how the `Restrict` tag/annotation works with EL expressions to provide role-based access control. Those features by themselves are already quite impressive, but we have not touched business rules yet. Business rules take access control to a whole new level, unseen in previous generations of Java security frameworks.

- Using business rules, you can put all security configuration in one file and simplify the `Restrict` tags/annotations. That is a huge plus when you have a large web site with many user roles and many potential entry points because all access rules can be reviewed and analyzed at once. It also allows nonprogrammers to develop rules using GUI tools that the JBoss Rules project provides.

- Business rules give you "per instance" access controls based on the current state of the application. Refer to Section 20.3.2., "Per Instance Access Rules", for more details.

Of course, the downside of using access rules is that you must bundle the JBoss Rules JAR files and configuration files in the application (see Section 20.3.3., "Configuring JBoss Rules"). But that is a small price to pay for such advanced features.

Let's begin by reimplementing the role-based access-control scheme in rules.

20.3.1. Simple Access Rules

Before we discuss the access rules, let's first explain how the `Restrict` tag/annotation really works under the hood. When you have an empty `Restrict`, it is equivalent to making a call to the `#{identity.hasPermission}` method. The shorthand version of the EL is `#{s:hasPermission(...)}`. To understand how this works, let's look at an annotation example we mentioned earlier:

```
@Stateful
@Name("manager")
public class ManagerAction implement Manager {


  ... ...

  @Restrict
  public String checkInventory () {
    // code
  }
}
```

The empty `@Restrict` annotation is equivalent to the following.

```
@Restrict#{s:hasPermission('manager',
               'checkInventory', null)}
```

The first call parameter is the component name (the `name`), and the second parameter is the method name (the `action`). They form the basis of the security rule. We ignore the third `null` parameter for now. To allow only users with the `admin` role to access this method, we have the following rule in the JBoss Rules configuration file:

```
package MyApplicationPermissions;

import org.jboss.seam.security.PermissionCheck;
import org.jboss.seam.security.Role;

rule CanUserCheckInventory
when
  c: PermissionCheck(name == "manager",
                  action == "checkInventory")
  Role(name == "admin")
then
  c.grant()
end;
```

The name of the rule can be arbitrary. The important point is that the rule is triggered when the `#{manager.checkInventory}` method is called, and access is granted when the current user has the `admin` role.

> **Check for Logged-In Users**
>
> If you want to grant access to all logged-in users, regardless of their roles, you can check whether the `Principal` object exists. The `Principal` object is created in the login process. To do that, use `exists Principal()` to replace the `Role(name == "admin")` line in the rule we discussed earlier.

The `<Restrict>` tag rules for web pages are similar. Because no component name and method name exist here, the default `name` is the JSF `view-id` of the page, and the default `action` is render. For instance, the following page configuration results in a `#{s:hasPermission('/inventory.xhtml', 'render', null)}` call when the `inventory.xhtml` page is accessed.

```
<pages>

  ... ...

  <page view-id="/inventory.xhtml">
    <restrict/>
  </page>

</pages>
```

This is the security rule for `admin`-only access to the page:

```
rule CanUserViewInventory
when
  c: PermissionCheck(name == "/inventory.xhtml",
                     action == "render")
  Role(name == "admin")
then
  c.grant()
end;
```

20.3.2. Per Instance Access Rules

So far, we have not mentioned the third argument on the `#{s:hasPermission(...)}` method call. By passing an object from the Seam stateful context to the security check method, you can make rules that grant access only when certain runtime conditions are met. For instance, in an e-commerce web site, the administrator might give a regular user one-time authorization to view the store inventory. The user has access to the inventory until an expiration time. The one-time authorization is stored in the `User` object in the current Seam session context. This is an example of the `User` class:

```
@Entity
public class User {

  // Returns whether one-time authentication
  // has been granted
  @Transient
  public boolean getAuth () {
    // ... ...
  }
  public void setAuth (boolean auth) {
    // ... ...
  }

  // Returns whether the one-time authentication
  // has expired
  @Transient
  public boolean getAuthExp () {
    // ... ...
  }

}
```

In the following example, the current `User` object in the session is passed to the security check.

```
@Stateful
@Name("manager")
public class ManagerAction implement Manager {

  ... ...

  @In
  User user;
```

```
@Restrict ("#{s:hasPermission('manager',
                     'checkInventory', user)}")
public String checkInventory () {
  // code
}
}
```

Then in the rule, we check the one-time authorization and expiration time before granting the access.

```
package MyApplicationPermissions;

import org.jboss.seam.security.PermissionCheck;
import org.jboss.seam.security.Role;
import myapp.User;

rule CanUserCheckInventory
when
  c: PermissionCheck(name == "manager",
                     action == "checkInventory")
  User(auth == "true", authExp == "false")
then
  c.grant()
end;
```

Per-instance access rules enable developers to control the application behavior dynamically. These are very useful in many applications.

20.3.3. Configuring JBoss Rules

If you just want to use the basic Seam security features such as user authentication and role-based access control, you do not need any additional libraries or configurations besides the ones listed in Chapter 3, *Recommended JSF Enhancements*. But if you need to use rule-based security features (i.e., to use the simple or per-instance security rules), you need to set up JBoss Rules support in Seam.

To use the JBoss Rules engine, you must bundle the JBoss Rules JARs, as well as the `security.drl` file, which is a plain-text file containing the security rules you saw earlier in this chapter, in the application EAR.

```
mywebapp.ear
|+ app.war
|+ app.jar
|+ drools-*.jar
|+ el-*.jar
|+ antlr-*.jar
|+ commons-jci-*.jar
|+ janino-*.jar
|+ jbpm-x.y.z.jar
|+ stringtemplate-x.y.z.jar
|+ jboss-seam.jar
|+ security.drl
|+ META-INF
```

Then you must tell Seam where to find the security rules. The following configuration in the `components.xml` file indicates that the security rules are in the `/security.drl` file in the EAR archive.

```
<components
    xmlns="http://jboss.com/products/seam/components"
    xmlns:core="http://jboss.com/products/seam/core"
    xmlns:drools="http://jboss.com/products/seam/drools"
    xmlns:security="http://jboss.com/products/seam/security">

    ... ...

  <drools:rule-base name="securityRules">
    <drools:rule-files>
      <value>/security.drl</value>
    </drools:rule-files>
  </drools:rule-base>

  <security:identity authenticate-method=
                "#{authenticator.authenticate}"/>
</components>
```

That's it for configuring the JBoss Rules engine. The template projects Seam Gen generated already have the JBoss Rules-based security configured and provide a skeleton `security.drl` file for you to enter your own rules.

VI

Testing Seam Applications

Developer testing has become a crucial component in modern software-development processes. As a POJO framework, Seam was designed from the ground up for easy testability. Seam goes beyond and above what other POJO frameworks do when it comes to testing. Seam actually provides its own testing framework based on TestNG, which makes it easy to write automated, out-of-the-container units and integration tests for Seam applications. In the next two chapters, you learn how easy it is to write test cases for Seam applications. We also explain how to set up the proper testing environment for out-of-the-container testing.

21

Unit Testing

The wide adoption of agile software-development methods, such as Test Driven Development (TDD), has made unit testing a central task for software developers. An average-sized web project can have hundreds, if not thousands, of unit test cases. Hence, testability has became a core feature for software frameworks.

Plain Old Java Objects (POJOs) are easy to unit test. You just instantiate a POJO using the standard Java `new` keyword, and run its methods in any unit-testing framework. It is no coincidence that the spread of agile methodologies and POJO-based frameworks happened at the same time in the last couple years. Scam is a POJO-based framework designed for easy unit testing.

Enterprise POJOs do not live in isolation. They must interact with other POJOs and infrastructure services (e.g., a database) to perform their tasks. The standard TDD and agile practice is to "mock" the service environment in the testing environment—that is, to duplicate the server APIs without actually running the server. However, the mock services are often difficult to set up and depend on the testing framework you choose. To address this challenge, Seam comes with a `SeamTest` class that greatly simplifies the mocking tasks. The `SeamTest` facility is based on the popular TestNG framework, and it mocks all Seam services in your development environment.

In this chapter, we discuss how to use the `SeamTest` class to write TestNG unit tests. Our test cases are written against the `stateful` example application discussed in Chapter 6, *A Simple Stateful Application*. To run the tests, enter the `stateful` project folder and run the command `ant test`. The build script runs all tests we have in the `test` directory and reports the results in the command console as follows:

```
$ant test

   ... ...

   [testng] PASSED: simulateBijection
```

```
[testng] PASSED: unitTestSayHello2
[testng] PASSED: unitTestSayHello
[testng] PASSED: testSayHello
[testng] PASSED: unitTestStartOver

[testng] ===============================================
[testng]     HelloWorld
[testng]     Tests run: 5, Failures: 0, Skips: 0
[testng] ===============================================
```

The test results are also available in HTML format in the `build/testout` directory (see Figure 21.1., "The test results for the stateful project").

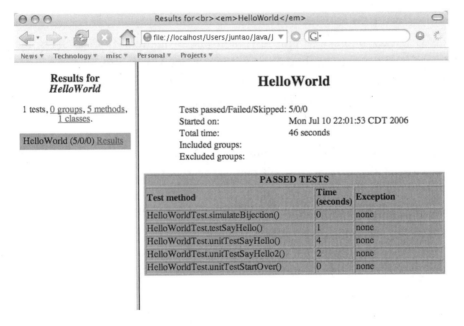

Figure 21.1. The test results for the stateful project

As we discuss in Appendix B, *Using Example Applications as Templates*, you can use the `stateful` project as a template and place your own test cases in the `test` directory. This way, you can reuse all configuration files, library JARs, and the build script. But for the curious, we explain exactly how the build script sets up the classpath and configuration files to run the tests in Appendix B, *Using Example Applications as Templates*.

> **What Is TestNG?**
>
> TestNG is a "next-generation" testing framework after JUnit. It supports many categories of developer tests, including unit tests, integration tests, end-to-end tests, etc. Compared with JUnit, TestNG tests are more flexible and easier to write.
>
> Like Seam, TestNG makes extensive use of Java annotations to simplify the code. That makes it a natural choice for Seam application developers. But more importantly, TestNG provides superior built-in support for mock objects, which are crucial for testing framework-managed applications. Seam takes advantage of this capability and comes with a custom mock framework in the SeamTest class. We cover the use of the SeamTest class in this chapter and the next.
>
> In this chapter, we provide a basic introduction to TestNG, to get you started with TestNG. All the examples should be fairly self-explanatory. If you are interested in learning more about TestNG, refer to the TestNG web site, http://testng.org/.

21.1. A Simple TestNG Test Case

Let's start with a simple method in the ManagerAction class to illustrate key elements in a TestNG unit test case.

```
public class ManagerAction implements Manager {

  public String startOver () {
    person = new Person ();
    confirmed = false;
    return "hello";
  }

  ... ...

}
```

The following method tests the `ManagerAction.startOver()` method. It instantiates a `ManagerAction` POJO, runs the `startOver()` method, and checks the return value is the string `hello`. It is extremely simply, but it has all the basic elements of a unit test.

```java
public class HelloWorldTest extends SeamTest {

  @Test
  public void unitTestStartOver() throws Exception {
    Manager manager = new ManagerAction ();
    assert manager.startOver().equals("hello");
  }

  ... ...

}
```

Notice the `@Test` annotation on the `unitTestStartOver()` method. It tells TestNG that this method is a test case and should be executed by the test runner. The `HelloWorldTest` class inherits from `SeamTest`, which gives test methods access to mock facilities built inside `SeamTest`. We do not use any mock service in this simple test case, but you will see its usefulness in the next section.

TestNG enables you to have multiple test classes and multiple test run configurations. In each test run configuration, you can choose to run one or several test classes. A test configuration is defined in an XML file in the classpath. In the `testing.xml` test configuration file, we tell TestNG that it should run the test cases in the `HelloWorldTest` class.

```xml
<suite name="HelloWorld" verbose="2" parallel="false">

  <test name="HelloWorld">
    <classes>
      <class name="HelloWorldTest"/>
    </classes>
  </test>

</suite>
```

Now we use TestNG's built-in ANT task to run the test configuration. With the correct classpath set up, we just need to pass in the test configuration file. This is a snippet from the `stateful` project's `build.xml` file:

```
<target name="test" depends="compile">

  <taskdef resource="testngtasks"
           classpathref="lib.classpath"/>

  ... ...

  <testng outputdir="${build.testout}">
    <classpath refid="lib.classpath"/>
    <classpath path="${build.test}"/>
    <xmlfileset dir="${test}"
                    includes="**/*.xml"/>
  </testng>

</target>
```

The test results appear on the console, as well as in HTML format in the `build/testout` directory, as we described before.

21.2. Simulating Dependency Bijection

Dependency bijection (see Chapter 1, *What Is Seam?*) is extensively used in Seam applications. Although bijection is easy for developers, it poses challenges for unit tests. Seam dependency bijection annotations can work directly on private data fields. Without getter/setter methods (or constructor methods), the test framework does not have access to those private fields and, hence, cannot wire together POJOs and services for testing. An example is the `person` field in the `ManagerAction` class; it is annotated with both `@In` and `@Out`, but it does not have getter/setter methods. How can the unit test case in TestNG manipulate the `ManagerAction.person` field?

```
@Stateful
@Name("manager")
@Scope (SESSION)
public class ManagerAction implements Manager {

  @In @Out
  private Person person;

  ... ...
}
```

This is where the mock facilities in the SeamTest class become useful. The SeamTest class provides the getField() and setField() methods to simulate bijection and operate directly on Seam component's private fields. The following example shows how to use the get-Field() and setField() methods. We first inject a Person object and test whether the injection succeeds. Then we run the ManagerAction.startOver() method, which refreshes the person field, and test the result to be outjected. It is important to cast the getField() result to the proper object type.

```
public class HelloWorldTest extends SeamTest {

  @Test
  public void simulateBijection() throws Exception {
    Manager manager = new ManagerAction ();
    Person in = new Person ();
    in.setName ("Michael Yuan");

    // Inject the person component
    setField (manager, "person", in);
    Person out = (Person) getField(manager, "person");
    assert out != null;
    assert out.getName().equals("Michael Yuan");

    // Run a test method that updates and outjects
    // the person component
    assert manager.startOver().equals("hello");

    // Check the new person component outjected
    out = (Person) getField(manager, "person");
    assert out != null;
    assert out.getName() == null;
  }

  ... ...
}
```

Accessing Private Fields?

The Java specification does not allow access to private fields from outside the class. How does SeamTest do it, then? The SeamTest class runs its own embedded Seam runtime, which instruments the class bytecode to get around the regular JVM restriction.

21.3. Mocking the Database and Transaction

Almost all Seam applications store their data in relational databases. Developers must unit-test database-related functionalities. However, database testing outside the server container is difficult. You must mock all the persistence-related container services, including creating a fully functional EJB3 `EntityManager`, connecting to an embedded database, and managing a database transaction. The `SeamTest` class, together with the JBoss Embeddable EJB3 modules, makes it easy to mock the database services. See Section 21.4., "Loading the Test Infrastructure", for more details on how to set up the test environment to load the proper infrastructure.

The first thing you need to do is create an `EntityManager`. The `resources/META-INF/persistence.xml` file contains information on how to connect to the embedded database (see Chapter 25, *Tomcat Deployment*, for more details).

```
<persistence>
   <persistence-unit name="helloworld">
      <provider>
      org.hibernate.ejb.HibernatePersistence
      </provider>
      <jta-data-source>java:/DefaultDS</jta-data-source>
      <properties>
      ... ...
      </properties>
   </persistence-unit>
</persistence>
```

You should first create an `EntityManagerFactory` by passing the persistence unit name in the `persistence.xml` file to a static factory method. From the `EntityManagerFactory`, you can create an `EntityManager` and then inject it into your Seam component using the `SeamTest.setField()` method discussed in the previous section.

```
EntityManagerFactory emf =
    Persistence.createEntityManagerFactory("helloworld");
EntityManager em = emf.createEntityManager();

Manager manager = new ManagerAction ();
setField(manager, "em", em);
```

> **Persistence Context Name**
>
> In a Seam Gen-generated project, the persistence unit name defaults to the project name itself. So if you are porting the book's example applications to a Seam Gen-generated project, don't forget to change the persistence unit name for the `createEntityManagerFactory()` method before you run the tests.

Now you can test any database methods in your Seam POJO. All database operations are performed against an embedded HSQL database bundled in the test environment. You do not need to set up this database yourself if you use the project template in the book's source code bundle (see Appendix B, *Using Example Applications as Templates* and Chapter 25, *Tomcat Deployment*). The only catch is that if you write any data into the database, you must enclose the `EntityManager` operations inside a transaction such as the following:

```
em.getTransaction().begin();
String outcome = manager.sayHello ();
em.getTransaction().commit();
```

The following is a complete listing of the `unitTestSayHello()` test case, which tests the `ManagerAction.sayHello()` method in `stateful`. It ties together everything we've discussed.

```
public class HelloWorldTest extends SeamTest {

  @Test
  public void unitTestSayHello() throws Exception {

    Manager manager = new ManagerAction ();

    EntityManagerFactory emf =
      Persistence.createEntityManagerFactory("helloworld");
    EntityManager em = emf.createEntityManager();
    setField(manager, "em", em);

    Person person = new Person ();
    person.setName ("Thomas Heute");
    setField(manager, "person", person);
    setField(manager, "confirmed", false);

    em.getTransaction().begin();
```

```
      String outcome = manager.sayHello ();
      em.getTransaction().commit();

      assert outcome.equals("fans");

      List <Person> fans = manager.getFans();
      assert fans!=null;
      assert fans.get(fans.size()-1)
              .getName().equals("Thomas Heute");

      person = (Person) getField (manager, "person");
      assert person != null;
      assert person.getName().equals("Thomas Heute");

      em.close();
   }

   ... ...
}
```

21.4. Loading the Test Infrastructure

As we discussed in Section 21.1., "A Simple TestNG Test Case", we define the tests in the `test/testng.xml` file and run the tests in the `testng` ANT task. The Java source code for all the test cases is located in the `test` directory.

To run the tests, especially the mock database tests (see Section 21.3., "Mocking the Database and Transaction") and integration tests (see Chapter 22, *Integration Testing*), the testng test runner must first load the JBoss Embeddable EJB3 container and the Seam runtime. All the Seam configuration files for the application must be on the classpath (or in `META-INF` and `WEB-INF` directories on the classpath), just as they would be in a real application server.

> **Using Seam Gen**
>
> Projects that Seam Gen generates already have the test infrastructure properly set up. You just need to put the `*Test.xml` (i.e., the `testng.xml` equivalent) files and the test case source files in the `test` directory and run `ant test`. You can use the `EntityManager` and other EJB3 services in the test cases.

You can use the same configuration files for testing as for deployment, except for the WEB-INF/components.xml file. The test/components.xml file is copied to the test classpath. Consider the following example; it differs from the deployment version in two aspects. First, you do not need the EAR name prefix in the EJB3 bean JNDI name pattern because no EAR file exists in the tests. Second, you need an additional core:ejb component so that Seam can load the JBoss Embedded EJB3 container when it starts up.

```xml
<components ...>

  ... same as deployment ...

  <core:init
    jndi-pattern="#{ejbName}/local"
    debug="false"/>

  <core:ejb installed="true"/>

</components>
```

To load the JBoss Embeddable EJB3 container, you also need to put its support library JARs and configuration files on the test classpath. Those files are located in the lib/embeddedejb3 and lib/embeddedejb3/conf directories in the sample code bundle. Obviously, we also need JSF, Hibernate, and Seam JARs on the classpath. These are the relevant parts of the build.xml file for running the tests:

```xml
<property name="lib" location="../lib" />
<property name="testlib"
          location="../lib/embeddedejb3" />
<property name="applib" location="lib" />
<path id="lib.classpath">
  <fileset dir="${lib}" includes="*.jar"/>
  <fileset dir="${testlib}" includes="*.jar"/>
  <fileset dir="${applib}" includes="*.jar"/>
</path>

<target name="test" depends="compile">

  <taskdef resource="testngtasks"
           classpathref="lib.classpath"/>

  <mkdir dir="${build.test}"/>

  <javac destdir="${build.test}"
          debug="true">
```

```
    <classpath>
      <path refid="lib.classpath"/>
      <pathelement location="${build.classes}"/>
    </classpath>
    <src path="${test}"/>
  </javac>

  <copy todir="${build.test}">
    <fileset dir="${build.classes}"
            includes="**/*.*"/>
    <fileset dir="${resources}"
            includes="**/*.*"/>
    <fileset dir="${testlib}/conf"
              includes="*.*"/>
  </copy>

  <copy todir="${build.test}/WEB-INF"
                          overwrite="true">
    <fileset dir="${test}"
            includes="components.xml"/>
  </copy>

  <testng outputdir="${build.testout}">
    <classpath refid="lib.classpath"/>
    <classpath path="${build.test}"/>
    <xmlfileset dir="${test}"
                includes="testng.xml"/>
  </testng>

</target>
```

The beauty of this test setup is that the test runner bootstraps the entire runtime environment for Seam. Thus, you can run not only unit tests, but also integration tests that fully utilize the JSF EL to simulate real-world web interactions.

22

Integration Testing

Unit tests are useful, but they have limitations. By definition, unit tests focus on POJOs and their methods. All the mock infrastructure was there to make it possible to test those POJOs in relative isolation. That means we do not get to test whether the POJO interacts correctly with the framework itself. For instance, how do you test whether an outjected component has the correct value in Seam runtime context? How do you know that the JSF interactions and EL expressions have the desired effects? Here is where we need integration testing to test live POJOs inside the Seam and JSF runtime. Unlike the white-box unit tests, the integration tests test the application from the user's point of view.

Integration tests can also be much simpler than unit tests, especially when the tests involve database operations and other container services. In integration tests, we test live Seam components instead of the test-instantiated POJOs in unit test cases. An embedded Seam runtime started by `SeamTest` manages those live Seam components. The embedded Seam runtime provides the exact same services as the Seam runtime in JBoss AS servers. You do not need to mock the bijection or manually set up the `EntityManager` and transaction for database access.

If you use the book's example projects as a template (e.g., the stateful example) or use Seam Gen to generate your projects, you are ready to go with the integration tests. You can just add your own test cases, as described shortly, to the `test` directory and run `ant test`. No extra configuration and setup is needed. If you choose to set up your own project from scratch, you need to bootstrap the JBoss Embeddable EJB3 container, as we did in Section 21.4., "Loading the Test Infrastructure".

In and out of Server Container Testing

A simple form of integration testing is to just deploy the application in JBoss AS and run the tests manually through a web browser. But for developers, the keyword for easy testability is automation.

> Developers should be able to run integration tests unattended and view the results in a nicely formatted report. Ideally, the tests should run directly inside the development environment (i.e., JDK 5.0 or directly inside an IDE) without starting any server or browser.

The biggest challenge in testing live Seam components is to simulate the JSF UI interactions. How do you simulate a web request, bind values to Seam components and then invoke event-handler methods from the test case? Fortunately, the Seam testing framework has made all those easy. In the next section, we start from a concrete test example. As in Chapter 21, *Unit Testing*, we use the `stateful` sample application as an example.

22.1. A Complete Test Script

In a Seam web application, we access Seam components through #{} EL expressions in JSF pages. To access those components from TestNG test cases, the Seam test framework does two things: First, it provides a mechanism to simulate (or "drive") the entire JSF interaction lifecycle from the test code. Second, it binds test data to Seam components via JSF EL expressions or reflective method calls. Let's check out those two aspects in our test code.

22.1.1. Simulating JSF Interactions

In each web request/response cycle, JSF goes through several steps (phases) to process the request and render the response. Using the `Script` inner classes inside `SeamTest`, you can simulate test actions in each JSF phase by overriding the appropriate methods. The test runner then just calls those lifecycle methods in the order of JSF lifecycle phases. The following snippet shows the basic structure of a typical script to test the submission of a web form.

```
public class HelloWorldTest extends SeamTest {

  @Test
  public void testSayHello() throws Exception {

    new Script() {

      @Override
      protected void updateModelValues()
                            throws Exception {
```

```
      // Bind simulated user input data objects
      // to Seam components
    }

    @Override
    protected void invokeApplication() {
      // Invoke the UI event handler method for
      // the HTTP POST button or link
    }

    @Override
    protected void renderResponse() {
      // Retrieve and test the response
      // data objects
    }

  }.run();

}

... ...
}
```

The `updateModelValues()` method updates Seam data components based on the values in the user input fields. The `invokeApplication()` method invokes the event-handler method for the form submission button. It makes use of the data component constructed in the `update-ModelValues()` stage. The `renderResponse()` method checks the outcome of the event-handler method, including any component that is to be outjected. In the next several sections, we look at those methods in more detail.

JSF Lifecycle Phases

JSF has five phases in a request/response cycle. You can refer to a JSF book to understand exactly what the server does in each phase. In this chapter, we demonstrate the three most commonly used JSF phases. Each JSF lifecycle phase has a corresponding method in the `SeamTest.Script` class. You need to override a lifecycle method only if you need to perform tasks in its corresponding lifecycle phase.

22.1.2. Using JSF EL Expressions

But how exactly do you "bind the test data to Seam components" and "invoke Seam event-handler methods"? In regular JSF, we use EL expressions to bind data and actions, which JSF resolves when the form is submitted. In the test script, we can also use JSF EL expressions. The Seam testing framework resolves these.

You can use the `getValue()` and `setValue()` methods in `SeamTest` to bind value objects to Seam components via EL expressions. The `SeamTest.invokeMethod()` method invokes a Seam component method specified in an EL expression. The following example shows the complete test script. In `updateModelValues()`, we bound the string `"Michael Yuan"` to the `#{person.name}` component. In `invokeApplication()`, we invoke the `#{manager.sayHello}` event-handler method. Then, in the `renderResponse()` method, we retrieve the `#{manager.fans}` component and verify its content.

```java
public class HelloWorldTest extends SeamTest {

  @Test
  public void testSayHello() throws Exception {

    new Script() {

      @Override
      protected void updateModelValues()
                          throws Exception {
        setValue("#{person.name}", "Michael Yuan");
      }

      @Override
      protected void invokeApplication() {
        assert getValue ("#{person.name}")
                    .equals("Michael Yuan");
        assert invokeMethod("#{manager.sayHello}")
                    .equals("fans");
      }

      @Override
      protected void renderResponse() {
        List <Person> fans =
            (List<Person>) getValue(
                              "#{manager.fans}");
        assert fans!=null;
        assert fans.get(fans.size()-1)
            .getName().equals("Michael Yuan");

        assert getValue("#{person.name}")
```

```
                            .equals("Michael Yuan");
        }

    }.run();

  }

  ... ...
}
```

That's it for the test script. The EL expression enables us to write test cases that closely resemble the JSF page. We can test Seam components and EL expressions all together. However, in some cases, we just want to test the behavior of Seam components without the EL binding. In that case, we can access Seam components directly through a reflective API.

22.2. Accessing Seam Components Without the EL

In this section, we rewrite the earlier test script to use Seam API calls instead of EL expressions.

22.2.1. Obtaining a Seam Component

In a Seam test case, we can retrieve any Seam component by its name via the static `Component.getInstance()` method. The `Boolean` parameter indicates whether Seam should try to create the component if it does not exist yet.

```
@Override
protected void updateModelValues()
                    throws Exception {
  Person person =
(Person) Component.getInstance("person", true);
  assert person!=null;
  ... ...
}
```

In this test, Seam instantiates a new `Person` object and makes it available under the component name `person`.

22.2.2. Binding Values to the Component

When we have a component object, we can bind test values to it via the regular setter methods:

```
@Override
protected void updateModelValues()
                    throws Exception {
  Person person =
(Person) Component.getInstance("person", true);
  assert person!=null;
  person.setName("Michael Yuan");
}
```

The `updateModelValues()` method asserts that the `person` component is not `null` and then sets its property using the simulated user input.

22.2.3. Invoking UI Event Handler Method

After the data component is updated with the data in the current request, Seam invokes the UI event-handler method to process the request. At this phase, the test script invokes the `invoke-Application()` method. In this example, we obtain the `manager` stateful session bean and call its `sayHello()` method. Notice that the `person` component is already injected into the `manager` component at this stage.

```
@Override
protected void invokeApplication() {
  Manager manager =
(Manager) Component.getInstance("manager", true);
  String outcome = manager.sayHello();
  assert outcome.equals("fans");
}
```

We assert that with the input name `"Michael Yuan"`, the `manager.sayHello()` method successfully returns the `"fans"` string to direct JSF to display the `fans.xhtml` page according to the navigation rules.

22.2.4. Checking the Response

After the `manager.sayHello()` event-handler method exits, the `fans` property in the `manager` component should be updated with the newly saved person name. Then Seam performs any necessary outjection. In our example, the `person` component is outjected, although it is not altered in the `sayHello()` method. Here we test those component states when the next JSF page is rendered.

```
@Override
protected void renderResponse() {

  Manager manager =
(Manager) Component.getInstance("manager", false);
  List <Person> fans = manager.getFans();
  assert fans!=null;
  assert fans.get(fans.size()-1)
              .getName().equals("Michael Yuan");

  Person person =
(Person) Component.getInstance("person", false);
  assert person!=null;
  assert person.getName().equals("Michael Yuan");
}
```

Because both the `person` and `manager` components were already created in the previous phases, we pass the `false` argument to the `Component.getInstance()` methods here.

> **Do Not Use `getField()`/`setField()` in Integration Tests**
>
> In the integration test script, Seam components such as `person` and `manager` are real, live components in the embedded Seam runtime. They are not POJOs instantiated by the test case. Thus, you cannot use the `getField()` and `setField()` methods to access their data fields, as we did in Chapter 21, *Unit Testing*. But then, you do not need those methods to get around bijection here, either—injection happens automatically, and you can get any outjected component via a simple `Component.getInstance()` call. In other words, in the integration test script, we should use Seam components the same way we would use them from a JSF page.

VII

Production Deployment

Seam applications can deploy in all Java EE 5.0- and J2EE 1.4-compliant application servers, as well as the Tomcat servlet/JSP server. In this part, we show you how to deploy Seam applications in JBoss AS 4.x (with or without the EJB3 module), JBoss AS 5.x, Glassfish 1.x, WebLogic 9.x, and Tomcat 5.5.x. We also cover important deployment issues such as how to use a production database, how to tune for performance and scalability, and how to set up a server cluster.

23

Java EE 5.0 Deployment

As developers, you have a variety of choices when it comes to the deployment environment for Seam applications.

If you can deploy in a Java EE 5.0-compliant application server, you have no problem. Seam is designed to work in that environment. The book examples are fully tested on the EJB3 profile of JBoss AS 4.0.5+. With minimal modifications to configuration files and JAR files, your Seam application could easily run in JBoss AS 5.0 and Sun's GlassFish Application Server.

If you do not have a Java EE 5.0 application server but have access to a J2EE 1.4 server, you can write your applications in Seam POJOs instead of EJB3 beans. This approach is discussed in Chapter 24, *Seam Without EJB3*. But as we mentioned, Seam POJOs are not as feature rich as EJB3 components (see Section 2.4.1., "Seam POJO Components").

Finally, Tomcat fans can deploy both EJB3-based and POJO-based Seam applications in plain Tomcat servers. The Tomcat deployment uses the JBoss Microcontainer to load the necessary services. We discuss that approach in Chapter 25, *Tomcat Deployment*.

In this chapter, we focus on Java EE 5.0 deployment of Seam applications.

23.1. JBoss AS 4.0.5

Strictly speaking, JBoss AS 4.0.5 is not a Java EE 5.0-compliant application server. But it has the important pieces: EJB3 and JSF support. To deploy Seam applications in JBoss AS 4.0.5, you must install the server from the GUI installer and choose the EJB3 profile. See Appendix A, *Installing and Deploying JBoss AS*, for more details. All the examples in this book are configured to run in the JBoss AS 4.0.5 EJB3 profile.

23.2. JBoss AS 4.2.x and 5.x

JBoss AS 4.2.x and 5.x embed the JSF reference implementation (RI) instead of the Apache MyFaces implementation embedded in JBoss AS 4.0.5. The JSF RI implements JSF 1.2 specification. To deploy Seam applications in JBoss AS 4.2.x and 5.x, you need to configure the web.xml file in app.war/WEB-INF/ and comment out the MyFaces listener.

```
<!-- MyFaces -->
<!--
<listener>
  <listener-class>
org.apache.myfaces.webapp.StartupServletContextListener
  </listener-class>
</listener>
-->
```

Next, you need to enable the SeamELResolver in order for Seam to resolve component names correctly in web pages. To do that, add the following element in your faces-config.xml file in app.war/WEB-INF/. Also, you need to update the XML namespaces in faces-config.xml to JSF 1.2. Below is an example.

```
<faces-config version="1.2"
    xmlns="http://java.sun.com/xml/ns/javaee"
    xmlns:xsi="http://www.w3.org/2001/XMLSchema-instance"
    xsi:schemaLocation="http://java.sun.com/xml/ns/javaee
http://java.sun.com/xml/ns/javaee/web-facesconfig_1_2.xsd">

  <application>
    <el-resolver>
      org.jboss.seam.jsf.SeamELResolver
    </el-resolver>
  </application>

  <lifecycle>
    <phase-listener>
      org.jboss.seam.jsf.SeamPhaseListener
    </phase-listener>
  </lifecycle>

  ... more config ...

</faces-config>
```

Finally, since the JSF 1.2 RI libraries already bundle the `el-ri.jar` and `el-api.jar` files, you can remove those JARs from your EAR archive and remove their references from the `mywebapp.ear/META-INF/application.xml` file.

23.3. GlassFish

GlassFish is Sun's open-source Java EE 5.0 application server. Every Seam release since the 1.0 GA has been tested on GlassFish. In this section, we cover what configuration files you must change to make the book examples (and Seam Gen-generated projects) run on GlassFish. This is more involved than running Seam applications on JBoss AS.

First, we highly recommend that you use Hibernate as the Java Persistence API (JPA) provider in GlassFish. By default, GlassFish uses TopLink Essentials (a.k.a. the watered-down "lesser TopLink") for JPA implementation. It might be fine for basic JPA needs, but Seam makes good use of Hibernate-specific features, such as Hibernate validators and filters. In fact, it would be foolish not to use the Hibernate JPA with Seam, considering how easy it is to install Hibernate JPA in GlassFish: By including Hibernate JARs in your EAR, you can enable Hibernate JPA for a single application. Or you can simply copy Hibernate JARs to GlassFish's `lib` directory and enable Hibernate JPA for all applications. To use the Hibernate JPA, just choose the proper persistence provider in your `persistence.xml`, as we do later.

If you have to use the "lesser TopLink" JPA, we also have a toplink build target in the `examples/glassfish` project. But be aware that you need to load the database manually for the hotel data because TopLink does not read the `import.sql` file.

All the changes from a JBoss deployment to a GlassFish deployment concern the configuration files and library JARs only.

Because GlassFish uses the JSF 1.2 RI not MyFaces, you should make the same changes we discussed in Section 23.2., "JBoss AS 4.2.x and 5.x". They include: commenting out the context listener for MyFaces in `web.xml`, adding a `SeamELResolver` in `faces-config.xml`, and removing the `el-ri.jar` and `el-api.jar` files from the EAR and `application.xml`.

GlassFish requires you to declare all EJB3 session bean reference names in the `web.xml` file for the web application to access the beans. This is a rather tedious process. You must add the following lines in `web.xml` for each session bean in your application.

```
<ejb-local-ref>
  <ejb-ref-name>
    projectname/ManagerAction/local
  </ejb-ref-name>
  <ejb-ref-type>Session</ejb-ref-type>
  <local>Manager</local>
  <ejb-link>ManagerAction</ejb-link>
</ejb-local-ref>
```

Then if you need to inject an EJB3 session bean (A) into another session bean (B) using the `@In` annotation, you also need to declare bean A in the JAR file containing bean B. That must be done if bean A and bean B are in the same JAR file. You must add the `ejb-local-ref` element to the `META-INF/ejb-jar.xml` file bundled in the JAR file containing bean B. That is tedious and is a pretty big inconvenience of GlassFish.

```
<ejb-jar ...>
  <enterprise-beans>
    <session>
      <ejb-name>BeanA</ejb-name>
      <ejb-local-ref>
        <ejb-ref-name>
          projname/BeanB/local
        </ejb-ref-name>
        <ejb-ref-type>Session</ejb-ref-type>
        <local>BeanBInterface</local>
        <ejb-link>BeanB</ejb-link>
      </ejb-local-ref>
    </session>

    ... more injections ...

  </enterprise-beans>

  ... ...

</ejb-jar>
```

You also need to tell Seam the session bean naming pattern you just used in `web.xml` so that Seam can locate those beans. Make sure you have the following in the `components.xml` file:

```
<core:init
  jndi-pattern="java:comp/env/projectname/#{ejbName}/local"
  debug="true"/>
```

To use the Hibernate JPA with GlassFish's built-in JavaDB (Derby database), you need a `persistence.xml` file similar to the following. To use other databases, refer to the GlassFish manual.

```
<persistence ...>
  <persistence-unit name="bookingDatabase">
    <provider>
      org.hibernate.ejb.HibernatePersistence
    </provider>
    <jta-data-source>jdbc/__default</jta-data-source>
    <properties>
      <property name="hibernate.dialect"
          value="org.hibernate.dialect.DerbyDialect"/>
      <property name="hibernate.hbm2ddl.auto"
               value="create-drop"/>
      <property name="hibernate.show_sql"
               value="true"/>
      <property name="hibernate.cache.provider_class"
    value="org.hibernate.cache.HashtableCacheProvider"/>
    </properties>
  </persistence-unit>
</persistence>
```

Finally, you need to bundle the following JAR files in your EAR in addition to any library files you already need for JBoss AS deployment:

- `hibernate*.jar`: Hibernate3, Annotation, EntityManager JARs

- `thirdparty-all.jar`: Combined third-party JARs for Hibernate JPA support outside of JBoss AS

- `jboss-archive-browsing.jar`: Required for Hibernate EntityManager

- `commons-beanutils-1.7.0.jar`: Required by Seam outside of JBoss AS

- `commons-digester-1.6.jar`: Required by Seam outside of JBoss AS

Now the application should deploy in GlassFish.

24

Seam Without EJB3

JBoss Seam was originally designed to be a framework on top of Java EE 5.0—to bridge the gap between JSF and EJB3. However, Seam is also highly flexible and can stand on its own. In fact, Seam has no hard dependency on either JSF or EJB3. In Section 2.4.1., "Seam POJO Components", we already mentioned that you can use POJO components to replace EJB3 components. That is good news for developers who are not yet ready to move to EJB3. We can build Seam applications solely from POJOs, and such applications can be deployed in any J2EE 1.4 application server, such as the default configuration of JBoss AS (i.e., no AOP or EJB3 module installed), WebLogic AS, WebSphere AS, Oracle AS, and others. With a little help from the JBoss MicroContainer, you can easily run those non-EJB3 Seam applications in plain Tomcat servers (see Section 25.1., "Packaging a POJO Application for Tomcat").

Running POJOs instead of EJB3 components has two trade-offs: slightly increased configuration complexity and reduced infrastructure services. The increased configuration is needed to bootstrap and wire essential services—in particular, the `EntityManager` and transaction manager—into the POJOs. The EJB3 container used to do this transparently. The reduced infrastructure service is the result of POJOs that cannot consume EJB container services. See Section 2.4.1., "Seam POJO Components", for a more complete explanation.

In this chapter, we use two example applications to show exactly how Seam POJO applications are developed and configured. Both are ported from the `integration` example (see Chapter 10, *Validating Input Data*, Chapter 11, *Clickable Data Tables*, and Chapter 12, *Bookmarkable Web Pages*). Both use JSF as the web framework.

- The `jpa` example does not have a dependency on the EJB3 session beans or the EJB3 container. It uses Seam POJOs to replace EJB3 session bean components. But it does use the Java Persistence API (JPA, a.k.a. EJB3 entity bean API) for database entity objects. Because the JPA is a standalone API that can be used in Java SE, it probably can be considered as a non-EJB3 API. This example uses Hibernate JPA as the JPA provider.

- The `hibernate` example shows how to eliminate all dependencies on EJB3 container and JPA. It uses the Hibernate API to access the database.

We use the simplest code examples here to focus on the configuration of Seam POJOs. You probably already know how to develop EJB3-based Seam applications, so we primarily discuss the difference between Seam POJO configuration and EJB3 bean configuration. This way, you can easily port your existing EJB3 examples for deployment outside the EJB3 container. If you want to check out more complex and more complete examples, refer to `examples/jpa` and `examples/hibernate` in the Seam distribution. Without further ado, let's check out our new POJO-based examples.

24.1. Seam POJO with JPA

Because the JPA is the same as the EJB3 entity bean and `EntityManager` API, the only difference between the EJB3-based `integration` and the POJO-based `jpa` example is the `manager` component, which provides UI event-handler methods. In the `integration` example, the `manager` component is an EJB3 session bean. In the `jpa` example, it is a POJO.

24.1.1. A Seam POJO Example

The Seam POJO component is actually simpler than the EJB3 session bean. No interface needs to be implemented, and the only required annotation is `@Name` to give it a Seam name.

```
@Name("manager")
public class ManagerPojo {

  ... ...

}
```

However, Seam POJO components are stateful and have a conversational scope by default (see Chapter 5, *An Introduction to Stateful Framework* and Chapter 7, *Conversations*). That means a new `ManagerPojo` object is created each time the user clicks on the Say Hello button and is destroyed when the updated response page is fully rendered. To mimic the stateless object behavior as in the original Hello World example, we declare the `ManagerPojo` object to have an `APPLICATION` scope, which basically makes it a singleton in the application.

```
@Name("manager")
@Scope (APPLICATION)
public class ManagerPojo {

  ... ...

}
```

Finally, the `@PersistenceContext` annotation in the `integration` example makes the EJB3 container inject an `EntityManager` object. But because we no longer have the EJB3 container here, we just inject a Seam-managed JPA `EntityManager` using the Seam `@In` annotation. It works the same way as the EJB3 container-managed `EntityManager`. This is the complete code for the `ManagerPojo` class:

```
@Name("manager")
public class ManagerPojo {

  @In (required=false) @Out (required=false)
  private Person person;

  @In (create=true)
  private EntityManager em;

  Long pid;

  @DataModel
  private List <Person> fans;

  @DataModelSelection
  private Person selectedFan;

  public String sayHello () {
    em.persist (person);
    return "fans";
  }

  @Factory("fans")
  public void findFans () {
    fans = em.createQuery(
               "select p from Person p")
            .getResultList();
  }

  public void setPid (Long pid) {
    this.pid = pid;
```

```
  if (pid != null) {
    person =
      (Person) em.find(Person.class, pid);
  } else {
    person = new Person ();
  }
}

public Long getPid () {
  return pid;
}

public String delete () {
  Person toDelete = em.merge (selectedFan);
  em.remove( toDelete );
  findFans ();
  return null;
}

public String update () {
  return "fans";
}
}
```

24.1.2. Configuration

Turning EJB3 session bean components into Seam POJOs is an essential step in getting rid of the application's dependency on EJB3. However, to deploy the application outside the EJB3 container, we need to configure Seam to take over some of the essential services that the EJB3 container handles for us. In this section, we show you how to configure the `jpa` POJO application for deployment in the default J2EE 1.4-compatible profile of JBoss AS 4.0.5.

We focus on the difference between Seam POJO and EJB3 configuration here. Hence, you can change any Seam EJB3 application from session beans to POJOs, and then make the changes highlighted here to make it deployable in J2EE.

> **Seam Gen for POJO Application**
>
> If you select the WAR application option in Seam Gen setup (see Section 4.2.1., "Set Up Seam Gen"), Seam Gen will generate the correct default configuration files for Seam POJO deployment inside the JBoss AS.

First, in the `faces-config.xml` file, you must use the `TransactionalSeamPhaseListener` to bootstrap the Seam runtime with Seam-managed transaction manager and persistence context. We can no longer count on the EJB3 container to manage those for us now.

```
<faces-config>

  <lifecycle>
    <phase-listener>
org.jboss.seam.jsf.TransactionalSeamPhaseListener
    </phase-listener>
  </lifecycle>

</faces-config>
```

Next, you need to set up the persistence context and `EntityManager` to use in a non-EJB3 environment. In the `persistence.xml` file (in `app.jar/META-INF/`), you must specify a cache provider and a mechanism to look up the JTA transaction manager—the EJB3 container automatically does that for session beans, but we are dealing with POJOs here. Note that you also need to explicitly specify the transaction type to be JTA for Seam to work properly.

```
<persistence>
  <persistence-unit name="helloworld"
                    transaction-type="JTA">
    <provider>
      org.hibernate.ejb.HibernatePersistence
    </provider>
    <jta-data-source>
      java:/DefaultDS
    </jta-data-source>
    <properties>
      <property name="hibernate.dialect"
          value="org.hibernate.dialect.HSQLDialect"/>
      <property name="hibernate.hbm2ddl.auto"
          value="create-drop"/>
      <property name="hibernate.show_sql" value="true"/>

      <property name="hibernate.cache.provider_class"
value="org.hibernate.cache.HashtableCacheProvider"/>
      <property
name="hibernate.transaction.manager_lookup_class"
value="org.hibernate.transaction.JBossTransactionManagerLookup"/>
    </properties>
  </persistence-unit>
</persistence>
```

> **On Other Application Servers**
>
> To deploy Seam POJOs on non-JBoss application servers, you only need to customize the `persistence.xml` file for the particular application server. You typically need to change the JNDI binding for the data source, the Hibernate dialect for the database, and, most important, the transaction manager lookup class. For instance, for deployment on WebLogic, you would need the `WeblogicTransactionManagerLookup` class.

For Seam to build an `EntityManager` and inject it into the POJO, we must bootstrap it in the `components.xml` file. The `core:entity-manager-factory` component scans the `persistence.xml` files and instantiates the persistence unit named `helloworld` (see the previous code listing). Then the `core:managed-persistence-context` component builds an `EntityManager` from the `helloworld` persistence unit. The `EntityManager` is named `em`. That ensures that the `@In (create=true) EntityManager em;` statement in `ManagerPojo` works because it injects the `em` named `EntityManager` to the field variable with the same name. Because the application has no EJB3 components, you do not need to specify the `jndiPattern` attribute on the `core:init` component.

```
<components ...>

  <core:init debug="true"/>

  <core:manager conversation-timeout="120000"/>

  <core:entity-manager-factory name="helloworld"/>

  <core:managed-persistence-context name="em"
       entity-manager-factory="#{helloworld}"/>

</components>
```

No more need exists for EJB3-specific configuration, such as `ejb-jar.xml` and the `jndi-pattern` property in `components.xml`.

24.1.3. Packaging

For J2EE 1.4 deployment, you can always package your application in EAR format as we did in Section 2.5., "Configuration and Packaging". However, because our `jpa` POJO application does not have any EJB components, we can package it in a simple WAR file. In a WAR file, you put all the framework JAR files, as well as `app.jar`, which contains the application POJO classes and `persistence.xml`, in the `WEB-INF/lib` directory. The only caveat is that because the J2EE-compatible profile of JBoss AS installs only the core Hibernate library, without annotation or JPA support, we need to include distribution JAR files from Hibernate 3.2.1 GA. This is the packaging structure of the `jpa.war` file:

```
jpa.war
|+ index.html
|+ hello.xhtml
|+ fans.xhtml
|+ ... ...
|+ WEB-INF
   |+ lib
      |+ jboss-seam.jar
      |+ jboss-seam-ui.jar
      |+ jboss-seam-debug.jar
      |+ jsf-facelets.jar
      |+ el-api.jar
      |+ el-ri.jar
      |+ hibernate3.jar
      |+ hibernate-annotations.jar
      |+ hibernate-entitymanager.jar
      |+ ejb3-persistence.jar
      |+ app.jar
         |+ META-INF
            |+ persistence.xml
         |+ ManagerPojo.class
         |+ Person.class
         |+ seam.properties
   |+ web.xml
   |+ faces-config.xml
   |+ components.xml
   |+ jboss-web.xml
   |+ navigation.xml
   |+ pages.xml
```

Seam Gen for POJO Application

If you select the WAR application option in Seam Gen setup (see Section 4.2.1., "Set Up Seam Gen"), Seam Gen will generate a project template and build script for POJO WAR deployment as we show in the `jpa.war` example. The Seam Gen-built WAR application can be deployed in JBoss AS but might lack some library JARs for deployment in other application servers.

The `jboss-web.xml` file replaces the `jboss-app.xml` in the EAR file to configure the scoped classloader and root URL context. The `jboss-web.xml` file is not required but is nice to have when multiple applications are deployed in the same server. This is an example of the `jboss-web.xml` file:

```
<jboss-web>
  <context-root>/jpa</context-root>
  <class-loading
      java2ClassLoadingCompliance="false">
    <loader-repository>
      jpa:loader=jpa
      <loader-repository-config>
        java2ParentDelegation=false
      </loader-repository-config>
    </loader-repository>
  </class-loading>
</jboss-web>
```

On Other Application Servers

The library JARs we listed here in `jpa.war` are for JBoss AS deployment. If you plan to deploy your WAR file in a non-JBoss application server, you will probably need more dependency JARs. For instance, for WebLogic AS 9.2 deployment, you need the My-Faces JARs, the Apache Commons JARs, and several other third-party JARs bundled in `thirdparty-all.jar` in the sample code bundle. Refer to the `jpa` example in the Seam official distribution for the necessary JARs for different application servers.

> The `jboss-web.xml` file is obviously a JBoss-specific configuration file. The application works fine without it, and the root URL just defaults to the WAR filename. For other application servers, you can refer to their manuals to find out how to configure equivalent options in the previous `jboss-web.xml`.

24.2. Using Hibernate POJOs and API

If you do not want to use the JPA for persistence objects, you can use Hibernate POJOs and data access APIs. JPA is a complete ORM solution, and Hibernate implements all JPA features, including all optional features such as caching and filtering. The Hibernate JPA also provides complete support for Hibernate ORM annotations beyond the JPA standard (e.g., the Hibernate validator we discussed in Chapter 10, *Validating Input Data*). The Hibernate JPA should be sufficient for most application needs. However, as an open-source framework at the forefront of ORM innovation, some Hibernate features are not yet standardized. In particular, JPA does not yet support these features:

* The JPA query language is not as rich as that in Hibernate. For instance, JPA does not support Hibernate's query-by-criteria or query-by-example.

* Hibernate offers more methods to manage objects with detached state; JPA supports only one `merge()` operation in the EntityManager.

* The object type system in Hibernate is much richer than that in JPA.

* Hibernate gives you more control over the size of the extended persistence context.

If you need to use those features, you must use the Hibernate API directly. You also need to use the Hibernate API directly if you are working with legacy Hibernate code (e.g., a large number of XML mapping files and queries in existing applications).

> **Using Hibernate API in EJB3 Applications**
>
> Because Hibernate is a superset of JPA, sometimes you might want to use the Hibernate `Session` instead of the JPA `EntityManager` in

> your EJB3 session bean components. Just follow the next example
> to build a managed Hibernate `Session` and inject it into your EJB3
> session bean.

A Hibernate POJO is the same as a JPA entity bean because Hibernate supports the same annotations as JPA. Of course, for earlier Hibernate versions, you can use XML files instead of
annotations to map POJOs to database tables. In this example, we take the annotation approach and leave the `Person` class unchanged from the `integration` example.

24.2.1. Using the Hibernate API

To use the Hibernate API to manage the database objects, we inject a Hibernate `Session` instead of an `EntityManager` into the `ManagerPojo` class. The API methods in the Hibernate
`Session` is roughly equivalent to methods in the `EntityManager`; they have only slightly different method names. This is the Hibernate version of the `ManagerPojo` class:

```
@Name("manager")
@Scope (APPLICATION)
public class ManagerPojo {

  @In (required=false) @Out (required=false)
  private Person person;

  @In (create=true)
  private Session helloSession;

  Long pid;

  @DataModel
  private List <Person> fans;

  @DataModelSelection
  private Person selectedFan;

  public String sayHello () {
    helloSession.save (person);
    return "fans";
  }

  @Factory("fans")
  public void findFans () {
    fans = helloSession.createQuery(
                  "select p from Person p")
                      .list();
```

```
}

public void setPid (Long pid) {
  this.pid = pid;

  if (pid != null) {
    person = (Person)
      helloSession.get(Person.class, pid);
  } else {
    person = new Person ();
  }
}

public Long getPid () {
  return pid;
}

public String delete () {
  Person toDelete =
    (Person) helloSession.merge (selectedFan);
  helloSession.delete( toDelete );
  findFans ();
  return null;
}

public String update () {
  return "fans";
}

}
```

24.2.2. Configuration

When the Hibernate session `helloSession` component is bootstrapped (and injected), Seam looks for the `hibernate.cfg.xml` file, instead of the `persistence.xml` file, in the JAR files in its classpath. This is the structure for the `app.jar` file in the Hibernate application:

```
app.jar
|+ ManagerPojo.class
|+ Person.class
|+ seam.properties
|+ hibernate.cfg.xml
```

The `hibernate.cfg.xml` file has pretty much the same options as the `persistence.xml` file. It builds a Hibernate session factory and registers it under the JNDI name `java:/helloSession`. Note that you must put the database entity POJO class name in a `mapping` element. If you have multiple entity POJO classes in your application, use multiple `mapping` elements. The `mapping` elements tell Hibernate to read the ORM annotations on those classes and map them to database tables.

```
<hibernate-configuration>
  <session-factory name="java:/helloSession">
    <property name="show_sql">false</property>
    <property name="connection.datasource">
      java:/DefaultDS
    </property>
    <property name="hbm2ddl.auto">
      create-drop
    </property>
    <property name="cache.provider_class">
      org.hibernate.cache.HashtableCacheProvider
    </property>
    <property name="transaction.flush_before_completion">
      true
    </property>
    <property name="connection.release_mode">
      after_statement
    </property>
    <property name="transaction.manager_lookup_class">
org.hibernate.transaction.JBossTransactionManagerLookup
    </property>
    <property name="transaction.factory_class">
org.hibernate.transaction.JTATransactionFactory
    </property>

    <mapping class="Person"/>
  </session-factory>
</hibernate-configuration>
```

Finally, you must bootstrap the `helloSession` component in the `components.xml` file. The `core:hibernate-session-factory` component sets up the session factory, and the `core:managed-hibernate-session` component creates a Hibernate session named `helloSession` that can be injected into `ManagerPojo`. Note that the Hibernate session component name must match the JNDI name in `hibernate.cfg.xml` so that Hibernate knows which session factory it is supposed to use to create the session.

```
<components ...>

  <core:init debug="true"/>

  <core:manager conversation-timeout="120000"/>

  <!-- Bootstrap Hibernate -->
  <core:hibernate-session-factory/>
  <core:managed-hibernate-session
      name="helloSession" auto-create="true"/>

</components>
```

You can now package the application in a WAR format, as we discussed earlier (Section 24.1.3., "Packaging").

25

Tomcat Deployment

Besides full-blown Java EE application servers, many developers want a simpler way to deploy applications on "lightweight" servers such as the Tomcat web server. In this chapter, we discuss how to run Seam applications on plain Tomcat servers. The approach is to use the JBoss MicroContainer to bootstrap necessary services from your own application, much like the Spring framework does for service wiring.

> **JBoss MicroContainer Is Key for Service Bootstrapping**
>
> The JBoss MicroContainer (`http://www.jboss.com/products/jbossmc`) is an XML-based dependency injection framework at the core of the JBoss application server. It can also be used as a stand-alone framework. Hence, we can use the JBoss MicroContainer to load dependency services in non-JBoss application server environments.
>
> To understand exactly how the JBoss MicroContainer works, refer to its documentation. In this chapter, we cover only settings to load Seam services.

Using the JBoss MicroContainer bootstrapping, it is possible to run Seam EJB3 applications in Java SE without any container. This is especially useful for test-driven development of Seam applications (see Chapter 21, *Unit Testing* and Chapter 22, *Integration Testing*). We cover this use case at the end of the chapter.

Before we start, let's emphasize that JBoss AS is by far the best server to run Seam applications. We do not recommend that you run production Seam applications in plain Tomcat. We discuss the Tomcat build in this chapter for educational purposes so that you can use the same techniques to run Seam applications in other Java application servers.

> **"Lightweight" Containers?**
>
> Some may argue that running Seam applications on a simple Java server, such as Tomcat, would reduce the runtime footprint and result in better performance. That is simply not true. First, JBoss AS offers much better performance compared with plain Tomcat because JBoss AS supports sophisticated clustering and caching features. Second, to run Seam applications outside of JBoss AS, the application must bootstrap all necessary JBoss services itself, so you must bundle several JBoss library JAR files inside the application. The runtime memory footprint of a Tomcat application is not that different from the equivalent JBoss application. Furthermore, you cannot share those JBoss libraries between applications deployed in Tomcat. That is a severe disadvantage if you need to run multiple Seam applications in the same Tomcat server.

You must have JDK 5 and Tomcat 5.5+ to run Seam applications. If you have not done so, download Tomcat from `http://tomcat.apache.org/` and install it by unzipping the downloaded archive. You must also set the `JAVA_HOME` environment variable to your JDK 5 installation directory.

The example projects for this chapter are adopted from the `integration` example discussed earlier in the book. The `tomcatjpa` example shows how to build a Tomcat WAR application for Seam POJO applications without EJB3 session beans, and the `tomcatejb3` example shows how to build a Seam EJB3 application for Tomcat. To run the examples, just build the projects and copy the `tomcatjpa.war` or `tomcatejb3.war` files from `build/jars` to the `webapps` directory in your Tomcat installation, and then run `bin/startup.sh` to start Tomcat. The applications are then accessible from `http://localhost:8080/tomcatjpa/` and `http://localhost:8080/tomcatejb3/` URLs respectively.

> **Seam Gen Does Not Support Tomcat Deployment**
>
> The WAR application option in Seam Gen (see Section 4.2.1., "Set Up Seam Gen") is designed to support Seam POJO applications inside JBoss AS (see Chapter 24, *Seam Without EJB3*) but not embedded EJB3 applications in Tomcat.

25.1. Packaging a POJO Application for Tomcat

In Chapter 24, *Seam Without EJB3*, we covered how to build Seam POJO applications for deployment in J2EE 1.4 application servers. We discussed how to build a WAR deployment archive for the application (Section 24.1.3., "Packaging"). Of course, those WAR files are not yet deployable in the plain Tomcat server, for two reasons: First, Seam requires a few third-party library JARs that are bundled in JBoss AS but not in Tomcat. Second, Seam requires a JTA-based transactional data source, which is not available in Tomcat.

In this section, we resolve those two issues. The complete example is in the `tomcatjpa` project in the source code bundle.

25.1.1. Bundling Support JARs

In the WAR file, you can add all support library JARs in the `WEB-INF/lib` directory. As it turns out, Tomcat requires quite a few JARs to run Seam. To see the complete list of JARs, build the `tomcatjpa` project and look into the contents in `build/jars/tomcatjpa.war` (run `jar xvf tomcatjpa.war` to expand the archive). Those JARs are divided into the following categories:

- JSF support libraries—By default, Tomcat does not support any web framework beyond servlets and simple JSP. We must add JSF implementation JARs such as `myfaces*.jar`. If you need to use Facelets or Ajax4jsf or any other JSF component library, you must add their JARs as well.

- Hibernate support libraries—The `hibernate3.jar`, `hibernate-annotations.jar`, `hibernate-entitymanager.jar`, and `ejb3-persistence.jar` files are from the Hibernate 3.2 release. It supports the Hibernate core, annotations, and JPA `EntityManager`.

- JBoss MicroContainer libraries—The JBoss MicroContainer is used to bootstrap a JTA data source for Seam. We need all JARs from the JBoss MicroContainer distribution, as well as JARs for the JBoss transaction, the JDBC driver, the embedded HSQL database engine, etc. You can find a complete list of JARs required for the MicroContainer in the `lib/microcontainer` directory in the source code bundle.

- Seam libraries—The `jboss-seam-*.jar` file provides support for the JBoss Seam framework.

- Third-party utility libraries—Seam requires a few third-party utility JARs: the Apache Commons JARs (i.e., `commons-*.jar`), as well as dynamic code-generation/-manipulation library JARs `cglib.jar` and `javassist.jar`.

```
tomcatjpa.war
|+ index.html
|+ hello.xhtml
|+ fans.xhtml
|+ ... ...
|+ WEB-INF
   |+ lib
      |+ jboss-seam*.jar
      |+ jsf-facelets.jar
      |+ el-*.jar
      |+ hibernate*.jar
      |+ ejb3-persistence.jar
      |+ commons-*.jar
      |+ cglib.jar
      |+ javassist.jar
      |+ myfaces*.jar
      |+ ... Microcontainer JARs ...
      |+ app.jar
         |+ META-INF
            |+ persistence.xml
         |+ ManagerPojo.class
         |+ Person.class
         |+ seam.properties
   |+ classes
      |+ jboss-beans.xml
      |+ jndi.properties
      |+ log4j.xml
   |+ web.xml
   |+ faces-config.xml
   |+ components.xml
   |+ jboss-web.xml
   |+ navigation.xml
   |+ pages.xml
```

The MicroContainer requires the configuration files in the WEB-INF/classes directory, as we discuss in Section 25.1.2., "Configuring the Transactional DataSource".

25.1.2. Configuring the Transactional DataSource

So far, we have included MicroContainer JARs in the WAR and instantiated the Seam component to bootstrap the MicroContainer. But we still need a few configuration files to make the MicroContainer load the JTA data source from the embedded HSQL database and then register it under the JNDI name `java:/DefaultDS`.

The MicroContainer requires three configuration files. They must be placed in the classpath of the application. In our example, we put those files in the `WEB-INF/classes` directory in the WAR application archive. Let's now examine them one by one.

The most important MicroContainer configuration file is the `jboss-beans.xml` file, shown here. It first sets up a local JNDI server because the Tomcat JNDI server is read-only. It then sets up a JTA transaction manager and, finally, a data source with the appropriate connection settings and JNDI name. In the following example, a HSQL data source is registered under `java:/DefaultDS` for use in `persistence.xml` or `hibernate.cfg.xml`. You can easily edit the `jboss-beans.xml` file to support alternate databases.

```xml
<deployment ...>

  <bean name="Naming"
        class="org.jnp.server.SingletonNamingServer"/>

  <bean name="TransactionManagerFactory"
class="org.jboss.seam.microcontainer.TransactionManagerFactory"/>
  <bean name="TransactionManager" class="java.lang.Object">
    <constructor factoryMethod="getTransactionManager">
      <factory bean="TransactionManagerFactory"/>
    </constructor>
  </bean>

  <bean name="helloDatasourceFactory"
class="org.jboss.seam.microcontainer.DataSourceFactory">
    <property name="driverClass">
      org.hsqldb.jdbcDriver
    </property>
    <property name="connectionUrl">
      jdbc:hsqldb:.
    </property>
    <property name="userName">sa</property>
    <property name="jndiName">
      java:/DefaultDS
    </property>
    <property name="minSize">0</property>
    <property name="maxSize">10</property>
    <property name="blockingTimeout">
```

```
      1000
   </property>
   <property name="idleTimeout">
      100000
   </property>
   <property name="transactionManager">
     <inject bean="TransactionManager"/>
   </property>
 </bean>
 <bean name="helloDatasource"
       class="java.lang.Object">
   <constructor factoryMethod="getDataSource">
     <factory bean="helloDatasourceFactory"/>
   </constructor>
 </bean>

</deployment>
```

Next, you need to include the `jndi.properties` file in the application classpath (i.e., `WEB-INF/classes`) to set up a local JNDI server because the Tomcat default JNDI server is read-only. Note that we break the file into four lines for printing convenience; in reality, each of the two property name and value pairs should be on the same line.

```
java.naming.factory.initial
  org.jnp.interfaces.LocalOnlyContextFactory
java.naming.factory.url.pkgs
  org.jboss.naming:org.jnp.interfaces
```

Finally, the `log4j.xml` file on the classpath configures the logging for the MicroContainer.

```
<log4j:configuration
    xmlns:log4j="http://jakarta.apache.org/log4j/"
    debug="false">

  <appender name="CONSOLE"
        class="org.apache.log4j.ConsoleAppender">
    <errorHandler class=
"org.jboss.logging.util.OnlyOnceErrorHandler"/>
    <param name="Target" value="System.out"/>

    <layout class="org.apache.log4j.PatternLayout">
      <param name="ConversionPattern"
      value="%d{HH:mm:ss,SSS} %-5p [%c{1}] %m%n"/>
```

```
   </layout>
  </appender>

  <root>
   <priority value="INFO"/>
   <appender-ref ref="CONSOLE"/>
  </root>

</log4j:configuration>
```

25.1.3. Bootstrapping the JBoss MicroContainer

In the `WEB-INF/components.xml` file, we must instantiate the built-in `core:microcontainer` component to bootstrap the MicroContainer services. Add the following element to the `components.xml` file:

```
<components>

  ... ...

  <core:microcontainer installed="true"/>

</components>
```

The whole process works like this: When Tomcat deploys the WAR file, it loads the `web.xml` file, which, in turn, loads Seam as a `listener`. The Seam runtime looks into the `components.xml` file when initializing Seam services. It finds out that it needs to load the JBoss MicroContainer. The JBoss MicroContainer then uses configuration files in the `WEB-INF/classes` directory to instantiate service objects from the bundled JAR files.

25.2. Packaging an EJB3 Application for Tomcat

So far, we have showed that you can build a Tomcat-deployable WAR file for Seam POJO applications. Those applications do not require an EJB3 container to run. However, as we also mentioned, without the EJB3 container, you lose access to all the great EJB3 container services that complement Seam (Section 2.4.1., "Seam POJO Components").

So what if you want to take advantage of EJB3 container services but still do not want to run a fully certified Java EE 5.0 application server? Well, with the JBoss Embeddable EJB3, you can have the best of both worlds. Again, the JBoss MicroContainer does the magic.

Embeddable EJB3 for Out-of-Container Testing

Using the JBoss MicroContainer and EJB3 libraries, you can bootstrap a complete EJB3 container in a plain Java SE environment. This is useful when you need to test EJB3 applications outside the application server (see more in Section 21.4., "Loading the Test Infrastructure").

In this section, we walk through the `tomcatejb3` example to show you exactly what is needed to run the JBoss Embeddable EJB3 with Seam.

Building Tomcat WAR files for Seam: Official Examples

The official example applications in the Seam distribution support Embeddable EJB3-based Tomcat deployment as well. You can build the Tomcat WAR file via the `ant tomcat` command.

25.2.1. Bundling Necessary JARs in the WAR File

As we described in Section 25.1.1., "Bundling Support JARs", we need quite a few JARs to support Seam and MicroContainer deployment in Tomcat. For the Embeddable EJB3, we also need the complete set of JBoss EJB3 JAR files, as well as other JARs for container services that the MicroContainer would bootstrap. To make JAR management easier, we have consolidated the JAR files into several `*-all.jar` files: JBoss EJB3 JAR files, including all MicroContainer JARs, are consolidated in a single `jboss-ejb3-all.jar` file; all third-party support libraries for EJB3 (including `cglib.jar` and `javassist.jar`, as mentioned before) are packaged in the `thirdparty-all.jar` file; and Hibernate libraries are packaged in `hibernate-all.jar`. Additionally, Seam requires a few Apache Commons JARs and the `jstl.jar` file to work. All the Embeddable EJB3-related JARs are in the `lib/embeddedejb3` directory in the book's source code bundle.

The following listing shows the structure of the `tomcatejb3.war` file. All the library JAR files are in the `WEB-INF/lib` directory. Of course, you must add more libraries here if you need additional framework support (e.g., jBPM).

```
tomcatjpa.war
|+ index.html
|+ hello.xhtml
|+ fans.xhtml
|+ ... ...
|+ WEB-INF
   |+ lib
      |+ jboss-seam*.jar
      |+ jsf-facelets.jar
      |+ el-*.jar
      |+ myfaces*.jar
      |+ jboss-ejb3-all.jar
      |+ thirdparty-all.jar
      |+ hibernate-all.jar
      |+ commons-*.jar
      |+ jstl.jar
      |+ app.jar
         |+ META-INF
            |+ ejb-jar.xml
            |+ persistence.xml
         |+ ManagerPojo.class
         |+ Person.class
         |+ seam.properties
   |+ classes
      |+ ... files from lib/embeddedejb3/conf ...
   |+ web.xml
   |+ faces-config.xml
   |+ components.xml
   |+ jboss-web.xml
   |+ navigation.xml
   |+ pages.xml
```

Next, let's look at the Embeddable EJB3 configuration files in `WEB-INF/classes`.

25.2.2. Bundling Embeddable EJB3 Configuration Files

We already know that the `jboss-beans.xml` file loads services in the MicroContainer. For the Embeddable EJB3, there is already a set of preconfigured `jboss-beans.xml` files to load up the services available in an EJB3 container. Those files are located in the `lib/embeddedejb3/conf` directory in the source code bundle and are packaged in the `WEB-INF/classes` dircctory in `tomcatejb3.war`.

- The `embedded-jboss-beans.xml` file is the main configuration file for the JBoss Micro-Container, which bootstraps all the infrastructure services beneath Seam. For instance, it constructs the initial JNDI properties, the transaction manager, the security manager, the default data source, etc. The XML syntax in this file is rather dense. Fortunately, you do not typically need to change this file for your applications.

- The `jboss-jms-beans.xml` and `security-beans.xml` files are also JBoss MicroContainer configuration files to set up the JMS messaging provider (with persistent data stores) and the JAAS security manager. Again, you do not typically need to change those files.

- The `ejb3-interceptors-aop.xml` file defines interceptor services that are required for EJB3 beans. You do not need to change this file.

- The `default.persistence.properties` and `jndi.properties` files define properties for the underlying persistence engine and the JNDI classes.

- The `log4j.xml` file replaces the `server/default/conf/log4j.xml` file in JBoss AS. It configures how the application logs to the console and various logging files.

- The `login-config.xml` file is the same security authentication file in the EAR file. You can modify it if you want to use Java EE-managed security.

Refer to the JBoss Embeddable EJB3 documentation for how to customize the configuration files.

25.2.3. Bootstrapping the JBoss MicroContainer

With the JAR files and configuration files properly set up, you must tell the application to start up the embedded Seam/EJB3 services when it is deployed. That is done by setting the `installed` property on the `core:ejb` component to `true` in the `WEB-INF/components.xml` file, as follows. Because no more EAR file exists, we no longer need the `projname` prefix in the JNDI pattern for locating EJB3 beans.

```
<components ...>
  <core:init jndi-pattern="#{ejbName}/local"
             debug="true"/>

  <core:manager conversation-timeout="120000"/>

  <core:ejb installed="true"/>

</components>
```

25.2.4. Using an Alternative Data Source

The `embedded-jboss-beans.xml` file configures the default data source, registered under the JNDI name `java:/DefaultDS`, for the application. But what if you need to use an alternative database? The standard data source configuration in JBoss AS (discussed in Chapter 26, *Using a Production Database*) would not work because Tomcat does not support the `*-ds.xml` file for data source definition. You could edit the `embedded-jboss-beans.xml` file and change the database setting in it (see Section 25.1.2., "Configuring the Transactional Data-Source"), or you could add the `jboss-beans.xml` configuration file to provide an alternative data source. The following is an example `jboss-beans.xml` file inside the `META-INF` directory of the EJB3 JAR file (i.e., the `app.jar` file, in our examples). It creates a data source registered under the JNDI name `java:/bookingDatasource`. You can change the database driver, connection URL, and many other settings.

```xml
<deployment xmlns:xsi=...>

  <bean name="bookingDatasourceBootstrap" class=
"org.jboss.resource.adapter.jdbc.local.LocalTxDataSource">
    <property name="driverClass">
      org.hsqldb.jdbcDriver
    </property>
    <property name="connectionURL">
      jdbc:hsqldb:.
    </property>
    <property name="userName">sa</property>
    <property name="jndiName">
      java:/bookingDatasource
    </property>
    <property name="minSize">0</property>
    <property name="maxSize">10</property>
    <property name="blockingTimeout">
      1000
    </property>
    <property name="idleTimeout">
      100000
    </property>
    <property name="transactionManager">
      <inject bean="TransactionManager"/>
    </property>
    <property name="cachedConnectionManager">
      <inject bean="CachedConnectionManager"/>
    </property>
    <property name="initialContextProperties">
      <inject bean="InitialContextProperties"/>
    </property>
  </bean>
```

```
<bean name="bookingDatasource"
        class="java.lang.Object">
  <constructor factoryMethod="getDatasource">
    <factory
      bean="bookingDatasourceBootstrap"/>
  </constructor>
</bean>

</deployment>
```

The JBoss MicroContainer automatically picks up all `jboss-beans.xml` files in the application's classpath during bootstrapping. You can use those `jboss-beans.xml` files to provide alternatives for other default services in embedded Seam/EJB3 as well. The JBoss MicroContainer is flexible when it comes to services wiring, so use it!

26

Using a Production Database

Seam is an ideal solution for developing database-driven web applications. But so far in this book, for the sake of simplicity, we have not showed how to use a production-quality relational database in our example applications. Instead, all our examples use the HSQL database engine embedded inside the JBoss AS to store data. The advantage of using HSQL is that we do not need extra configuration in the application; it is the default `java:/DefaultDS` data source in the server environment.

However, in a real-world web application, we almost always need to use a production database, such as MySQL, Oracle, Sybase, or MS SQL, to store application data. Fortunately, it is actually very easy to configure alternative database back ends for a Seam application. In this chapter, we show you exactly how to set up a MySQL database back end for the Seam Hotel Booking example.

26.1. Installing and Setting Up the Database

Obviously, you have to install your favorite production database server first. The database server can reside on its own computer or share the same computer as the JBoss AS instance. Most database servers also support multiple databases and multiple users. Each database is a collection of relational tables for a user or an application. Each user has a username/password combo and has the privilege to read or write in a set of databases. For this exercise, you should install the latest MySQL server and then create a database named `seamdemo` for the Seam Hotel Booking example application. You should grant read/write privilege to the `seamdemo` database for the user `myuser` with the password `mypass`.

Next, you should initialize the database. You need to create the table structures and populate the tables with initial data (e.g., the hotel names and locations in this example). To do that for the Seam Hotel Booking example, run the `productiondb/seamdemo.sql` script on the MySQL command line against the `seamdemo` database. The following is a snippet from the `seamdemo.sql` script file:

```
DROP TABLE IF EXISTS `Booking`;
CREATE TABLE `Booking` (
  `id` bigint(20) NOT NULL auto_increment,
  `creditCard` varchar(16) NOT NULL default '',
  `checkinDate` date NOT NULL default '0000-00-00',
  `checkoutDate` date NOT NULL default '0000-00-00',
  `user_username` varchar(255) default NULL,
  `hotel_id` bigint(20) default NULL,
  PRIMARY KEY  (`id`),
  KEY `FK6713A0396E4A3BD` (`user_username`),
  KEY `FK6713A03951897512` (`hotel_id`)
);

DROP TABLE IF EXISTS `Hotel`;
CREATE TABLE `Hotel` (
  `id` bigint(20) NOT NULL auto_increment,
  `address` varchar(100) NOT NULL default '',
  `name` varchar(50) NOT NULL default '',
  `state` char(2) NOT NULL default '',
  `city` varchar(20) NOT NULL default '',
  `zip` varchar(5) NOT NULL default '',
  PRIMARY KEY  (`id`)
);
INSERT INTO `Hotel` VALUES (...),(...)...

DROP TABLE IF EXISTS `User`;
CREATE TABLE `User` (
  `username` varchar(255) NOT NULL default '',
  `name` varchar(100) NOT NULL default '',
  `password` varchar(15) NOT NULL default '',
  PRIMARY KEY  (`username`)
);
INSERT INTO `User` VALUES (...),(...)...
```

Automatic Initialization

The database initialization step is not absolutely necessary. For instance, in the HSQL-based examples early in the book, we configured Seam to automatically create the table schema based on the entity bean annotations (see the last section in this chapter). We then placed an `import.sql` file in the EJB3 JAR file. The SQL `INSERT` statements in the `import.sql` file are automatically executed when the application is deployed.

See the MySQL administration documentation on how to install the server, create databases, manage users, and run SQL scripts from the command line.

In the following sections, we explain how to set up the JBoss AS to use the production database. The process can be easily automated by Seam Gen (see Chapter 4, *Rapid Application Development Tools*). But we recommend you read the rest of this chapter to understand exactly what goes on behind the Seam Gen automated project generator.

26.2. Installing Database Driver

Next, you need to install a JDBC driver for the database. The driver allows Seam applications to interact with the database using standard JDBC APIs, which is required for the EJB3 persistence engine in Seam to function.

You can find JDBC drivers for your database on the database vendor's web site. For MySQL database, you can download the driver for free from `www.mysql.com/products/connector-j`. This is just a JAR file, which you need to copy into the `server/default/lib` directory of the JBoss AS installation (replace `default` with any alternative server configuration you are using).

26.3. Defining a DataSource

For the application to reference the database as a data source, you must create a data source configuration file. Different application servers have different ways of doing it. In the Seam Hotel Booking example, the `productiondb/booking-ds.xml` file configures the MySQL data source for JBoss AS. It contains the URL to access the database server, the database name, and the username and password of the user who would access the database on behalf of the Java application. You must copy this file to the `server/default/deploy` directory of your JBoss AS. Then all your applications can access the `seamdemo` database on this MySQL server via a DataSource object obtained from the `java:/bookingDatasource` JNDI name.

```
<datasources>
  <local-tx-datasource>
    <jndi-name>bookingDatasource</jndi-name>
    <connection-url>
      jdbc:mysql://localhost:3306/seamdemo
    </connection-url>
    <driver-class>
```

```
      com.mysql.jdbc.Driver
    </driver-class>
    <user-name>myuser</user-name>
    <password>mypass</password>
  </local-tx-datasource>
</datasources>
```

Alternative Data Sources in Tomcat Deployment

Tomcat does not have a standard way of configuring data sources because it does not support JTA data sources out of the box. To use an alternative database in a Tomcat-deployed Seam application, you must configure it in the Microcontainer configuration files (see Section 25.1.2., "Configuring the Transactional DataSource" and Section 25.2.4., "Using an Alternative Data Source").

26.4. Configuring the Persistence Engine

The `persistence.xml` file in the EJB3 JAR file's `META-INF` directory configures the underlying persistence engine for Seam. In the source code, you can find this file under the `resources/META-INF` directory.

The `persistence.xml` file specifies that the `EntityManager` object in this Seam application persists all entity beans to the `java:/bookingDatasource` database. Recall that this DataSource points to the `seamdemo` database on the production MySQL server. The `persistence.xml` file also configures the `EntityManager` to use the MySQL dialect of the SQL language when updating the database. The `hibernate.hbm2dll.auto=none` property specifies that the table schema is not automatically created when the application is deployed. If the property has the value `create-drop`, the database tables are created at application deployment and deleted at undeployment (or server shutdown). Finally, if the value is `update`, the database schema is updated or created, but the content is not deleted. Often on a production system, a database user does not have the privileges to create or drop tables.

```
<persistence>
  <persistence-unit name="bookingDatabase">
    <provider>
```

```
      org.hibernate.ejb.HibernatePersistence
    </provider>
    <jta-data-source>
      java:/bookingDatasource
    </jta-data-source>
    <properties>
      <property name="hibernate.dialect"
  value="org.hibernate.dialect.MySQLDialect"/>
      <property name="hibernate.hbm2ddl.auto"
                value="none"/>
    </properties>
  </persistence-unit>
</persistence>
```

That's it! That's all you need to set up a MySQL back-end database for the Seam Hotel Booking example application. Setting up other production databases, such as Oracle and MS SQL, is similarly easy.

27

Performance Tuning and Clustering

Seam drastically improves application developer productivity via extensive use of annotated POJOs, dependency bijection, and runtime service interceptors. Developers write less code because Seam generates and executes much of the boilerplate code behind the scenes. However, the developer "convenience" comes with a price: The more work Seam needs to do, especially at runtime, the slower the system performs. Today, as computer hardware performance continues to improve and price continues to drop, improving developer productivity is a higher priority than raw performance.

However, for high-volume web applications, we must carefully evaluate and try to compensate for the performance impacts from the Seam runtime. For starters, we should tune our Seam applications to make the most of existing hardware. If a single server is insufficient, we should also understand how to scale a Seam application by leveraging a server cluster. In this chapter, we discuss how to tune and scale Seam applications.

Annotation and Performance

Different Seam annotations are processed at different stages of the application lifecycle, and they have big implications on performance. Basic configuration annotations such as `@Stateful` and `@Name` are processed at application deployment. They increase only the application startup time and do not impact runtime performance. In fact, in other enterprise Java frameworks, this type of deployment information is specified in XML files. XML parsing is often slower than annotation processing. Thus, Seam does not have additional performance overhead.

> However, some annotations, such as the dependency bijection an-
> notations (e.g., `@In` and `@Out`), trigger Seam runtime interceptors be-
> fore and after each method call or property access. They do have a
> performance impact.

27.1. Tuning Performance on a Single Server

You should follow the following common JBoss best practices to tune a Seam application on
a single server.

27.1.1. Avoid Call by Value

When installing the JBoss AS from the GUI installer, you are asked whether you want to enable Call by Value and Deployment Isolation (see Figure 27.1., "Choose Call by Value or
Call by Reference"). Seam automatically generates dynamic proxy objects to make calls from
JSF components to EJB3 session beans. If you enable Call by Value, the call parameters and
return values are serialized in the process. The benefit is that the JSF and EJB3 tiers of the application are properly separated. This is useful when you have multiple versions of the same
Java classes deployed in the same server or when you need to port applications from other application servers to JBoss AS.

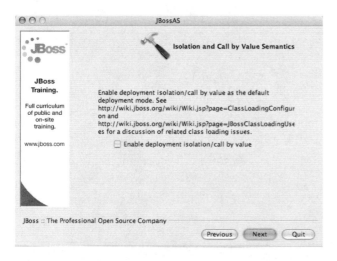

Figure 27.1. Choose Call by Value or Call by Reference

However, the Call by Value method is also slow. Because object serialization and deserialization are very CPU intensive, a Call by Value method call could be 10 times slower than a regular Call by Reference call. Most Seam applications are designed to run inside the same JVM on JBoss AS, so we recommend that you not check the selection box in Figure 27.1., "Choose Call by Value or Call by Reference".

27.1.2. JVM Options

First, always start the JVM using the `-server` option. It does a number of optimizations up front, which trades faster runtime performance for longer startup time.

Next, it is important to give the JVM as many resources as possible. The most important resource for the JVM is the amount of RAM. Because all server-side state data (e.g., HTTP sessions and stateful session beans) are stored in the RAM, it is crucial for high-load servers (i.e., lots of concurrent users) to have a large amount of RAM. On a typical server box, you should allocate at least 75 percent of the physical RAM to the JVM. You can do that via JVM startup options in the `JAVA_OPTS` property in the `bin/run.conf` file (use the `bin\run.bat` file for Windows). We use the same value for the `-Xmx` (maximum RAM) and `-Xms` (minimum RAM) options to force the JVM to use the specified amount of RAM. For instance, the `-Xmx6g -Xms6g` option starts the JVM with 6GB of RAM.

Sixty-four-bit Systems

On a 32-bit system, the JVM has access to only a maximum of 2GB of RAM. On a 64-bit system, including AMD64 and Intel EMT64, you can allocate far more RAM to the JVM. But you must use a 64-bit JVM to take advantage of the additional RAM.

However, a too-large memory heap could also hurt performance because it takes too long for the garbage collector to sweep through it. We have observed the JVM behaving erratically under stress when the heap is several gigabytes big. In this case, especially when the system has multiple CPUs, we recommend that you run multiple JBoss AS instances or simply multiple virtual machines (e.g., VM-Ware) on the same server. You can use a load balancer to distribute the load to those virtual machines (see later in this chapter).

Modern JVMs use very sophisticated algorithms to run garbage collection. Garbage collection should run in parallel to other tasks so that the heap is continuously being cleaned up. That avoids the long server pause when the garbage collector stops other processes to clean up a large heap. To run the parallel garbage collector, you can specify the `-XX:+UseParallelGC -XX:+UseParallelOldGC` option for the JVM.

Finally, performance tuning is often application specific and requires empirical observations. You can tweak many other JVM options for improving performance and debugging. For instance, you can fine-tune the garbage-collection algorithm in the JVM to minimize the GC pause in your specific use case. Different JVMs (e.g., the Sun JVM, BEA JRockit JVM, and IBM JVM) also have different options for performance tuning. We recommend that you read a JVM tuning guide for more information.

27.1.3. Reducing Logging

By default, both Seam and MyFaces log a lot of information. Much of the information is for application developers and has little use in a production environment. The excessive logging I/O operations could really be the bottleneck on a high-load server. To reduce logging on a production server, you can increase the logging level for the `org.jboss` classes to the `INFO`. Just uncomment the following lines in the `server/default/conf/log4j.xml` file. That gets rid of much of the logging from Seam.

```xml
<log4j:configuration>

  ... ...

  <category name="org.jboss">
    <priority value="INFO"/>
  </category>

  <category name="javax.faces">
    <priority value="INFO"/>
  </category>

</log4j:configuration>
```

27.1.4. Tuning the HTTP Thread Pool

In JBoss AS, a separate thread answers each HTTP request. When the application has many concurrent users, much of the CPU time is spent managing those threads. Optimizing thread management is a key in improving the application performance under high load.

To avoid excessive thread creation and termination, JBoss AS maintains a pool of threads. When a new HTTP request comes in, the server retrieves a worker thread from the pool to process the request. After the response is rendered, the worker thread is returned to the pool and made available to process another HTTP request. You can specify a maximum size for the thread pool. If all the threads in the pool are currently being used, new requests must wait until a thread finishes its work and becomes available. To fully utilize CPU resources, the size of the thread pool should be at least five times the number of available CPUs on the server. However, too many threads can impede performance: The CPU then must spend more time switching contexts between threads instead of processing requests.

Another constraint on thread pool size is the number of HTTP keepalive connections (see the associated sidebar). Each keepalive connection corresponds to an active user. You can configure the maximum number of keepalive connections on the server. If all connections are keepalive, the number of connections is essentially the number of concurrent users the server can handle. Additional users then receive the connection timeout error. However, each keepalive connection also ties up a worker thread, so your thread pool size must be at least as big as the number of keepalive connections. For a high-load server, you might have a large number of keepalive connections, which would require too many threads to be effective.

An obvious fix is to have a modest number of keepalive connections and then a modestly larger thread pool. The spare threads, which are not tied to the keepalive connections, are used to service users overflowing the keepalive limit. This way, some users get the keepalive connection and enjoy better performance, whereas others have slower regular connections but still get service. You can optimize the right mix of threads and keepalive connections only through trial and error for your specific server needs.

> **Keepalive Connections**
>
> A keepalive connection allows a web browser to reuse the same network connection for multiple HTTP requests. It eliminates the overhead for creating and destroying multiple connections. All modern web browsers use HTTP keepalive connections by default.

> However, for a connection be a keepalive, the server also must support it. As you can see here, the server has the flexibility to decide which users get keepalive connections, depending on its own load.

The two thread-related settings just discussed are in the HTTP `Connector` element in the `server/default/deploy/jbossweb-tomcat55.sar/server.xml` file. The `maxThreads` attribute determines the size of the thread pool, and the `maxKeepAliveRequests` attribute determines the maximum number of keepalive connections. If the `maxKeepAliveRequests` attribute is `-1`, the server will allow an unlimited number of keepalive request until the thread pool is exhausted.

```
<Server>

  <Service name="jboss.web"
      className="org.jboss.web.tomcat.tc5.StandardService">

    <Connector port="8080"
        address="${jboss.bind.address}"
        maxThreads="250"
        maxKeepAliveRequests="100"
        strategy="ms"
        maxHttpHeaderSize="8192"
        emptySessionPath="true"
        enableLookups="false"
        redirectPort="8443" acceptCount="100"
        connectionTimeout="20000"
        disableUploadTimeout="true"/>

  </Service>

</Server>
```

27.1.5. Choosing Between Client- and Server-Side State Saving

JSF can save its internal component state in the user's HTTP session (server-side state saving) or in the browser as hidden form fields (client-side state saving). Server-side state saving consumes the server's memory and is generally harder to scale because of the need to replicate the session data in a cluster (see later in this chapter). Client-side state saving, on the other hand, distributes the state-management load to the users' browsers.

However, when it comes to CPU performance, client-side state saving is much slower because of the need to serialize objects. Thus, you must decide whether memory or CPU is the more likely bottleneck of your application and choose the appropriate state-saving method. You can select the state-saving method in the application's WEB-INF/web.xml file. Make sure that you turn off serialization when the state object is saved in the session.

```
<webapp>

  ... ...

  <context-param>
    <param-name>
      javax.faces.STATE_SAVING_METHOD
    </param-name>
    <param-value>server</param-value>
  </context-param>

  <context-param>
    <param-name>
      org.apache.myfaces.SERIALIZE_STATE_IN_SESSION
    </param-name>
    <param-value>false</param-value>
  </context-param>

</webapp>
```

The Server-Side State Saving Bug in MyFaces

JBoss AS 4.x uses Apache MyFaces as the default JSF implementation. However, MyFaces 1.1.3 and earlier have a bug that sometimes causes server errors when using the server-side state saving. MyFaces 1.1.4+, which is the default in JBoss AS 4.0.5+, has remedied this problem. If you use an earlier version of JBoss AS, we strongly recommend that you upgrade the MyFaces module in it.

27.1.6. Using a Production Data Source

JBoss AS's default datasource java:/DefaultDS points to the embedded HSQL database shipped with the server. Although the HSQL database is fine for application development, it is unsuitable for production environments. It is a major performance bottleneck and becomes unstable under high load. Be sure to set up a datasource with a production database for your applications. Refer to Chapter 26, *Using a Production Database*, for more on how to set up the production datasource.

> **Data Access Is the Bottleneck**
>
> In most real-world applications, the database access layer is likely the performance bottleneck. Thus, you must optimize the database access as much as possible.

27.1.7. Using a Second-Level Database Cache

Seam applications use EJB3 entity beans to model relational database tables. In most applications, only a small subset of the database records are frequently used. To improve performance, we should cache entity beans representing those frequently accessed records in the application memory, instead of making repeated database round-trips for the same bean objects.

To use the entity bean cache, you must annotate the bean class. All bean instances from the class are automatically cached after the first access until the `EntityManager` updates the underlying database table.

```
@Entity
@Name("person")
@Cache(usage=CacheConcurrencyStrategy.READ_ONLY)
public class Person implements Serializable {

  private long id;
  private String name;

  @Id @GeneratedValue
  public long getId() { return id;}
  public void setId(long id) { this.id = id; }

  public String getName() { return name; }
  public void setName(String name) {
    this.name = name;
  }
}
```

In the `persistence.xml` file for those entity beans, specify the distributed JBoss TreeCache as the cache implementation.

```xml
<entity-manager>
  <name>myapp</name>
  <jta-data-source>java:/DvdStoreDS</jta-data-source>
  <properties>
    ... ...
    <property name="hibernate.cache.provider_class"
      value="org.jboss.ejb3.entity.TreeCacheProviderHook"/>
    <property
      name="hibernate.treecache.mbean.object_name"
      value="jboss.cache:service=EJB3EntityTreeCache"/>
  </properties>
</entity-manager>
```

The cached objects are stored in "regions." Each region has its own size and cache expiration settings. Instances of the `Person` entity bean are stored in a cache region named `/Person` (the cache region name matches the fully qualified Java class name for the entity bean). The regions are configured in the JBoss AS's `server/default/deploy/`
`ejb3-entity-cache-service.xml` file.

```xml
<server>
  <mbean code="org.jboss.cache.TreeCache"
      name="jboss.cache:service=EJB3EntityTreeCache">
    <depends>jboss:service=Naming
    <depends>jboss:service=TransactionManager
    ... ...
    <attribute name="EvictionPolicyConfig">
      <config>
        <attribute name="wakeUpIntervalSeconds">
          5
        </attribute>

        <region name="/_default_">
          <attribute name="maxNodes">
            5000
          </attribute>
          <attribute name="timeToLiveSeconds">
            1000
          </attribute>
        </region>

        <region name="/Person">
          <attribute name="maxNodes">
```

```
          10
        </attribute>
        <attribute name="timeToLiveSeconds">
          5000
        </attribute>
      </region>

      <region name="/FindQuery">
        <attribute name="maxNodes">
          100
        </attribute>
        <attribute name="timeToLiveSeconds">
          5000
        </attribute>
      </region>

      ... ...

    </config>
  </attribute>
  </mbean>
</server>
```

In addition to caching entity bean instances, we can cache EJB3 query results in the previously described cache regions. For instance, the following code caches the query result in the /FindQuery cache region. For the query cache to be effective, you must cache the entity bean of the query result as well. In this case, we must cache the Person entity bean for the query cache to be effective:

```
List <Person> fans =
  em.createQuery("select p from Person p")  .
    .setHint("org.hibernate.cacheRegion",
             "/FindQuery")
    .getResultList();
```

For more information on using second-level database cache JBoss EJB3, refer to the JBoss documentation.

27.1.8. Using Database Transactions Carefully

In Chapter 9, *Transactions*, we discussed both database transactions and nontransactional extended persistence context. Without a transaction manager, we typically flush the persistence context at the end of the conversation and send all database updates in a batch. That offers two performance advantages to the transactional approach:

- The database updates are flushed in a batch at the end of the conversation instead of being flushed at the end of each request/response cycle (i.e., the end of the thread). That reduces unnecessary database round-trips during the conversation.

- The nontransactional database update is significantly faster than a transactional one.

Of course, the drawback is that if the database (or connection to the database) fails in the middle of the update batch, the database is only partially updated.

A good compromise is to build up the database changes in stateful Seam components throughout the conversation and then use a single transactional method at the end of the conversation to update the `EntityManager`. This way, we avoid the round-trips in the conversation and still take advantage of the transactional support when we actually access the database. See more details on this technique in Section 9.3., "Atomic Conversation (Web Transaction)".

27.2. Clustering for Scalability and Failover

With proper optimization, a Seam application can handle most low- to medium-load scenarios on a single commodity server. However, true enterprise applications must also be scalable and fail-tolerant.

- Scalability means that we can handle more load by adding more servers. It "future-proofs" our applications. A cluster of X86 servers is probably much cheaper than a single mainframe computer that handles a comparable load.

- Fail tolerance means that when a server fails (e.g., because of hardware problems), its load is automatically transferred to a failover node. The failover node should already have the user state data (e.g., conversational contexts); thus, the user will not experience any disruption. Fail tolerance and high reliability are crucial requirements in many enterprise environments.

As an enterprise framework, Seam was designed from the ground up to support clustering. In the rest of this section, we discuss how to optimize your clustering settings. Detailed instructions on JBoss AS clustering setup are beyond the scope of this book. You can find more details in the "Clustering" chapter of the JBoss server guide.

Installing the Clustered Profile

Make sure that you selected the `ejb3-clustered` profile in the JBoss AS installer (or JEMS installer). This profile contains the necessary library JARs and configuration files to run clustered EJB3 (and, hence, Seam) applications.

27.2.1. Sticky Session Load Balancing

All HTTP load balancers support "sticky sessions": Requests in the same session must be forwarded to the same JBoss node unless there is a failover. You must turn on sticky sessions in your setup. In an ideal world, all nodes in a replicated cluster have the same state; thus, the load balancer can forward any request to any node. But in a real cluster, the network and CPU resources are limited. It takes time to actually replicate the state from node to node. Without sticky sessions, the user gets random HTTP 500 errors when the request hits a node that does not yet have the latest replicated state.

Apache Tomcat Connector

Apache Tomcat Connector (a.k.a. mod_jk 1.2—see `http://tomcat.apache.org/connectors-doc/`) is a popular software-based load balancer for Tomcat (and, hence, JBoss AS). It uses an Apache web server to receive user requests and then forward on to the JBoss AS nodes via the AJP v1.3 protocol. An important setting is that the maximum number of concurrent users in the load-balancer Apache server must match the sum of concurrent users in the JBoss AS nodes.

We recommend that you use the worker or mpm_winnt MPM in Apache together with mod_jk. The older prefork MPM is not thread-based and performs poorly when there are many concurrent users.

27.2.2. State Replication

In a failover cluster, state replication between nodes is one of the biggest performance bottlenecks. A JBoss AS cluster has three separate replication processes going on. All the following configuration files are relative to the `server/default/deploy` directory.

* The HTTP session data replication is configured via the `tc5-cluster.sar/META-INF/jboss-service.xml` file.

* The EJB3 stateful session bean (i.e., Seam stateful component) replication is configured via the `ejb3-clustered-sfsbcache-service.xml` file.

* The EJB3 entity bean cache (i.e., distributed second-level cache for the database) replication is configured via the `ejb3-entity-cache-service.xml` file.

All three configuration files are similar: They all use the JBoss TreeCache service to cache and replicate objects. We recommend that you set the `CacheMode` attribute `REPL_ASYNC` for asynchronous replication. In the asynchronous replication mode, the server node does not wait for replication to finish before it serves the next request. This is much faster than synchronous replication, which blocks the system at several wait points.

The `ClusterConfig` element in each configuration file specifies the underlying communication protocol stack for the replication traffic. Through the JGroups library, JBoss AS supports many network protocol stacks for `ClusterConfig`. It is important to optimize the stack to archive the best performance. From our experiments, we believe that the TCP/IP NIO stack is the best choice for most small clusters. Refer to the JBoss AS documentation for more on the clustering protocol stack.

27.2.3. Failover Architectures

The simplest cluster architecture includes all server nodes in a single cluster and gives all nodes an identical state through replication. Although the single-cluster architecture is simple, it is generally a bad idea in real-world applications. Because each node replicates its state to all other nodes in the cluster, the replication workload increases geometrically with the number of nodes in the cluster. This is clearly not a scalable architecture when the cluster grows beyond four to eight nodes. For good performance, we recommend partitioning the cluster into two node pairs.

Using the buddy replication feature in JBoss Cache 1.4.0, you can group the nodes into pairs. You can also set up the load balancer to retry the correct failover node when a node in a pair fails.

If the load balancer hits both nodes in the buddy pair (using sticky sessions, of course), the failover node receives twice the traffic when the other node fails. That is not an elegant failover because the user would expect congestion. An alternative architecture is asymmetric failover: The load balancer hits only one node in each buddy pair, and the other node is reserved as a replicated failover node. You need more redundant hardware in this setup, but the cluster has the same computational capabilities during the failover.

Performance tuning is a complex subject, especially in a cluster. You must carefully evaluate your application needs and devise the best strategy. The information in this chapter is intended merely to provide some simple guidelines.

Installing and Deploying JBoss AS

JBoss Seam is developed and tested on the latest JBoss Application Server (AS). It is built on top of many JBoss services, such as JBoss AOP (Aspect Oriented Programming), Hibernate, EJB3, JSF, JBoss Cache, and JBoss Transaction Manager. Seam provides a simple, unified programming model for accessing all those heavy-duty enterprise services.

The build scripts for all example applications in this book build EAR files that can be deployed in the JBoss AS (see Appendix B, *Using Example Applications as Templates*, on how to build the example applications). Seam requires JBoss AS 4.0+ with the latest EJB3 module (you'll learn how to install this shortly). You must use JDK 5.0 to run the JBoss AS.

> **Running Seam Applications Outside the JBoss AS**
>
> Although the JBoss AS is the best server to run Seam applications, you can also run Seam applications outside the JBoss AS if you have to do so. See Chapter 25, *Tomcat Deployment*, for more.

A.1. JDK 5.0 Is Required

You can run the `java -version` command from your operating system's command line to check the version of your current JDK installation. If you are running a JDK earlier than 5.0, you need to upgrade. Linux/UNIX and Windows users can download the latest JDK from Sun's `http://java.sun.com/j2se/1.5.0/download.jsp` web site. Mac OS X users should download the beta version of Apple JDK 5.0 from the `http://www.apple.com/java/` site.

To run JBoss AS successfully, you also need to set the `JAVA_HOME` environment variable and point it to your JDK 5.0 installation directory. On a Windows system, you can do that via the system Control Panel tool (i.e., click on the following items from the desktop: Start, Control

Panel, System, Advanced, Environment Variables). On a UNIX/Linux/Mac OS X system, you can do it via shell scripts.

A.2. Installing JBoss AS

The easiest way to install a Seam-compatible JBoss AS with the latest JSF and EJB3 modules is to use the JBoss Enterprise Middleware Suite (JEMS) GUI installer. You can download the installer from the `http://labs.jboss.com/portal/jemsinstaller/downloads` web page. Run the installer with the `java -jar jems-version-installer.jar` command. You will go through a series of screens to consent to the license terms and select an installation directory (see Figure A.1., "Select an installation directory.").

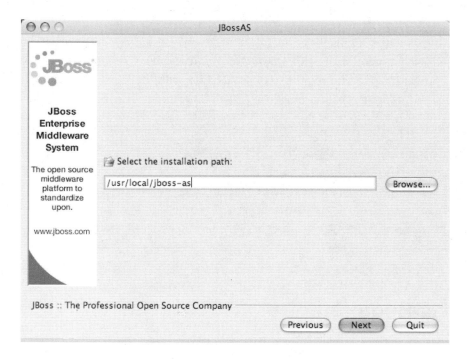

Figure A.1. Select an installation directory.

When the installer prompts you to select a server configuration, select either `ejb3` or `ejb3 with Clustering` (see Figure A.2., "Select an EJB3-compatible configuration to install."). Seam requires EJB3 support.

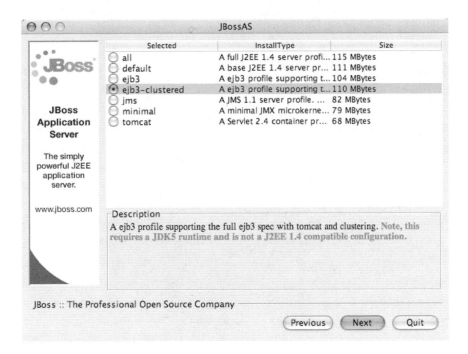

Figure A.2. Select an EJB3-compatible configuration to install.

> **JBoss AS 4.2.x and 5.x**
>
> This `ejb3` profile selection only applies to JBoss AS 4.0.5. For JBoss AS 4.2.x and 5.x, the default profile already includes EJB3 libraries.

You are asked to choose a configuration name for this installation; leave it as default (see Figure A.3., "Use default as the configuration name."). This way, you will be able to start the server without extra command-line arguments.

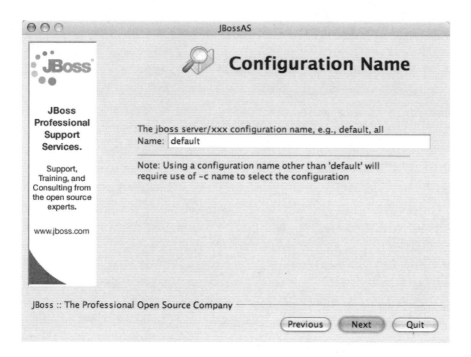

Figure A.3. Use default as the configuration name.

The installer also gives you options to secure JMX remote invokers. Those invokers enable remote users to look into your running server and even do things with it. Secure all those and give a username/password combo to protect those resources (see Figure A.4., "Secure all JMX invokers.").

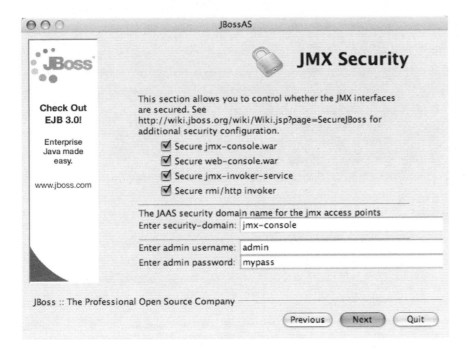

Figure A.4. Secure all JMX invokers.

What About the Seam Library?

An independent Seam container needs to be loaded for each Seam application, so be sure to include the `jboss-seam.jar` file in the application EAR file. The same goes for the `jboss-seam-ui.jar` file and the `jsf-facelets.jar` file—you must include them in your EAR file (in fact, in the WAR file) to support Seam-specific UI tags and Facelets. See Appendix B, *Using Example Applications as Templates*, for more details.

A.3. Deploying and Running Applications

To deploy a Seam application, you only need to copy the EAR application file (i.e., the build target from the source code) into the JBoss AS's `server/default/deploy` directory. To start the server, run `bin/run.sh` (or `bin\run.bat` on Windows). You can now access the Seam web application URL `http://localhost:8080/myapp/`. Of course, replace `myapp` with the application URL configured in your EAR (or WAR) file.

> **Ant**
>
> To build the example Seam application from source code, you should also have Apache Ant 1.6+ installed. Refer to the Ant documentation on how to install and use it.

B

Using Example Applications as Templates

In Chapter 4, *Rapid Application Development Tools*, we covered how to use Seam Gen to generate an application template for your Seam project. The Seam Gen template contains common configuration files, a build script, all support libraries, and even a sample application. It supports Eclipse/NetBeans IDE integration, out-of-the-container testing, and fast edit-save-reload development cycles. It is the best place to start building your Seam applications.

But the Seam Gen template project has a rather large footprint because it needs to include all support library JARs inside the project. It also lacks flexibility to support non-JBoss deployments. For the readers of this book, an alternative is to use the book's sample projects as templates for your own projects. This is more involved than Seam Gen, but it gives you more flexibility—and perhaps helps you learn more about Seam in the process. In this appendix, we discuss how to customize the book's sample applications.

The projects in the book source code bundle rely on library JARs in the `../lib` directory. Make sure that the `lib` directory in the source code bundle is side by side with the project directories of your Seam projects.

B.1. Simple EJB3-Based Web Applications

The `integration` example is the best starting place for a EJB3-based Seam web application. This is the directory structure of the source project:

```
mywebapp
|+ src
   |+ Java Source files
|+ view
   |+ web pages (.xhtml), CSS, and images
|+ resources
   |+ WEB-INF
      |+ web.xml
      |+ components.xml
```

```
            |+ faces-config.xml
            |+ navigation.xml
            |+ pages.xml
        |+ META-INF
            |+ persistence.xml
            |+ application.xml
            |+ jboss-app.xml
            |+ ejb-jar.xml
        |+ seam.properties
|+ lib
    |+ App specific lib JARs
|+ test
    |+ components.xml
    |+ testng.xml
    |+ Java source for test cases
|+ nbproject
    |+ NetBeans integration and support
|+ build.xml
```

To customize the project for your application, follow these steps:

- Add Seam components and other classes in the `src` directory.

- Add web pages, images, and other web resources in the `view` directory.

- Place required third-party library files in the `lib` directory. For instance, you can include the Ajax4jsf JARs, as we did in Chapter 16, *Enabling AJAX for Existing Components*. Modify the `build.xml` script if you need the JARs to be bundled outside of `app.jar`.

- Change the `resources/WEB-INF/navigation.xml` file to define the navigation rules (i.e., pageflow) in the new application.

- Edit the `resources/WEB-INF/pages.xml` file to include page parameters for RESTful pages (see Chapter 12, *Bookmarkable Web Pages*), page actions, and stateful navigation rules (see Chapter 19, *Stateful Pageflows*).

- Change the `resources/META-INF/persistence.xml` file to specify custom persistence options for the new application, if any (see Chapter 26, *Using a Production Database*, for some examples).

- Change the application name as follows:

- Change the project name `"integration"` in the `build.xml` file to your own project name (e.g., `"mywebapp"`).

- Change the `resources/META-INF/application.xml` file to reflect your application's context root URL.

- Change the class loader name in `resources/META-INF/jboss-app.xml` to a unique name that fits your application.

- Change the JNDI name pattern in the `resources/WEB-INF/components.xml` file to match your application name (i.e., `"mywebapp"`).

JSP vs. Facelets XHTML

The `integration` project template uses Facelets as the presentation technology. We highly recommend using Facelets in your Seam applications (see Section 3.1., "An Introduction to Facelets"). But if you really want to use JSP for web pages, you can use the `helloworld` example as the template. The setup is similar to the `integration` project setup we discuss here.

Then run `ant` in the project directory to build the application. The build result is in the `build/jars/mywebapp.ear` file. This is the structure of the EAR archive:

```
mywebapp.ear
|+ app.war
   |+ web pages (.xhtml), CSS, images
   |+ WEB-INF
      |+ web.xml
      |+ components.xml
      |+ faces-config.xml
      |+ navigation.xml
      |+ pages.xml
      |+ lib
         |+ jsf-facelets.jar
         |+ jboss-seam-ui.jar
         |+ jboss-seam-debug.jar
|+ app.jar
   |+ Java classes
   |+ seam.properties
   |+ META-INF
```

```
        |+ persistence.xml
        |+ ejb-jar.xml
|+ el-api.jar
|+ el-ri.jar
|+ jboss-seam.jar
|+ META-INF
   |+ application.xml
   |+ jboss-app.xml
```

If you have unit tests or integration tests for the application, you can put the test cases (the
.java files) and the testng.xml file in the test directory in the project. An alternative com-
ponents.xml file is already in the test directory. The difference between test/com-
ponents.xml and resources/WEB-INF/components.xml is that the test version does not have
the application name in its JNDI pattern and it installs the embeddable EJB3 container (see
Section 21.4., "Loading the Test Infrastructure")—because the tests are run outside the application server container. So if you customize the resources/WEB-INF/components.xml file
in your application, you must make the same changes to the test/components.xml file. This
is an example test/components.xml file:

```
<components ...>

  // same as resources/WEB-INF/components.xml

  <core:init
    jndi-pattern="#{ejbName}/local"
    debug="false"/>

  <core:ejb installed="true"/>

</components>
```

When you run ant test in the project directory, the build script runs all the tests defined in
the test/testng.xml file and outputs the test results both on the console and in the build/
testout directory.

For your reference, we list the complete build.xml script here:

```
<project name="Project Name"
        default="main" basedir=".">
```

```xml
  <description>Project Name</description>
  <property name="projname" value="mywebapp" />

  <property file="../build.properties"/>
  <property name="jboss.deploy"
location="${jboss.home}/server/default/deploy"/>

  <property name="lib" location="../lib" />
  <property name="testlib"
            location="../lib/embeddedejb3" />
  <property name="applib" location="lib" />
  <path id="lib.classpath">
    <fileset dir="${lib}" includes="*.jar"/>
    <fileset dir="${testlib}" includes="*.jar"/>
    <fileset dir="${applib}" includes="*.jar"/>
  </path>

  <property name="resources"
            location="resources" />

  <property name="src" location="src" />
  <property name="test" location="test" />
  <property name="view" location="view" />

  <property name="build.classes"
            location="build/classes" />
  <property name="build.jars"
            location="build/jars" />
  <property name="build.test"
            location="build/test" />
  <property name="build.testout"
            location="build/testout" />

  <target name="clean">
    <delete dir="build"/>
  </target>

  <target name="main"
          depends="compile,war,ejb3jar,ear"/>

  <target name="compile">
    <mkdir dir="${build.classes}"/>
    <javac destdir="${build.classes}"
      classpathref="lib.classpath"
      debug="true">
      <src path="${src}"/>
    </javac>
  </target>

  <target name="test" depends="compile">
    <taskdef resource="testngtasks"
      classpathref="lib.classpath"/>
```

```xml
    <mkdir dir="${build.test}"/>

    <javac destdir="${build.test}"
        debug="true">
      <classpath>
        <path refid="lib.classpath"/>
        <pathelement
            location="${build.classes}"/>
      </classpath>
      <src path="${test}"/>
    </javac>

    <copy todir="${build.test}">
      <fileset dir="${build.classes}"
              includes="**/*.*"/>
      <fileset dir="${resources}"
              includes="**/*.*"/>
      <fileset dir="${testlib}/conf"
              includes="*.*"/>
    </copy>
    <copy todir="${build.test}/WEB-INF"
                              overwrite="true">
      <fileset dir="${test}"
              includes="components.xml"/>
    </copy>

    <testng outputdir="${build.testout}">
      <classpath refid="lib.classpath"/>
      <classpath path="${build.test}"/>
      <xmlfileset dir="${test}"
                  includes="testng.xml"/>
    </testng>

</target>

<target name="war" depends="compile">
  <mkdir dir="${build.jars}"/>
  <war destfile="${build.jars}/app.war"
      webxml="${resources}/WEB-INF/web.xml">
    <webinf dir="${resources}/WEB-INF">
      <include name="faces-config.xml" />
      <include name="components.xml" />
      <include name="navigation.xml" />
      <include name="pages.xml" />
    </webinf>
    <lib dir="${lib}">
      <include name="jboss-seam-ui.jar" />
      <include name="jboss-seam-debug.jar"/>
      <include name="jsf-facelets.jar" />
    </lib>
    <fileset dir="${view}"/>
```

```xml
      </war>
  </target>

  <target name="ejb3jar" depends="compile">
    <mkdir dir="${build.jars}"/>
    <jar destfile="${build.jars}/app.jar">
      <fileset dir="${build.classes}">
        <include name="**/*.class"/>
      </fileset>
      <fileset dir="${resources}">
        <include name="seam.properties" />
      </fileset>
      <fileset dir="${applib}">
        <include name="*.jar" />
      </fileset>
      <metainf dir="${resources}/META-INF">
        <include name="persistence.xml" />
        <include name="ejb-jar.xml" />
      </metainf>
    </jar>
  </target>

  <target name="ear">
    <mkdir dir="${build.jars}"/>
    <ear destfile="${build.jars}/${projname}.ear"
appxml="${resources}/META-INF/application.xml">
      <fileset dir="${build.jars}"
          includes="*.jar, *.war"/>
      <metainf dir="${resources}/META-INF">
          <include name="jboss-app.xml" />
      </metainf>
      <fileset dir="${lib}">
        <include name="jboss-seam.jar"/>
        <include name="el-api.jar" />
        <include name="el-ri.jar" />
      </fileset>
    </ear>
  </target>

  <target name="deploy">
    <copy file="${build.jars}/${projname}.ear"
          todir="${jboss.deploy}"/>
  </target>

  <target name="undeploy">
    <delete
        file="${jboss.deploy}/${projname}.ear"/>
  </target>

</project>
```

B.2. POJO-Based Web Applications

If you want to use Seam POJOs and forgo the EJB3 session beans, you can choose the `jpa` or `hibernate` projects as templates (see Chapter 24, *Seam Without EJB3*). Those projects build applications into WAR files that are deployable in the J2EE 1.4-compliant profile of the JBoss AS 4.0.5+. With a little tuning, you can build WAR files deployable in any J2EE 1.4 application server (e.g., WebLogic, Sun Application Server).

The following listing shows the structure of the `jpa` project. For the Hibernate version, just replace `resources/META-INF/persistence.xml` with `resources/hibernate.cfg.xml`.

```
mywebapp
|+ src
   |+ Java Source files
|+ view
   |+ web pages (.xhtml), CSS, and images
|+ resources
   |+ WEB-INF
      |+ web.xml
      |+ components.xml
      |+ faces-config.xml
      |+ navigation.xml
      |+ pages.xml
      |+ jboss-web.xml
   |+ META-INF
      |+ persistence.xml
   |+ seam.properties
|+ lib
   |+ App specific lib JARs
|+ test
   |+ components.xml
   |+ testng.xml
   |+ Java source for test cases
|+ nbproject
   |+ NetBeans integration and support
|+ build.xml
```

To customize the project for your application, follow these steps:

- Add Seam components and other classes in the `src` directory.

- Add web pages, images, and other web resources in the `view` directory.

- Place required third-party library files in the `lib` directory. For instance, you can include the Ajax4jsf JARs, as we did in Chapter 16, *Enabling AJAX for Existing Components*. Modify the `build.xml` script if you need the JARs to be bundled outside of `app.jar`.

- Change the `resources/WEB-INF/navigation.xml` file to define the navigation rules (i.e., pageflow) in the new application.

- Edit the `resources/WEB-INF/pages.xml` file to include page parameters for RESTful pages (see Chapter 12, *Bookmarkable Web Pages*), page actions, and stateful navigation rules (see Chapter 19, *Stateful Pageflows*).

- Change the `resources/META-INF/persistence.xml` file to specify custom persistence options for the new application, if any (see Chapter 26, *Using a Production Database*, for some examples). For Hibernate applications, modify the `resources/hibernate.cfg.xml` file as needed.

- Change the application name as follows:

  - Change the project name `"jpa"` in the `build.xml` file to your own project name (e.g., `"mywebapp"`).

  - Change the `resources/WEB-INF/jboss-web.xml` file to reflect your application's context root URL as needed.

Run `ant` in the project directory to build the `build/jars/mywebapp.war` application archive. Required application library JARs are included in the `WEB-INF/lib` directory. This is the content of the WAR file:

```
mywebapp.war
|+ web pages (.xhtml), CSS, and images
|+ WEB-INF
   |+ lib
      |+ jboss-seam.jar
      |+ jboss-seam-ui.jar
      |+ jboss-seam-debug.jar
      |+ jsf-facelets.jar
      |+ el-api.jar
      |+ el-ri.jar
      |+ hibernate3.jar
      |+ hibernate-annotations.jar
      |+ hibernate-entitymanager.jar
      |+ ejb3-persistence.jar
```

```
    |+ app.jar
       |+ META-INF
          |+ persistence.xml
       |+ Java classes
       |+ seam.properties
  |+ web.xml
  |+ faces-config.xml
  |+ components.xml
  |+ jboss-web.xml
  |+ navigation.xml
  |+ pages.xml
```

Running tests in the POJO project is the same as running tests in the EJB3 project. This is the `build.xml` script to build the WAR application from the Seam POJO project:

```xml
<project name="My Project"
         default="main" basedir=".">

  <description>Project Name</description>
  <property name="projname" value="mywebapp" />

  <property file="../build.properties"/>
  <property name="jboss.deploy"
    location="${jboss.home}/server/default/deploy"/>

  <property name="lib" location="../lib" />
  <property name="testlib"
            location="../lib/embeddedejb3" />
  <property name="applib" location="lib" />
  <path id="lib.classpath">
    <fileset dir="${lib}" includes="*.jar"/>
    <fileset dir="${testlib}" includes="*.jar"/>
    <fileset dir="${applib}" includes="*.jar"/>
  </path>

  <property name="resources" location="resources"/>

  <property name="src" location="src" />
  <property name="test" location="test" />
  <property name="view" location="view" />

  <property name="build.classes"
            location="build/classes" />
  <property name="build.jars" location="build/jars"/>
  <property name="build.test" location="build/test"/>
  <property name="build.testout"
            location="build/testout" />
```

```xml
<target name="clean">
  <delete dir="build"/>
</target>

<target name="main" depends="compile,pojojar,war"/>

<target name="compile">
  <mkdir dir="${build.classes}"/>
  <javac destdir="${build.classes}"
         classpathref="lib.classpath"
         debug="true">
    <src path="${src}"/>
  </javac>
</target>

<target name="test" depends="compile">

  <taskdef resource="testngtasks"
           classpathref="lib.classpath"/>

  <mkdir dir="${build.test}"/>

  <javac destdir="${build.test}"
         debug="true">
    <classpath>
      <path refid="lib.classpath"/>
      <pathelement
        location="${build.classes}"/>
    </classpath>
    <src path="${test}"/>
  </javac>

  <copy todir="${build.test}">
    <fileset dir="${build.classes}"
                     includes="**/*.*"/>
    <fileset dir="${resources}" includes="**/*.*"/>
    <fileset dir="${testlib}/conf" includes="*.*"/>
  </copy>
  <copy todir="${build.test}/WEB-INF"
                              overwrite="true">
    <fileset dir="${test}"
             includes="components.xml"/>
  </copy>

  <testng outputdir="${build.testout}">
    <classpath refid="lib.classpath"/>
    <classpath path="${build.test}"/>
    <xmlfileset dir="${test}"
                includes="testng.xml"/>
  </testng>

</target>
```

```
<target name="pojojar" depends="compile">
  <mkdir dir="${build.jars}"/>

  <jar destfile="${build.jars}/app.jar">
    <fileset dir="${build.classes}">
      <include name="**/*.class"/>
    </fileset>
    <fileset dir="${resources}">
      <include name="seam.properties" />
    </fileset>
    <fileset dir="${applib}">
      <include name="*.jar" />
    </fileset>
    <metainf dir="${resources}/META-INF">
      <include name="persistence.xml" />
    </metainf>
  </jar>
</target>

<target name="war" depends="pojojar">
  <mkdir dir="${build.jars}"/>

  <war destfile="${build.jars}/${projname}.war"
       webxml="${resources}/WEB-INF/web.xml">
    <webinf dir="${resources}/WEB-INF">
      <include name="faces-config.xml" />
      <include name="components.xml" />
      <include name="navigation.xml" />
      <include name="pages.xml" />
      <include name="jboss-web.xml" />
    </webinf>
    <lib dir="${lib}">
      <include name="jboss-seam.jar" />
      <include name="jboss-seam-ui.jar" />
      <include name="jboss-seam-debug.jar" />
      <include name="jsf-facelets.jar" />
      <include name="el-api.jar" />
      <include name="el-ri.jar" />
      <include name="hibernate3.jar" />
      <include name="hibernate-entitymanager.jar" />
      <include name="hibernate-annotations.jar" />
      <include name="ejb3-persistence.jar" />
    </lib>
    <lib dir="${build.jars}"
         includes="app.jar"/>
    <fileset dir="${view}"/>
  </war>
</target>

<target name="deploy">
  <copy file="${build.jars}/${projname}.war"
```

```
        todir="${jboss.deploy}"/>
  </target>

  <target name="undeploy">
    <delete
        file="${jboss.deploy}/${projname}.war"/>
  </target>

</project>
```

B.3. Tomcat Applications

If you need to deploy Seam applications to Tomcat servers, you can use the `tomcatejb3` and `tomcatjpa` projects as templates. The `tomcatejb3` project uses the JBoss Embeddable EJB3 container to load EJB3 session beans in the Tomcat environment. The `tomcatjpa` project uses the JBoss MicroContainer to bootstrap JTA data sources needed for database access in Seam POJOs. Refer to Chapter 25, *Tomcat Deployment*, for more details. As with the POJO projects (`jpa` and `hibernate`), the Tomcat projects build the application into WAR files. Thus, they have similar setups and you can follow the same steps in Section B.2., "POJO-Based Web Applications" to customize a Tomcat project template. This is the structure of the `tomcatejb3` project:

```
mywebapp
|+ src
   |+ Java Source files
|+ view
   |+ web pages (.xhtml), CSS, and images
|+ resources
   |+ WEB-INF
      |+ web.xml
      |+ components.xml
      |+ faces-config.xml
      |+ navigation.xml
      |+ pages.xml
      |+ jboss-web.xml
   |+ META-INF
      |+ persistence.xml
   |+ seam.properties
|+ lib
   |+ App specific lib JARs
|+ test
   |+ testng.xml
   |+ Java source for test cases
```

```
|+ nbproject
   |+ NetBeans integration and support
|+ build.xml
```

The Tomcat WAR files contain more library JARs and configuration files than the J2EE 1.4-based POJO WAR files. This is the WAR file structure for a Tomcat WAR with embeddable EJB3 support:

```
tomcatjpa.war
|+ web pages (.xhtml), CSS, and images
|+ WEB-INF
   |+ lib
      |+ jboss-seam*.jar
      |+ jsf-facelets.jar
      |+ el-*.jar
      |+ myfaces*.jar
      |+ jboss-ejb3-all.jar
      |+ thirdparty-all.jar
      |+ hibernate-all.jar
      |+ commons-*.jar
      |+ jstl.jar
      |+ app.jar
         |+ META-INF
            |+ ejb-jar.xml
            |+ persistence.xml
         |+ Java class files
         |+ seam.properties
   |+ classes
      |+ ... files from lib/embeddedejb3/conf ...
   |+ web.xml
   |+ faces-config.xml
   |+ components.xml
   |+ jboss-web.xml
   |+ navigation.xml
   |+ pages.xml
```

We will not list the content of the build.xml file here because it is largely the same as that in Section B.2., "POJO-Based Web Applications".

B.4. More Complex Applications

The two applications we have discussed in this appendix are simple web applications. If your application uses advanced Seam features, you must package in additional JAR files and configuration files in the EAR or WAR archives.

The JBoss Rules JARs and configuration files are needed to support the rule-based web security framework in Seam. Refer to Chapter 20, *Rule-Based Security Framework*, for more details.

The jBPM JAR and configuration files are needed to support business processes and stateful pageflows in Seam applications. Refer to Chapter 18, *Managing Business Processes*, for more details.

PDF support requires the `jboss-seam-pdf.jar` file and the `itext-*.jar` file in the `WEB-INF/lib` directory of the WAR archive. Refer to Section 3.4.1., "Generate PDF Reports", for more details.

Facelets-based email template support requires the `jboss-seam-mail.jar` file in the `WEB-INF/lib` directory of the WAR archive. Refer to Section 3.4.2., "Template-Based Email", for more details.

Wiki text support requires the `antlr-*.jar` file in the `WEB-INF/lib` directory of the WAR archive. Refer to Section 3.4.3., "Display Rich Text", for more details.

Index

PRENTICE
HALL